Public Sector Management

6th edition

Norman Flynn

Los Angeles | London | New Delhi
Singapore | Washington DC

First published 2012

SAGE Publications Ltd
1 Oliver's Yard
55 City Road
London EC1Y 1SP

SAGE Publications Inc.
2455 Teller Road
Thousand Oaks, California 91320

SAGE Publications India Pvt Ltd
B 1/I 1 Mohan Cooperative Industrial Area
Mathura Road
New Delhi 110 044

SAGE Publications Asia-Pacific Pte Ltd
3 Church Street
#10-04 Samsung Hub
Singapore 049483

Library of Congress Control Number: 2011936992

British Library Cataloguing in Publication data

A catalogue record for this book is available from the British Library

ISBN 978-0-85702-873-0
ISBN 978-0-85702-874-7 (pbk)

Typeset by C&M Digitals (P) Ltd, Chennai, India
Printed by MPG Books Group, Bodmin, Cornwall
Printed on paper from sustainable resources

MIX
Paper from
responsible sources
FSC® C018575

Personal dedication: to Letrishka, Mickaela, Alastair and Rachel

Brief Contents

Contents

Acknowledgements

We are grateful to the following for permission to reproduce copyright material:

Chapter 1
- Figure 1.1 reproduced from the National Audit Office (2011) *National Health Service Landscape Review*, HC 708, Session 2010–11.
- Table 1.1 reproduced from the Office of National Statistics, *Civil Service Statistics*, licensed under the Open Government Licence v.1.0.
- Figure 1.2 from page 2 of *Local Government Financial Statistics, England*, No 20, 2010, Office for National Statistics/Department of Communities and Local Government licensed under the Open Government Licence v.1.0.
- Figure 1.3 from page 3 of *Local Government Financial Statistics, England*, No 20, 2010, Office for National Statistics/Department of Communities and Local Government licensed under the Open Government Licence v.1.0.

Chapter 2
- Extract from '*Conservative Party Manifesto 2010*' reproduced with kind permission from The Conservative Party.
- Extract from article by Samuel Brittan, writing in *Financial World* (published by the ifs School of Finance in association with CSFI) in October 2010.

Chapter 3
- Figures 3.1, 3.2 and 3.3 reproduce from the *Public Finances Databank*, HM Treasury, licensed under the Open Government Licence v.1.0.
- Figures 3.4, 3.5 and 3.6 reproduce from the Office of Budget Responsibility 2010-2011 estimates, licensed under the Open Government Licence v.1.0.
- Table 3.1 reproduced from 'Public Expenditure Statistical Analysis', 2010, HM Treasury, CM780, Table 9.15, p.132, licensed under the Open Government Licence v.1.0.
- Figure 3.8 reproduced from the *Public Finances Databank*, HM Treasury, licensed under the Open Government Licence v.1.0.

Chapter 4
- Table 4.1 reproduced from Paul Spicker (2011), *How Social security Works*, Bristol: Polity Press.
- Figure 4.1 reproduced from Government Statistics Service *Community Care Statistics* 2009–2010, Figure 5.1, licensed under the Open Government Licence v.1.0.

- Table 4.2, 4.3 and 4.4 reproduced from *Social Trends 40 – Education and Training*, page 32, Table 3.7, Office for National Statistics licensed under the Open Government Licence v.1.0.
- Figure 4.3 reproduced from the National Audit Office, *Criminal Justice System: Landscape Review*, 2010, page 8.
- Figure 4.4 reproduced from the National Audit Office, *Criminal Justice System: Landscape Review*, 2010, page 12.
- Table 4.5 reproduced from Roberts, R. (2011), 'Justice harm and Official Statistics', in Silvestri, A. (ed), *Lessons for the Coalition: An end of term report on New labour and criminal justice*, London: Centre for Crime and Justice Studies, pp. 68–78.
- Figure 4.5 reproduced from the 'Compendium of Reoffending Statistics and Analysis: Executive Summary', *Ministry of Justice Statistics Bulletin* (November 2010), page 2, licensed under the Open Government Licence v.1.0.
- Figure 4.6 reproduced from the Department of Communities and Local Government, 'House Building Statistics 2010', Table 209, licensed under the Open Government Licence v.1.0.
- Table 4.7 reproduced from the Department of Communities and Local Government, 'House Building Statistics 2010', Table 101, licensed under the Open Government Licence v.1.0.

Chapter 5
- Tables 5.1 and 5.2 reproduced from HM Treasury, *Budget* (June 2010), licensed under the Open Government Licence v.1.0.
- Table 5.3 from HM Treasury, *Spending Review 2010*, cm7942, page 10, licensed under the Open Government Licence v.1.0.
- Tables 5.4, 5.5 and 5.6 reproduced from *Budget Scotland 2011*, from the Scottish Government website licensed under the Open Government Licence v.1.0.
- Table 5.7 reproduced from *Northern Ireland Budget 2010*, from the Northern Ireland government website, licensed under the Open Government Licence v.1.0.
- Table 5.8 reproduced from *Budget Wales 2011*, from the Wales Government website, licensed under the Open Government Licence v.1.0.
- Figure 5.3 reproduced from the National Audit Office (2011) '*National Health Service Landscape Review*', HC 708, Session 2010–11.
- Table 5.9 reproduced from HM Treasury, 'Spending Review 2010', CM 7872, June 2010, licensed under the Open Government Licence v.1.0.
- Figure 5.4 reproduced from the National Audit Office (2010), '*A Short Guide to Structured Cost Reduction*', page 3.

Chapter 6
- Figure 6.1 and Table 6.1 reproduced from HM Treasury (2001), 'Outcome-Focused Management in the United Kingdom', General Expenditure Policy, page 2, Figure 1 'cascading PSAs into detailed business planning', licensed under the Open Government Licence v.1.0.

- Figure 6.2 reproduced from the National Audit Office (2010) *Taking the Measure of Government Performance*, HC 284, Session 2010–2011.
- Figure 6.3 reproduced from Department of Health (2008), *Developing the NH Performance Regime*, page 15, Figure 3, licensed under the Open Government Licence v.1.0.

Chapter 7
- Table 7.1 reproduced from Central Office of Information (2010), *Reporting on Progress Central Government Websites 2009–2010*, pp. 18–20, licensed under the Open Government Licence v.1.0.
- Table 7.2 reproduced from the National Audit Office (2010) Government of the Internet: Progress in Delivering Information and Services Online, HC 529 Session 2006–7, 13 July 2007.
- Extract from the National Audit Office report (May 2011), *The National Programme for IT in the NHS: AN update on the delivery of detailed care records systems*, HC 188 Session 2011–2012, p.13.
- Figure 7.1 reproduced from the Public Accounts Committee (2007) report 2006-2007, *The National Programme for IT in the NHS*, licensed under the Open Government Licence v.1.0.
- Extracts from the Cabinet Office (2002), 'Open Source Software use with UK Government', licensed under the Open Government Licence v.1.0.

Chapter 8
- Extracts from Cabinet Office, (2008) Excellence and Fairness: Achieving World lass Public Services, London: HMSO, pp.12–13, licensed under the Open Government Licence v.1.0.

Chapter 9
- Extract from OFSTED report (2008), Elizabeth Garrett Anderson Language College, licensed under the Open Government Licence v.1.0.
- Reproduced from TMG's, '*Imprisoned by bureaucracy*' by Philip Johnston, 16 January 2001, p. 15.
- Extract from HM Inspector of Prisons (1999), *Report on Wandsworth Prison*, licensed under the Open Government Licence v.1.0.
- Extract from HM Inspector of Prisons (2006), *Report on Wandsworth Prison*, licensed under the Open Government Licence v.1.0.
- Extract from HM Inspector of Prisons (2009), *Report on Wandsworth Prison*, licensed under the Open Government Licence v.1.0.

Chapter 10
- Extracts from Health Committee of Parliament report on Health Action Zones report licensed under the Open Parliament Licence v1.0.

- Figure 10.2 reproduced from Department of Communities and Local Government (2010), 'The New Deal for Communities: Evaluation: Final Report', *Vol.7, p.8*, licensed under the Open Government Licence v.1.0.
- Extracts reproduced from Department of Communities and Local Government (July 2009), 'Long-term evaluation of local area agreements and local strategic partnerships, report on the 2008 survey of all English local strategic partnerships', pp. 74–75, licensed under the Open Government Licence v.1.0.

Chapter 11

- Extract reproduced from Office of the Deputy Prime Minister (2003), 'Local Government Act 1999: Part 1, Best Value and Performance Improvement', ODPM Circular, 03/2003 p.6, licensed under the Open Government Licence v.1.0
- Figure 11.2 reproduced from Office of Fair Trading (March 2010), 'Choice and Competition in Public Services', p.12, licensed under the Open Government Licence v.1.0.

Chapter 12

- Extracts reproduced from the House of Commons Health Committee, 'Commissioning', 4th Report of Sessions 2009-2010, p.3 and p.9, licensed under the Open Government Licence v.1.0.
- Table 12.2 reproduced from Department from Local Government and Communities (2008), *The National Procurement Strategy for Local Government*, Final Report.
- Extract reproduced from Association of Directors of Social Services and National Council for Voluntary Organisations (1995), *Community Care and Voluntary Organisations: Joint Policy Statement*, London: ADSS?/NCVO, para. 14e, p.7.
- Extract reproduced from the National Audit Office (1995), *Contracting for Acute Health Care in England*, Report by the Comptroller and Auditor General, London: HMSO, p.19.

Chapter 13

- Figure 13.1 reproduced from Jim Broadbent and Richard Laughlin (2004), 'Striving for Excellence in Public Service Delivery: Experiences from an Analysis of the Private Finance Initiative', *Public Policy and Administration*, 19, p.82.
- 'Table 13.1 reproduced from Allyson Pollock, Jean Shaol and Neil Vickers (2002), *'Private finance and "value for money" in NHS hospitals: a policy in search of a rationale?'*, British Medical Journal Volume 324, May, pp. 1205–1209, with permission from BMJ Publishing Group Ltd.
- Figures 13.2 and 13.3 reproduced from Partnerships UK, 'Project database', licensed under the Open Parliament Licence v1.0.
- Office for National Statistics' *Productivity Handbook*, published by Palgrave Macmillan 2007, Chapter 9, page 135.

- Extract reproduced from Comptroller and Auditor General, *The Operational Performance of PFI Prisons*, HC 700, Session 2002-2003, 18th June 2010, pp. 6 & 9.
- Figure 13.4 reproduced from National Audit Office, 'The Department of Transport: The Failure of Metronet', HC 512, Session 2008-2009 (June 2009), p.5.
- Extract reproduced from the House of Commons Education and Skills Committee, 'Sustainable Schools: Are we building schools for the future?', 7th report, session 2006–2007, vol. 1 HC 140–1, July 2007, para 18, 31 & 68.
- Figure 13.5 reproduced from the Audit Commission Report (2003), *PFI in Schools*, p.14.
- Extract reproduced from House of Commons Public Accounts Committee (2009), 'Building Schools for the Future: renewing the secondary school estate', 27th report of 2008–2009, HC 274, licensed under the Open Parliament Licence v1.0.
- Extract reproduced from National Audit Office report (July 2010), 'HM Treasury: Financing PFI projects in the credit crisis and the Treasury's response', HC 287, Session 2010–2011, p.10, licensed under the Open Government Licence v.1.0.

Chapter 14

- Extract reproduced from Department for Transport and Office for Rail Regulation (2011), 'Reading the Potential of GB Rail, Report of the Rail Value for Money Study: Summary Report', p.42, licensed under the Open Government Licence v.1.0.

Links to all reports can be found on the companion website at www.sagepub.co.uk/ flynn6 or at the following websites:

National Audit Office http://www.nao.org.uk/
National Office for Statistics www.statistics.gov.uk
Department of Communities and Local Government www.communities.gov.uk
HM Treasury www.hm-treasury.gov.uk
Department of Health www.dh.gov.uk
The Scottish Government www.scotland.gov.uk
The Northern Ireland government www.northernireland.gov.uk
The Welsh Government www.wales.gov.uk
Central Office of Information www.coi.gov.uk/websitemetrics
Partnerships UK http://www.partnershipsuk.org.uk/PUK-Projects-Database.aspx
The Audit Commission www.audit-commission.gov.uk
Parliament UK www.parliament.the-stationery-office.co.uk

Companion Website

Go to the SAGE companion website for the sixth edition of *Public Sector Management* at www.sagepub.co.uk/flynn6 to find valuable resources.

For lecturers:
- Downloadable figures and tables from the sixth edition handily organised chapter-by-chapter and on PowerPoint slides.

For students:
- Free access to downloadable, full-text journal articles for further reading.
- Extensive thematically organised web links to policy documents, useful websites, and other relevant multimedia and social media resources.

PART ONE

INTRODUCTION

This is a book about management in the public sector in the United Kingdom. The public sector in the UK has been subjected to an unusual amount of attention by its politicians since the building of the foundations of the welfare state. Unlike the UK's European neighbours the constitution allows Prime Ministers and Ministers to change structures, create institutions, abolish tiers of government, change employment contracts and create control and incentive systems frequently and unhindered by statutory constraints. Some of the bigger changes, such as devolving government to Scotland, Wales and Northern Ireland or redrawing the boundaries and functions of local government, required legislation, but with a majoritarian parliamentary system, the reformers have normally got their way.

Change has itself become its own objective: incoming governments show that they are different from their predecessors by reorganising whatever came before. Since there is a small set of options for structures and systems, inevitably if this process goes on for long enough, old solutions become new again. In any case, what is presented as new is likely to be a new label on an old idea. No task force, special unit, change management initiative, process consultant could possibly promote an idea as tried and tested. Innovation, change, reform, improvement, delivery, restructuring, re-engineering are what makes careers progress.

There is also continuity. The functions of the state in the field of public services have largely not changed, with the exception of housing provision. The benefits system has had many reforms but the state still pays benefits to people who are unemployed, sick or with a disability. There is a state-funded and state-run healthcare system, free at the point of use, providing surgeries, clinics and hospitals universally. There is a state education system, providing for over 90% of the country's children. There is a criminal justice system, with police forces, courts, prisons and probation services. The shape of the institutions may have changed, the layers of management above the schools, prisons, hospitals, benefits offices may have been expanded, shrunk, split up, merged and reorganised but at the 'front end', the interface with the citizens, there is a degree of continuity.

What is the Public Sector?

The public sector can be defined in different ways. It could be seen as that part of the assets of the economy and society that is owned by the state. Or it could be those services that are provided collectively and funded in whole or in part from taxation. Or that part of the labour market in which people work for a public body, not a private company. While all sensible definitions, all produce fuzzy boundaries between what is private and what is public. If we look at ownership of assets, we see that the many assets, such as schools, prisons, hospitals, bridges built under Public–Private Partnerships (PPPs) are owned by a private company and leased to the state for a fixed term. So, is a school built under such a scheme part of the public sector? A similar ambiguity applies to public services: it is clear that a health procedure provided by the NHS, free at the point of provision, is a public service. But what about the same procedure in the same facility, paid for by a private insurance policy? And what about the leisure service, such as a swimming pool, where the swimmers pay an entrance fee that covers the full cost, and the facility is managed by a not-for-profit company that was established by the local authority?

Surely, a service provided by state employees is a clear and unambiguous definition of 'public'? Take Jobcentre Plus, for example, with its 86,000 employees? Services such as assessing and processing benefits, helping with job search, provided by directly employed staff, are surely public. Yes, but what if the computer system on which the service depends is provided by a contractor and maintained by the contractor's staff or even self-employed subcontractors? The same applies to all outsourced elements: if school catering is out-sourced, is it still part of the public education service?

The fuzziness of the boundary between public and private has implications for the way in which the public sector is run.

Funding and fees make a difference to management. Services provided free at the point of consumption have their own special characteristics: there must be a system of alloca-tion of services to people, other than price and market. Need and demand are indistin-guishable, rationing is essential and volume of service provided is determined by budget availability, not market success. Services provided through full cost recovery may also be subject to budget constraint, but the relationship between success in attracting service users and revenue generated is an important part of the management environment.

Employment also makes a difference. While public sector job contracts have become increasingly flexible and more like those in the private sector, whether people are directly employed by the organisation or working for a contractor makes a big difference to mana-gers: in some respects employing staff through outsourcing contractors can bring flexibility, as the contractual terms and conditions are not the same as employment contracts. The cooks working for the catering company cannot be managed in the same way as the cooks employed directly by the school, and the same applies for all occupations. In extreme cases, what might be seen as the core of the public sector is itself outsourced. Some local authority education departments, for example, have been outsourced to contractors and exercise the education authorities' planning, support and control functions. Health authorities hire contract medical staff from outsourcing nursing organisations, while nurs-ing is clearly a core function of the National Health Service. Outsourcing is not always at the edges.

The answer to our question 'what is the public sector?' has fuzzy edges, but a moder-ately distinct shape: it includes services that are provided as public goods, that are wholly or partly funded by taxation, that are managed through governance arrangements which involve some degree of public accountability and political control or influence. It also includes the whole process of collecting taxes to pay for those services, and all the transfer payments made to individuals and companies. Even given the fuzziness, we can say that public services account for about 20% of Gross Domestic Product. Transfer payments, including benefits and subsidies, such as farm subsidies, are not counted as part of GDP, but their total amount adds up to a further 20% of the size of GDP.

What is management?

Bertrand Russell once said that there are two types of occupation: one type involves moving matter in relation to other matter at or near the surface of the earth: the other type involves supervising those who move it.[1] This separation of people doing the work from those supervising the work is not universal: self-employed tradespeople, barristers and solicitors, dentists and general practitioners are among those occupations in which people supervise themselves. The separation is partly a function of scale: organising large numbers of workers may be easier with a separate supervisory level. Once the separation occurs, the question arises, what sort of people should be put into the supervisory or managerial positions? The question is very old and includes issues of professionals versus managers, the issue of what are the relevant competencies of managers and how can they be developed, and issues about the relationship between the management skills and the craft and professional skills of the people doing the work. Similar issues arise with the design of the information systems that underlie all organisations: should they be designed and implemented by a separate class of IT technical people, or should the managers or the professionals design the processes, and then call on the technical staff to design to their specification?

These issues are common to the private and the public sector. What distinguishes parts of the public sector is the specific nature of the tasks and processes required there. Some tasks and processes are common across the public and private divide: retail banks, for example, employ large numbers[2] of staff in branch networks and have interactions with individual customers both face to face and by telephone, email and website. Discretion at the front line is limited by rules, and supervision is carried out to ensure compliance. There is an information system whose purpose is both to provide or support customer service and to exercise control over the processes and the workers. This is all very similar to the tasks and methods of, for example, the Jobcentre Plus service: a network of physical service points, all with common branding; rules about what the recipients of the service can receive and the way they are dealt with; a hierarchy of supervision, with its hierarchy of targets, stretching down from a Board; an information system that provides support and contributes to the control of individuals' work. It is worth asking whether there is any difference between the management of a bank and the Jobcentre Plus service, especially at a time when the bank might well be in majority public ownership.

There are some differences: in the case of Jobcentre Plus, the people using the service have certain rights, to benefits and to the way they are allocated, which derive from their being a citizen and not a customer. In the case of the bank, customers have consumer rights, derived from law and from the fact that they decide to be a customer of a particular bank. If they are not satisfied with one retail bank they are free to go to another. Secondly, the way the benefits system is designed asks those working in it to use the system to help and encourage people to find and take a job, not just accept benefits. Individuals at the front line implement a policy of 'welfare to work' through which they, and the rules and entitlements, are supposed to affect individuals' behaviours. In addition, the accountability lines differ. While both organisations are managed by Boards of Directors, the Bank's Board is accountable to its shareholders, Jobcentre Plus to the people via the Minister and Parliament. The pressures from these two lines of accountability are different.

Another special aspect of those services which make up the public sector is that some of them have 'professionals' as their main service providers. Professions can be defined as those occupations in which the training and education includes the inculcation of ethics and codes of behaviour to which the members are expected to conform. Internal processes of registration, licensing, discipline and peer pressure take care of transgressions. The difference between the professions and other occupations is that the professions bring with them to any employer important aspects of their own management and supervision. Different professions have different degrees of internal control. Professionals work in both the private and public sectors, including lawyers, doctors, engineers. In some cases, such as the medical professions, a majority of members work for the NHS. Traditionally occupations such as teaching, social work, probation, most of whose members are public employees, have been considered less 'professional' than doctors, nurses and lawyers in the sense that they have enforceable codes of ethics and behavioural standards. When people who work in occupations that consider themselves to be professional and therefore self-regulating become subject to the sort of supervision normally applied to non-professional occupations they tend to react negatively. They do not like taking instructions from people who are not members of their profession. They tend not to respect the purported skills and processes associated with 'management'.

One answer to the question 'what is management?' therefore is 'management is what managers do', both compared to what 'workers' do and to what professionals do. The idea that management itself is a set of skills and processes that can be developed and applied apart from the actions of those doing the work is central to the proposition that organisations can and should be 'managed'. It is an idea of varying antiquity in the public sector.

The Structure of the Book

The book is in three parts. Part One puts public sector management in context. It starts with a chapter defining and identifying the public sector in the United Kingdom, the functions of the state and the shape of the institutions. Chapter 2 is about politics and different policies towards the public sector and its management, describing the different positions of the various parties in the United Kingdom. Chapter 3 is about public finance, how fiscal policy is made, what public money is spent on and where it comes from. It analyses the fiscal crisis that arose after the banking crash of 2008, and the sources of the deficit. Chapter 4 has a description of the major areas of policy that need to be managed, including income maintenance, community care, education, criminal justice, health and housing.

Part Two is concerned with management and is divided into the management of those services which are directly provided by employees and those which are outsourced or privatised. Part 2A covers the main aspects of financial management, performance management, information technology, customer–citizen orientation and service design, audit and inspection and collaboration among organisations. Part 2B is about managing outsourced services. It starts with a discussion of the uses of the market in public services, goes on to look at the contracting process, then turns to the special contractual form, the Public–Private Partnership. The last chapter is about regulation: the management of services that have been privatised but in which the government maintains the public interest. There is a more thematic introduction at the beginning of Part 2, on page 88.

Notes

1   Bertrand Russell, *In Praise of Idleness*, London: Routledge 1935.
2   Jobcentre Plus's 86,000 employees compares with Barclays Bank's 67,000, Royal Bank of Scotland retail division's 28,400 staff.

CHAPTER 1

The Public Sector in the United Kingdom

SUMMARY

This chapter starts with a discussion of the definition of the private and public sectors and how the boundary between the two has changed over time. It looks at the argument that there are 'public goods' that are distinct from other goods and services, and explains the extent of the public sector. It then looks at the specific characteristics of the public sector in the United Kingdom: the devolution of powers to Scotland, Wales and Northern Ireland, the fact that there is persistent and continuous reorganisation to the structures of the public sector, especially in the NHS and central government. It then describes the main institutions of the state: central government, the NHS, local authorities and their relationship with central government. It ends with a brief discussion of whether recent changes have resulted in a 'hollow state' as some theorists argue.

LEARNING POINTS

- The boundary between the public and private sectors is both permeable and changeable.
- The institutional forms that the state takes vary in the constituent countries of the United Kingdom.
- Governments reorganise structures very frequently.
- The UK is simultaneously decentralised in the cases of Scotland, Wales and Northern Ireland, but very centralised when it comes to central government control of local authorities, especially in England.
- The public sector represents a large part of the national economy and employment and was, until recently, growing.

PRIVATE AND PUBLIC SECTORS

The boundary between the public and private sectors changes with time and circumstances. During the period of post-war reconstruction, industries such as coal-mining, steel-making, motor manufacturing, shipbuilding, public transport including buses and trains, telecommunications, aircraft manufacturing, harbours, airports, oil, gas and electricity extraction, production and distribution were all publicly owned. In the same period, healthcare was taken into public ownership and the production of new housing was dominated by local authorities.

At the beginning of the 1980s there was a reversal of the process, as the state divested itself of industries and returned them to the private sector. There were a range of reasons for the privatisations, ideological, fiscal and pragmatic. There had always been politicians who opposed state ownership as a matter of principle, the principle that the profit motive was the only acceptable motive for business. At the end of the 1970s the Conservative governments were dominated by politicians who held this view, and the sale of state assets started, first with Cable and Wireless, then British Aerospace, British Petroleum, British Telecom, and later in the 1980s British Gas, the water industry in 1989, followed by electricity in 1990. The fiscal motivations were also important, as the cash raised from selling state assets could reduce the need for taxation, while the divestiture of (sometimes) loss-making industries reduced the burden of subsidy. The fiscal motivation contributed to the pragmatism of asset sales: even if there was not a strong ideological motive, faced with a choice between raising taxation or borrowing and making money by selling an asset, it would take a strong pro-public ownership ideology to resist the temptation. And so it proved through the 1990s, and into the Labour governments at the end of the 1990s: there was a growing consensus in favour of privatisation.

How the assets are owned and governed has an impact on decisions about asset acquisition, disposal and use. The estate, the land and buildings that an organisation has in ownership are an important element of any buildings-based service. Universities, for example, during the expansion period, acquired and disposed of land and buildings as part of their planned service delivery: some acquired assets far from their 'home' base and the resultant configuration of the estate had a fundamental impact on the types of research and teaching they could do, as well as how big they could be. Education authorities have had a responsibility to provide school places for the school-age population of their territories and have had to respond to the ebb and flow of pupils on the tides of demography and migration. Land acquisition and disposal has been an essential element of that response. The same is true of the health service, the prison service, the military and any service provided through land and buildings. Flexibility and responsiveness of asset use are greatly affected by the nature of the ownership: long leases under Public–Private Partnerships (PPPs), for example, lock the organisation into the asset for the period of the lease, however the requirement might change. Profits from changes in land values have traditionally provided public bodies with capital to make investments, an opportunity that only comes with unfettered land ownership.

The boundary between the public and the private was also pushed back in favour of the private by the sale of council houses to tenants through the 'right to buy' scheme, whereby tenants were offered big discounts and easy loans to buy the properties they lived in. This was largely an ideological and political choice, the judgment being that home-owners were likely to be more conservative than council tenants.

The third change in the boundary came with the increasing use of contracting with the private sector to provide services that remained public, such as highway maintenance, street cleaning, refuse collection. Beginning at the same time as the privatisations, the beginning of the 1980s, first local and health authorities and later the civil service were instructed to put out to tender an increasing list of services. This process of compulsory competitive tendering was extended to an increasing use of private finance and private management in new investment, especially in schools, hospitals and highways, through a process of Public–Private Partnerships, which we will examine in detail in Chapter 13. This process resulted, by 2011, in around 30% of all expenditure on public services being used to finance contracts for goods and services from the private sector.

The result of the three processes – privatisation, council house sales and outsourcing – shrank the numbers employed in the public sector by about 2 million in the two decades from 1980, to 5 million. Of these reductions, 1,355,000 were in the 'nationalised industries', 321,000 in local government and 200,000 in the civil service.

The shrinkage was reversed at the end of the 1990s, as the Labour governments increased public spending and public employment, especially in the NHS and education, but also in the civil service. From 1998 public sector employment rose every year to 2005, when it stood at 5,882,000, or 719,000 more than in 1998 and almost back to where it was before the great reductions started. The biggest increase was in the NHS, which put on 300,000 jobs.

This period of growth, which could be seen as a period of extending the boundary of the state, came to an end towards 2010, as fiscal deficits began to make the Labour governments look for reductions in numbers through greater use of information and communication technology and increased efficiency and productivity. With the change of government in 2010 and a fiscal deficit that the government decided to attack by cuts in spending as well as increases in taxation, the trend towards cutting the size of the state accelerated, as the Treasury called for cuts of 20–25% with their resulting cuts in jobs. While the details of these changes will be discussed in Chapter 3, a rough calculation of the scale of the spending cuts and the average cost of a public sector job puts the reduction of public employment between 2010 and 2014 at between 500,000 and 600,000, almost but not quite reversing the growth in employment implemented by the Labour governments between 1998 and 2005.

These ebbs and flows of employment numbers are the result of political and fiscal choices, but they do not explain the underlying issues about the boundary between the public and the private sectors. Public expenditure in the United Kingdom accounts for about 40% of Gross Domestic Product. This is not an entirely satisfactory definition of the scale of the public sector, since half of that spending is on transfers, subsidies and benefits which are not counted in the GDP figure. Expenditure on public services accounts for about 20% of GDP. Over the long term, is there an explanation for what is 'public' and what is 'private'?

Public goods and public services

There are four elements to the definition of what is public and what is private. The first is that certain things are 'public goods'. One feature of such goods and services is that they produce 'externalities', or benefits that accrue to people other than those who benefit directly. For example, education is said to benefit everyone living in a society of skilled and educated people. The other feature is that people cannot be excluded from certain benefits. Everyone benefits from clean air or street lighting. Because no one can be excluded, people should pay for such services collectively rather than individually. Even those politicians who believe that the state should do the minimum possible are normally willing to concede that these categories of services should be carried out by the public sector. Some people believe that no services are better provided by government and that even clean air is best achieved by property rights in air.

As a *justification* for the public sector, the 'public goods' argument suggests that the public sector should provide services where the market fails to do so, and the goods or services are required collectively, a decision made through the political process. As an *explanation* of what is public and what is private it is less convincing, since different services are in the public and private sectors in different societies and at different stages of development. Examples of the differences include the extensive provision of education through religious organisations but financed by the state in the Netherlands, the private provision of ambulances and fire protection in Denmark, public ownership of airlines in various countries. History and politics have more convincing explanations than a theory about public goods. Britain went through a period in which the ruling Conservative Party had an instinctive suspicion of public provision and a preference for markets and the private sector. The Labour Party abandoned its belief in state ownership as part of its modernisation programme and claims to be pragmatic in its approach to what should be private and what should be public.

The second distinction is how services are financed. Services are public services if they are financed mainly by taxation, rather than by direct payments by individual customers. One characteristic of most public services is that they are not available for sale and people cannot necessarily have more if they pay more. Even those services that are 'commercial', in the sense that money is exchanged at the point of consumption, are still public services in the sense that they are controlled through the political process, and accountability for service delivery is through politicians to the public rather than to shareholders.

The distinction is no longer absolute. People who receive homecare, for example, may pay for extra hours beyond those which they are assessed as needing. School children who do not pay for school visits may be left at school. Some public services are subject to charging: leisure facilities and car parks are normally charged for at cost or close to it. The NHS has charged for drugs since 1952 and patients in England and Scotland pay about 10% of the cost of drugs to the NHS.[1] NHS Trusts have private wings in which patients who pay may receive quicker treatment and better facilities than NHS patients. A high proportion of public services are 'free', at least at the point at which they are used: most of education and health, social security, criminal justice.

A third difference is who owns the facilities and by whom the service providers are employed. Traditionally public services were provided by public employees using publicly owned assets. Again, such a distinction is not absolute, after a period of contracting out and privatisation. Take public transport. In the United Kingdom outside London, bus transport is privately owned and deregulated. But there are still public service features. Everyone benefits from there being a public transport system, even car users whose freedom to drive is enhanced by other travellers taking buses. In London, buses are privately owned, but the routes are regulated by Transport for London and some routes are subsidised. Or, take refuse collection. Where private companies have won the right to collect rubbish, their employees are not public employees, the vehicles may or may not be owned by the local authorities but the details of the service are determined by the local authority.

The main defining characteristic is whether goods and services are sold only to people who pay for them and whether anyone with money can access them while other people are excluded. For people running and providing the services this distinction is important. In a business, the task is to attract customers, persuade them to pay a price that produces a profit and satisfy them enough to persuade them to remain customers. Public services have to attract people to use them, but they also have to enforce eligibility criteria where scarce resources have to be rationed in a way which does not apply in the private sector where scarce services are rationed by price. In the public sector, resources are rarely deliberately rationed by price. Prescription charges for drugs may deter poor people from taking medication, but there are safeguards to try to ensure that people in need do not have to pay and are not deterred. Nor do the managers and workers of public services have to satisfy people enough to persuade them to return. In those cases where the service is a monopoly, the service users have no choice. Even if they have a choice, it is not always the case that attracting more service users creates benefits for the organisation or its workers: often it just means more work. The motivation for satisfying customers is not to persuade them to return and generate more profit, but the value of public service.

It is really this last feature, the lack of a direct connection between ability to pay and access to the service, and the fact that there is not always a direct benefit from attracting customers, that makes management in the public sector distinct: marketing to generate sales is mostly irrelevant, unless artificial markets are created. Customer satisfaction as expressed by repeat business is not a relevant measure of success, nor is profitability. Motivations for good service are not themselves based on profit.

If these differences did not exist, then managing in the private and public sectors would be identical. Of course there are similarities: people's motivations in both sectors may have no connection with the well-being of the organisation or its customers; services in both sectors need to be designed and managed in similar ways; organisations have to be created to support the service process. Underlying these techniques, however, are the important differences in values and definitions of success.

DEVOLUTION AND DIFFERENCE

As well as being careful to define what we mean by the public sector, and to recognise the fact that the scale changes with time and that the boundaries are permeable, with cash flowing between the public and private sectors, we also need to consider the differences among the parts of the UK. The process of devolution has resulted in differences in policies, in institutional forms and policy and management processes in the constituent parts of the United Kingdom.

Scotland, Wales and Northern Ireland have their own national parliamentary and governmental institutions: only England has direct rule from Westminster, and no parliament or government of its own. The current devolution arrangements were brought in by Labour at the beginning of its first term of office. Referenda were held in Scotland and Wales in 1997 and by 1999 Scotland had a Parliament and Wales an Assembly. Similar plans were made for regional assemblies in England but when the first proposal was rejected in its referendum the plans were dropped. Scotland first had an Executive, then a Government from 2007, and Wales a 'Welsh Assembly Government' since 2005. Northern Ireland has an Assembly and an Executive, whose membership reflects the proportion of parties represented in the Assembly. The Scottish Parliament and Welsh Assembly are elected by proportional representation, unlike the UK Parliament. The powers allocated to the three devolved governments vary.

The Scotland Act of 1998 set out a list of reserved powers,[2] which were not to be devolved to Scotland. These included international relations, defence, treason, fiscal, economic and monetary policy, immigration and nationality, betting and gaming, emergency powers, various aspects of trade and industry and social security (except social welfare services). The exceptions left a wide range of powers for local decision, including the control over the big spending services, health and education, and most of the justice system. There was even provision for Scottish variation in income tax rates, a power that has not yet been used.

The National Assembly for Wales and the executive branch, the Welsh Assembly Government, have their fields of competence defined in the Government of Wales Act of 2006.[3] There are 20 'fields' for which they are responsible: agriculture, forestry and fishing; ancient monuments and buildings; culture; economic development; education; environment; fire and rescue; food; health and social services; highways and transport; housing; local government, the National Assembly; public administration; social welfare; sport and recreation; tourism; town and country planning; water and flood defence; the Welsh language. The main difference between Scotland and Wales is the omission of criminal justice from the Wales competencies.

The Northern Ireland Assembly and Northern Ireland Executive were created after the Belfast Agreement on devolution of powers and constitutional arrangements for the government of Northern Ireland. The Northern Ireland Act of 1998[4] set out a series of 'excepted' and 'reserved' matters, broadly similar to those in Scotland, with the exception of the criminal justice system. The Northern Ireland Act of 2009 transferred policing powers to the Assembly.

The devolution of powers to the three jurisdictions has created many differences in domestic policies and in governance and management arrangements. The differences include the structure of the health and social welfare services, the ownership and governance of the water and power systems, entitlements to services for elderly people, the requirement for students to pay university fees, the structure, including the distribution of functions, of local government, institutions and policies for economic development.

Devolution has incidentally created a constitutional anomaly, in that members of the UK Parliament representing Scottish, Welsh and Northern Irish constituencies can pass legislation affecting English citizens, while English MPs have no votes in the Scottish, Welsh and Irish Assemblies.

We will see in Chapter 5 that the budget processes in the devolved administrations are concerned only with expenditure, since fiscal policy is a reserved power for the Westminster government, with some marginal exceptions, and the aggregate amount of spending is decided outside the devolved administrations. This breaks the connection between taxation and elections: national politicians can blame the Westminster government for lack of funds (although spending per head in the devolved administrations is generally higher than that in England), rather than being compelled to ask the electorate for revenues to pursue policies and provide services. Since devolution does not include fiscal policy it frees politicians from choices about the connection between revenue and expenditure.

PERMANENT STRUCTURAL CHANGE

One hazard of writing a book about the public sector in the United Kingdom is that there will most likely have been another reorganisation between the completion of the manuscript and its publication. Since the mid-1970s reorganisation has been the chosen solution to a variety of problems: in 1974/75 local government was diagnosed as inefficient, so it was reorganised into bigger units to create economies of scale. The NHS has been in a constant state of reorganisation since 1947, with Regional Health Authorities created and then destroyed, funds given to General Practitioners to manage, then taken away from them and given to Primary Care Trusts, which in turn came up for destruction, and funds given back (again) to consortia of GPs to manage. New institutions are set up with very swift and cursory preparation, such as Education Action Zones or Strategic Partnerships. Ministries are amalgamated, split, re-named, abolished or created apparently at will. One of the first acts of the Gordon Brown premiership was to reorganise the departments. The Coalition set about abolishing organisations, including the Audit Commission and government regional offices, for example, among its first acts on taking power. It also proposed yet another reorganisation of the NHS, to continue the long tradition of never leaving the NHS alone. The National Audit Office report on central government reorganisation in 2010[5] found: 'There have been over 90 reorganisations of central government departments and their arm's length bodies between May 2005 and June 2009: over 20 a year on average. We estimate the gross cost of the 51 reorganisations covered by our survey to be £780 million, equivalent to £15 million for each reorganisation and just under £200 million a year (p. 4). This estimate excludes another 42 small reorganisations in the same period. The report also records: 'Central government has always reorganised, even though its fundamental activities change little. Since 1980, 25 departments have been created, including 13 which no longer exist (p. 4).

Apart from creating a lot of work for Human Resources departments, the constant reorganisation has consequences for public services. First, it diverts people's attention from the outside to the inside, from the service users to the organisation. Individuals' attention is focused on the possibility of being made redundant, of possible promotion, of likely relocation. Second, it confuses people who use the services: if the NHS, for example, creates, merges then abolishes Primary Care Trusts, how can patients or citizens relate to the PCTs or even understand which one is looking after their services or what they do? Some reorganisations are designed to improve customer service, for example by merging services that individuals receive but previously had to go to two or more locations to access.

To some extent the very front line may be less affected than the middle managers and upper reaches of the organisations, whose jobs are more likely to change. I interviewed a civil engineer who had been through many reorganisations of the bodies responsible for highways maintenance. His view was that what happened above his level had little impact on the technical activity of maintaining the highways, as opposed to the structures of resource allocation and accountability above that level. In large parts of public service, the way they are managed and delivered is relatively constant: benefits get assessed and paid; schools have classes, pupils and teachers; doctors and other medical professionals treat patients; police arrest, courts sit and prisons detain. Changes in the processes of management have big impacts on the way people work: changes in organisation structures rarely do. Take the 2011 reorganisation of the NHS, the before and after represented in Figure 1.1.[6]

If you look at the top three-quarters of the charts you will see big changes: Strategic Health Authorities disappear, 'Healthwatch' is created as a channel for patients' opinions, the Care Quality Commission starts to license providers, GP consortia take over almost all funding. Look at the bottom of the chart, and there are health professionals carrying on doing what health professionals have always done. The only change between the left and the right is that all NHS trusts become 'Foundation Trusts'.

This is a common phenomenon in reorganisations, whereby the levels or tiers above those of service delivery are reorganised, redefined, funded in new ways, told to produce strategies and plans in new ways while the business of providing services is still relatively unchanged at what has become known as the 'front line'.

The regime in prisons, for example, is set by custom and policy and is constrained by the resources, especially staff resources, available in each prison. Outside, or 'above' the prison in organisational terms, there have been many changes over the years: the Prison Service has had reorganisations, most recently consisting of a merger with the Probation Service into the National Offender Management Service.

General Practitioners, working in a one-to-one way with their registered patients, have been run as independent businesses, then working to Primary Care Trusts, themselves likely to be abolished in the current phase of reforms. One has to ask how much the rearrangement of

Current structure

Proposed structure

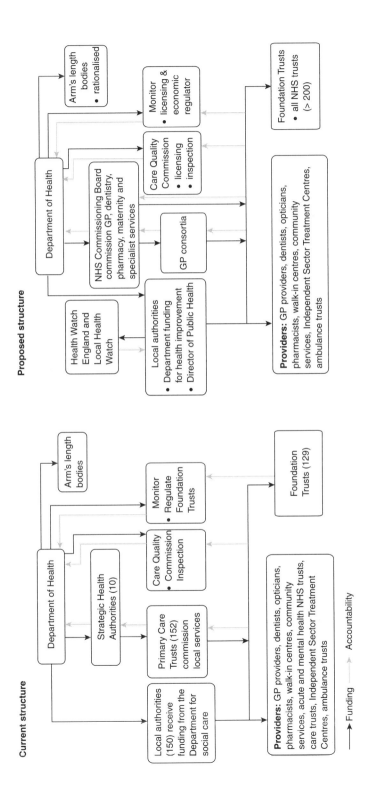

Figure 1.1 The NHS reorganisation

Source: NAO (2011) *National Health Service Landscape Review*

the middle and top tiers of organisations affects the everyday behaviour of the professionals working in the services and the people for whom the services are provided. The changes in management arrangements and structures are usually described as 'reforms', whatever type they are. Whether a change of name, a reorganisation, a merger or demerger is in reality a 'reform' should be subject to two tests: did the change make any measurable difference to the quantity or quality of service delivered to the users of the service? Did the change make any measurable or provable change to the behaviours of the staff delivering the service? If the change fails these tests, it should not be defined as a reform.

It is interesting to ask why successive governments feel the urge to reorganise. One reason lies in the constitution, which makes it relatively easy for governments to change organisational structures at national and local level. Other European states have constitutional protection for both sub-national governments and for civil servants, protection that is designed to stop arbitrary actions by governments. But this only explains why governments *can* make these changes, not why they *do*. The explanation probably lies in the very centralised nature of the UK system of government: Ministers are remote from the detail and often have no experience of running organisations, including local authorities. Structural change, because it is easy and is visible, seems an attractive option, whether or not it is likely to produce the desired outcomes, or indeed whether specific outcomes were ever defined.

CENTRAL GOVERNMENT

Central government in England and the devolved administrations consists of Departments, responsible for policy and high-level management control, Executive Agencies, responsible for the delivery of services (except in Northern Ireland), a range of non-departmental bodies with a variety of functions, and a set of inspectors, auditors and regulators with varying degrees of autonomy from central government.

At the centre of government are politicians doing jobs as Ministers of various ranks in their departments and an élite civil service. In 2011 there were 42 civil servants of the rank of Permanent Secretary, occupying the controlling positions in the civil service. The First Division Association, the trade union for senior civil servants, had 19,000 members, including 5,000 affiliates in the National Health Service. There were 19 Ministerial departments and 20 non-ministerial departments and about 65 Executive Agencies.

There were also 766 Non-Departmental Public Bodies[7] sponsored by the UK Government. These consist of 192 Executive NDPBs, 405 Advisory NDPBs, 19 Tribunal NDPBs and 150 Independent Monitoring Boards of Prisons, Immigration Removal Centres and Immigration Holding Rooms. The Executive NDPBs include the 56 Executive Agencies, where the majority of civil servants are employed.

Table 1.1 shows the numbers of civil servants employed in departments and other bodies in 2010.[8]

Table 1.1   Civil Service numbers employed by department 2010

	Q3 2010	
	Headcount	**Full-time equivalent**
Attorney General's departments		
Crown Prosecution Service	8,470	7,850
Crown Prosecution Service Inspectorate	40	40
Attorney General's Office	50	50
Serious Fraud Office	310	300
Treasury Solicitor	900	860
National Fraud Authority	50	50
Business, Innovation and Skills		
Business, Innovation and Skills	3,900	3,760
Advisory, Conciliation and Arbitration Service	940	880
Companies House	1,160	1,060
Insolvency Service	2,630	2,510
Office of Fair Trading	640	620
Office of Gas and Electricity Market	420	410
Postal Services Commission	50	50
National Measurement Office	70	70
UK Intellectual Property Office	900	840
Skills Funding Agency	1,870	1,820
Cabinet Office		
Cabinet Office excl. agencies	1,670	1,620
Other Cabinet Office agencies		
Central Office of Information	860	830
National School of Government	230	220
Office of the Parliamentary Counsel	110	110
Buying Solutions	380	360
Charity Commission		
Charity Commission	460	430
Department for Education		
Department for Education	2,930	2,800
Communities and Local Government		
Department for Communities and Local Government	2,600	2,520
Fire Service College	210	200
Ordnance Survey	1180	1150

(Continued)

Table 1.1   (Continued)

	Q3 2010	
	Headcount	**Full-time equivalent**
Planning Inspectorate	790	690
Queen Elizabeth II Conference Centre	50	50
Culture, Media and Sport		
Department for Culture, Media and Sport	480	460
Royal Parks	120	110
Defence		
Ministry of Defence	65,920	63,950
Defence Support Group	3,210	3,170
Defence Science and Technology Laboratory	3,830	3,720
Meteorological Office	1,870	1,800
UK Hydrographic Office	980	950
Energy and Climate Change		
Department for Energy and Climate Change	1,140	1,120
Environment, Food and Rural Affairs		
Department for Environment, Food and Rural Affairs	2,690	2,590
Centre for Environment, Fisheries and Aquaculture Science	560	530
Food and Environment Research Agency	910	840
Ofwat	230	220
Rural Payments Agency	2,830	2,630
Animal Health	1,640	1,540
Veterinary Laboratories Agency	1,260	1,160
Veterinary Medicines Directorate	160	150
Export Credits Guarantee Department		
Export Credits Guarantee Department	200	200
Foreign and Commonwealth Office		
Foreign and Commonwealth Office (excl. agencies)	5,960	5,900
Wilton Park Executive Agency	80	70
Government Equalities Office		
Government Equalities Office	110	110
Health		
Department of Health (excl. agencies)	2,620	2,540
Food Standards Agency	1,460	1,420
Medicines and Healthcare Products Regulatory Agency	1,010	960

	Q3 2010	
	Headcount	Full-time equivalent
NHS Business Services Authority	220	190
HM Revenue and Customs		
HM Revenue and Customs	74,780	67,550
Valuation Office	4,090	3,770
HM Treasury		
HM Treasury	1,370	1,360
Chancellor's other departments		
Debt Management Office	100	100
Government Actuary's Department	140	130
National Savings and Investments	150	140
Royal Mint	890	870
Home Office		
Home Office (excl. agencies)	3,180	3,070
Criminal Records Bureau	750	680
Identity and Passport Service	4,250	3,800
UK Border Agency	22,840	21,520
International Development		
Department for International Development	1,640	1,600
Justice		
Ministry of Justice (excl. agencies)	3,410	3,300
HM Courts Service	19,970	17,880
Land Registry	5,670	5,130
National Archives	610	580
The Office of the Public Guardian	440	420
Tribunals Service	3,210	2,960
Scotland Office	100	90
Wales Office	60	60
National Offender Management Service	50,830	48,770
UK Supreme Court	40	40
Northern Ireland Office		
Northern Ireland Office	120	120
Ofsted		
Ofsted	1,550	1,500

(Continued)

Table 1.1   (Continued)

	Q3 2010	
	Headcount	Full-time equivalent
Office of Qualifications and Examinations Regulation		
Office of Qualifications and Examinations Regulation	170	170
Security and Intelligence Services		
Security and Intelligence Services	5,840	5,590
Transport		
Department for Transport	2,130	2,070
Driver and Vehicle Licensing Agency	6,510	5,950
Driving Standards Agency	2,610	2,450
Government Car and Despatch Agency	280	270
Highways Agency	3,810	3,720
Maritime and Coastguard Agency	1,210	1,160
Office of Rail Regulation	300	290
Vehicle Certification Agency	150	140
Vehicle and Operator Services Agency	2,430	2,350
UK Statistics Authority		
UK Statistics Authority	4,030	3,270
Census Field	190	180
Work and Pensions		
DWP Corporate and Shared Services	13,090	12,200
Jobcentre Plus	86,540	77,750
Pensions and Disability Carers Service	15,360	13,720
Child Maintenance Enforcement Commission	9,250	8,160
The Health and Safety Executive	3,850	3,600
Scottish Government		
Scottish Government (excl. agencies)	5,570	5,320
Scottish Housing Regulator	60	60
Crown Office and Procurator Fiscal Service	1,840	1,730
General Register Scotland	320	300
HM Inspectorate of Education	220	200
Historic Scotland	1,120	1,040
National Archive for Scotland	150	140
Office of Accountant in Bankruptcy	160	150
Registers of Scotland	1,360	1,260
Scottish Court Service	1,670	1,520
Scottish Prison Service Headquarters	4,120	4,010
Scottish Public Pensions Agency	260	240

	Q3 2010	
	Headcount	Full-time equivalent
Social Work Inspection Agency	40	40
Student Awards Agency	170	160
Transport Scotland	410	410
Office for the Scottish Charity Regulator	50	50
Disclosure Scotland	180	170
Welsh Assembly		
Welsh Assembly Government	5,800	5,510
ESTYN	100	100
Total employment	**514,840**	**479,360**

Over 60% of the half a million civil servants work in the six biggest organisations, as shown in Table 1.2. These are big organisations by any standards, with all the management issues and problems that come from size.

Unlike many neighbouring countries' civil services, the way that UK civil servants are paid and managed is decentralised and devolved. Since the early 1990s[9] departments and agencies have been responsible for their own recruitment and have a degree of autonomy over pay. Civil servants are subject to the same employment law as workers in the private sector, rather than having special privileges and constitutional protection. In this basic respect, management of these large organisations is similar to managing people in large private organisations.

For these large groups of staff, especially Jobcentre Plus and HMRC, the management issues are probably akin to those in businesses such as supermarkets or banks: large numbers of staff in very dispersed locations; a set of activities that have to be governed by rules with small degrees of discretion for the service delivery workers; staff unlikely to be highly motivated by the job itself, because it is routine and boring. The way the work is done is designed by management and monitored by technology, whether length and number of phone calls, key strokes on computers, items scanned with the barcode scanner.

Table 1.2   Employment in the six biggest departments

Jobcentre Plus	86,540
HM Revenue and Customs	74,780
Ministry of Defence	65,920
National Offender Management Service	50,830
UK Border Agency	22,840
HM Courts Service	19,970
Total of these	**320,880**

THE NATIONAL HEALTH SERVICE

The NHS is reputed to be the largest organisation in Europe. In 2011, the health services in England, Scotland and Wales (and Health and Social Care Services in Northern Ireland) employed just under 1.5 million people, as shown in Table 1.3.[10]

The NHS has been reviewed and reorganised many times since it was founded. Organisational form has been used to solve many continuing dilemmas: what should be controlled locally and what centrally? How should local people be represented in decision making? Should the doctors be controlled by somebody other than doctors and if so how should this be done? How can access be organised so that people have the same chances of getting treated wherever they live? How should resources be allocated, to populations or to hospitals and other services? Resource allocation has always struggled with the fact that hospitals and doctors have been concentrated in the cities while the population is more dispersed, and many formulas have been designed to preserve or correct that imbalance.

The answers to these questions have been varied. There have been hierarchies of health authorities and various other bodies between the Department of Health and the patients. Local people have been represented on health authorities, although never through direct elections, and on community health councils. The two mechanisms that have been used to control the doctors have been some form of management through which someone other than a doctor has tried to tell them what to do, and changes to doctors' contracts and administered markets.

The evolution of the NHS has left different structures in the four countries of the UK. The four arrangements are set out in Table 1.4.[11,12] The differences are partly a result of scale: Scotland has unified Health Boards overseeing all health services in Scotland. In Northern Ireland health and social services are managed as one entity. Wales and England have hierarchical geographical structures and a separation of primary care from hospital care.

The NHS and Social Care Bill of 2011 proposed yet another reorganisation of the NHS, continuing the process of 'commissioning', whereby the services provided by hospitals were defined and 'purchased' by someone other than those who run the hospitals. This time, though, those charged with purchasing or commissioning services were to be allowed a more free choice of provider, subject to European competition laws and regulation by an independent regulator, with powers similar to those of the regulators of the public utilities and power industries.

Table 1.3 Employment in National Health Service 2011

NHS England	1,217,714
NHS Scotland	168, 051
NHS Wales	56, 482
Health and Social Care, Northern Ireland	53, 893
Total employees	**1,496,140**

Table 1.4   Overview of the structure of the NHS in the UK, 2004

Organisation	England	Wales	Scotland	NI
Government department	DH	NHSD	SEHD	DHSSPS
Strategic direction	SHAs	Regional Offices	NHS Unified Boards	HSS Boards
Primary care management	PCTs	LHBs	Primary Care operating division	LHSCGs
Hospital management	NHS Trusts	NHS Trusts	Secondary Care operating division	HSS Trusts
Community care management	PCTs and NHS Trusts	NHS Trusts	Operating divisions	HSS Trusts
Social services management	Local Authorities	Local Authorities and LHBs	SEHD and Local Authorities	HSS Trusts

This was an attempt to change the boundary between public and private sectors in the NHS, in the same way that it had previously been redefined by the privatisations and outsourcing in local government and the civil service.

LOCAL GOVERNMENT

Local government has not been subject to reorganisation in England to the same extent as the NHS. Apart from the creation of the Greater London Authority and the London Mayoralty in 2000, the structure of the English system has been stable since the series of restructurings in the 1970s. Scottish and Welsh local government was reorganised following a review in 1995, abolishing the old system of tiered local authorities and replacing it with 'unitary' authorities, responsible for all services. The current set-up varies by jurisdiction, with a single tier in Wales and Scotland, a single tier plus Area Boards for Health and Social Services in Northern Ireland and a mixture of single-tier and two-tier authorities in England. The arrangements are summarised in Table 1.5.

At the end of 2010, 2,885,000[13] people were employed in local authorities in the UK. The main change to local government during the Labour governments was to the internal organisation, with a move from the use of Committees to the Cabinet system, with a smaller executive group and, where local electorates voted for it, an elected Mayor, acting in an executive capacity, unlike the traditional, largely ceremonial mayoralty in traditional local authorities.

The system, by comparison with other European countries, gives very little autonomy to the local authorities, which are controlled both financially and managerially by central government, including the governments of Wales and Scotland.

Table 1.5   Local government structure in the United Kingdom

England	Wales
46 Unitary authorities in urban areas	22 Unitary authorities
36 Metropolitan District Councils	**Scotland**
32 London Boroughs and the Corporation of the City of London	32 Unitary authorities
34 County Councils in rural areas	**Northern Ireland**
238 District Councils in rural areas plus Parish and Town Councils	26 District Councils
1 Greater London Authority (Mayor and London Assembly)	9 Area Boards for Health and Social Services

LOCAL AUTHORITY FUNDING

Local authority spending is almost all directly controlled by central government. There is a formula by which the Department for Communities and Local Government calculates a spending level for each service for each local authority, the amount which the government says would provide a standard level of service (the Standard Spending Assessment or SSA). This level is then used to distribute the business rate, which is aggregated nationally and redistributed, the revenue support grant and the amount of council tax which authorities are expected to raise. Council Tax accounts on average for about 20% of local authority spending. Business rates are collected locally but pooled and redistributed according to population size. Revenue Support Grant is allocated on a formula and there are various grants dedicated to particular services, such as the Standards Fund for education, and monies for such things as services for asylum seekers. Successive governments increased the proportion of the total central government support that is ear-marked ('ring-fenced' is the normal metaphor) in this way, including education expenditure. Capital expenditure is subject to direct control, through a process of application, approval and now competition.

The Labour administration tried to raise the amount of central government support for local government spending. Support had been declining in real terms in the last three years of the previous administration and the incoming government announced plans to make it grow by 4% per year. Some of the money came with strings attached. Local authorities that achieved their Best Value targets were allowed extra central government support of up to 2.5% of their budget. The revised financial régime also includes a three-year planning period and a limit on the annual changes in the grant in an attempt to produce more predictability and stability. Figure 1.2 shows the sources of revenue and expenditures by economic category for local government in England, 2008–9.

Of total spending of £160 billion, specific grants account for £57.9 billion, or 36%. This is not a measure of the degree of central government policy control, but it is an indication of financial control. Council tax, the only local tax available to local authorities, and the redistributed non-domestic rate (NNDR in Figure 1.2), a tax on local businesses that is set nationally and then distributed to local authorities, each accounted for 13% of revenues in 2008–9.

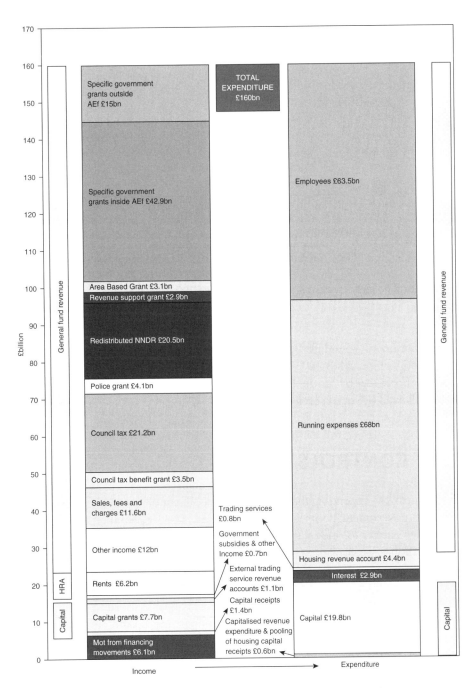

Figure 1.2 Local government revenue and expenditure, England 2008–9 (AEF = Aggregate External Finance)

Source: 'Local Government Financial Statistics, England', No. 20, 2010, National Statistics/Department of Communities and Local Government, p. 2

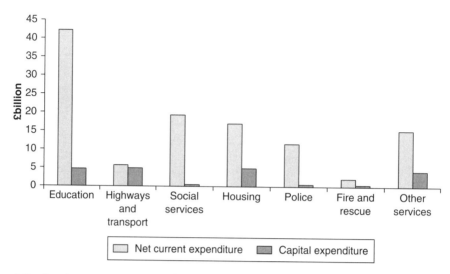

Figure 1.3   Local government expenditure on services 2008–9

The distribution of spending by service is shown in Figure 1.3 – Local government expenditure on services 2008–9.[14]

Figure 1.3 shows that by far the biggest local authority service, measured by spending, is education, followed by social services and housing.

DIRECT CONTROLS

As well as control over spending there are many aspects of policy and management through which central government controls local authorities. The legislation forcing competition determined the answer to one of the questions any organisation has to ask: how much of what we do should we consider contracting out? Changes in education legislation determined the proportion of the budget that education authorities can spend on activities other than that which goes on inside schools. Planning controls have been weakened by a process of upholding a greater proportion of appeals against local authority planning decisions. House building by local authorities has virtually stopped and housing management is subject to outsourcing.[15]

These direct controls have affected the way in which local authorities are managed. As individual departments and services are to a large extent controlled by regulations, managers have low discretion and are increasingly concerned with implementing national policies rather than managing the interface between local politicians and their organisations. In turn this leads to fragmentation of decision-making within the authorities.

Overall allocation of resources among the services is still subject to some local discretion. While SSAs are published for each service, these figures are only indicative. Within services decisions are circumscribed and this means that there is a reduced possibility for overall planning and management of the organisation as a corporate whole, which in any case is fragmented as a result of outsourcing. Contracts operate for a variety of services, whether they are carried out by the private sector or an in-house team. The contracting process makes the contracted parts relatively independent and subject to specific constraints. For example, if there is a five-year contract which specifies how a service is to be delivered, it is difficult to make any fundamental decisions about that service until the contract is up for renewal. The competition process also sets constraints. If the price for the contract is set through competition, management must ensure that costs are at or below the contract price. This has implications for staffing levels, wage and salary levels and, often, conditions of service: some of the major areas of managerial discretion are therefore dictated by the market, itself created by legislation and regulations.

Quangos and corporations

Quango, or quasi-non-governmental public body, is a term used to define those public bodies which are not elected, which are technically independent but whose members are appointed either directly or indirectly by government.

The Cabinet Office defined one category of such organisations: 'A non-departmental public body is a body which has a role in the processes of national government, but is not a government department or part of one, and accordingly operates to a greater or lesser extent at arm's length from Ministers'.[16] They include 211 executive Non-Departmental Public Bodies (NDPBs), 458 advisory NDPBs and 42 tribunals. As well as these, the category of quango includes 26 NHS bodies and 861 NDPBs, none of which are elected, plus school boards of governors (about one thousand grant maintained schools, accountable to the Department for Education (DfE)) and the 650 boards of further and higher education colleges and universities. Around 21,000 people are appointed to these non-elected bodies.

In many cases the quango is legally established as a company but carries out functions which would otherwise have been carried out by a department or by local authorities. Housing Action Trusts refurbish housing and estates. The use of companies for these functions has eroded local democracy in the sense that people are appointed rather than elected; it also fragments the actions taken by the state at local level since each body carries out its own mandate.

These arrangements have important implications for managers. One results from the authority and accountability of board members. Local authority members are directly elected and have a legitimacy as a result. Paid officials are accountable to them and understand where responsibility for decisions lies. Similarly the relationship between civil servants and ministers may cause occasional problems but generally people understand who is responsible for what. When working for an appointed board, the relationships are not so clear. Board members may be removed by ministers, for example, so a manager must take account of the minister's wishes as well as the board's. In some cases the boards are very part-time, so their relationship with the managers is not hierarchical, as between a company board and company managers: it can be more advisory with the paid managers having most of the power. Some school boards have this relationship with head teachers.

There is another form of organisation, the Public Corporation, governed by a Board. The most visible of these is the British Broadcasting Corporation.

HOLLOW STATE?

Theoreticians have suggested that there have been such fundamental changes to the scale, structure and function of the state that it needs to be defined in new ways. One stream of thought (for example Bob Jessop)[17] speaks of the 'hollowing out' of the state, whereby the state has contracted out many of its activities and withdrawn from others, and so is a hollow replica of its former self. Others speak of the transition from the 'welfare state' or the 'Keynesian welfare state' to the 'regulatory state'[18] where the state has shrunk to a set of regulators of activities previously carried out by the state and now done by private companies.

While there is some insight to be gained from these propositions, an examination of the scale and scope of the public sector suggests that the state is very much still in existence, still providing services and still employing people. Taking the public sector as a whole, employment stood at about 6 million at the end of 2010,[19] or around 20% of a total employed population of 29 million. UK public employment in 1989 was 5.3 million, so the trend is upwards not downwards, even after the Coalition's attempt to cut back the size of the state. As we look in detail at the way in which the various parts of the public sector are managed, we will see that there have been changes over the years, that there has been increased use of contracting and outsourcing, and the development of a regulatory regime for the privatised sectors. Talk of the death of the state, in these circumstances, seems premature. However, there are regulatory activities and interactions between the government and the private sector which form important elements of public management, more so than when the welfare state was designed 60 years ago.

CONCLUSIONS

We have seen that the public sector in the United Kingdom has a large number of varied institutions, and that the forms of organisation are different in each of the constituent countries. Governments have used structural reorganisation as a way of trying to bring about change, especially in the NHS and the Civil Service. These changes have important implications for managers in the public sector as they have to respond frequently not just to new structures but to new governance arrangements.

Further reading

June Burnham and Robert Piper, *Britain's Modernised Civil Service*. (London: Palgrave Macmillan, 2008). A history of the process and structural changes in the UK Civil Service.

Russell Deacon and Alan Sandry, *Devolution in the United Kingdom* (Edinburgh: Edinburgh University Press, 2007). Looks at the process of devolution and the impact on policy differences in the devolved administrations.

Christopher Ham, *Health Policy in Britain* (London: Palgrave Macmillan, 2009). Christopher Ham has been a lifelong student of health policy and organisation in the UK.

David Wilson and Chris Game, *Local Government in the United Kingdom* (London: Palgrave Macmillan, 2011). Analysis of the politics and organisation of local government.

DISCUSSION TOPICS

- Why are certain activities and services in the public sector and others in the private sector?
- Why do governments keep trying to make structural changes to the public sector?
- Are local authorities autonomous bodies?

NOTES

1 Prescriptions are free in Wales and Northern Ireland.
2 Scotland Act, 1998, Schedule 5.
3 Government of Wales Act, 2006, Schedule 5.
4 Northern Ireland Act, 1998, Schedule 2 Excepted Matters, Schedule 3 Reserved Matters.
5 National Audit Office, *Reorganising Central Government*, HC 452 Session 2009–2010 (2010).
6 National Audit Office, 2011, 'National Health Service Landscape Review', HC 708, Session 2010–11.
7 For details of government bodies and their functions, go to *Public Bodies*, published periodically by the Cabinet Office. Figures here come from the 2009 edition.
8 Office for National Statistics, Civil Service Statistics, accessed March 2010.
9 1991 Civil Service Order in Council extended departmental and agency responsibilities for staff to 95% of recruitment; 1992 Civil Service (Management Functions) Act gave delegated authority to Agencies and office holders in charge of departments.
10 Sources: NHS The Information Centre, *Monthly Statistics*, February 2011; NHS Scotland Information Services; Welsh Assembly 2010 *Health Statistics Wales;* Department of Health, Social Services and Public Safety, Northern Ireland, 2010.
11 Subject to the 2011 proposed further reorganisation in England.

12 Source: Royal College of General Practitioners Information Sheet No. 8 (2004) *The Structure of the NHS*.

13 Office for National Statistics, Statistical Bulletin *Public Sector Employment*, December 2010.

14 Source: *Local Government Financial Statistics England, No. 20, 2010*, Communities and Local Government/ National Statistics, p. 3.

15 The choice has a measure of local democratic control – tenants can vote for outsourcing or to stay with local authority management.

16 Cabinet Office Agencies and Public Bodies Team, 2005, *Public Bodies* 2005, Norwich: HMSO, p. vi.

17 Robert Jessop (2002), *The Future of the Capitalist State*. Cambridge: Polity Press.

18 For example, Mick Moran (2003), *The British Regulatory State*. Oxford: Oxford University Press; Roger King (2007), *The Regulatory State in an Age of Governance*. London: Palgrave Macmillan.

19 Ibid.

CHAPTER 2
Politics and the Public Sector

SUMMARY

This chapter asks whether there are significant differences among political parties with regard to the role and functioning of the public sector in the UK. It finds that while there is a broad consensus on the basic role of the state there are differences about its scale, relative to the private sector, and about the extent to which the state can solve society's problems. At their root, these differences reflect fundamental differences about individualism versus collectivism, but these are often masked by pragmatism in the case of social issues on the one hand and fiscal realities on the other. Differences can also be found in attitudes towards the market and the degree to which the state should be centralised or decentralised. The Coalition government has declared itself both pro-market and decentralist, using the slogan 'Big Society'.

LEARNING POINTS

- There are still political differences about the public sector, although they cannot necessarily be defined in terms of 'left' and 'right'.
- Devolution has opened the field to a variety of policies, no longer restricted to differences within Westminster.
- It is difficult to distinguish clearly policies that result from political principle and those that result from pragmatism.

POLITICAL DIFFERENCES

The main parties that currently send representatives to the House of Commons, Scottish Parliament and the Northern Ireland and Welsh Assemblies come from different political traditions and histories. While nationalist parties have national independence or autonomy as their foundation, they also have positions on policy, the role of the state, the place the public sector has in society. The differences among the English parties may seem small to an outsider, but they also have their foundations in different ideas about the relationship between the state and society. The Liberal Democrats might claim inheritance of the origins of the welfare state, while the Labour Party was certainly important to its consolidation and development after the Second World War. The Conservative party has had its various wings, from 'one nation', emphasising solidarity, to variations of the right wing position downplaying state action and preferring individualism, markets and low taxes. Within all the major parties there are differences and factions with a variety of attitudes and policies towards the public sector.

Many policies are commonly supported across parties, so to understand the difference that politics makes to the scope, shape and management of the public sector it is necessary first to identify what the differences in approach have been. For example, although the programme of privatisation of nationalised industries and public utilities was first set out by Conservatives, it was pursued with equal vigour by Labour governments. The gradual introduction of private companies providing services to and within the NHS, the use of the Private Finance Initiative to finance hospital and school building, the completion of the privatisation of the railway were all carried out under Labour but would have fitted into Conservative policy had that party been in power. We need to ask whether there are clear political differences in principle in policies towards the public sector among the major parties.

One example of policy differences is how higher education should be funded. When the Liberal Democrats' manifesto for the 2010 General Election proposed abolishing University tuition fees, it was following a path already set by the Scottish Nationalists for Scottish students, a path later followed by Plaid Cymru for students from Wales. Tuition fees had been introduced by the Blair government in 1998 and progressively increased from £1,000 per year to £3,290, reflecting a policy stance by Labour that an increasing proportion of higher education funding should come from student fees, which would be progressively increased. Their increase to a maximum of £9,000 per year by the Coalition government in 2010 represented an acceleration of the process. Prior to the election, those in favour of funding through fees included Labour and Conservatives, those against included Plaid Cymru, the Liberal Democrats and the Scottish Nationalists.

Another difference has been policy towards poverty. The Labour governments had explicit anti-poverty strategies, including a strategy for child poverty. The minimum wage, working family tax credits and Sure Start were all explicitly targeted at reducing poverty, with set targets for the number of children living below a defined poverty line. While the Conservative Party claims a concern for the welfare of every citizen, it is unlikely to have poverty reduction as a central policy aim, with an explicit set of policy instruments designed to implement it, although it does have explicit policies on service delivery to poor people.

Another discernible difference concerns the way that the performance of the public sector should be managed. The Scottish Nationalists and the Labour parties in Wales and England were comfortable with target setting, explicit agreements with civil service and local authorities about outcomes expected, and about the incentives to achieving those targets. The Coalition has been less keen on explicit targets and on performance measurement in general.

THE ROLE OF THE STATE

One important set of differences concerns fundamental questions about the preferred role of the state in society and the relationship between the citizen and the state. Historically there is an identifiable European tradition of some version of social democracy, whereby an agreement is reached by government, the owners of business and the representatives of workers on the role of the state in social welfare and labour protection, on the scale and use of taxation and on the management of the macro economy by government. While the agreement varied in its degree of formality in different European states, and varied in the exact shape of the institutions created to enact the agreements, there has been a discernible 'European' state, stretching from North to South, that is distinct from the shape of the state on other continents. It includes some form of social protection, against unemployment and sickness, organised and delivered through the state or state-backed institutions. It also involves a process of policy-making that includes consultation with and participation by those affected by policies and a degree of respect for entitlements, both of citizens and state employees. The organisational forms vary, especially the relative roles of national, provincial and municipal governments, with different degrees of delegation or decentralisation in different states. On this dimension, the UK is at the centralised end of the scale.

Within this overall state form, there have been political differences that have been definable on a spectrum from 'right' to 'left', the right preferring small state, low taxation, low levels of regulation and public services, the left taking a more interventionist approach, willing to tax and spend a higher proportion of GDP, and taking the side of the workers more than the employers, but all within a narrowly defined range of policy options. The left is normally represented by socialist or social democratic parties, the right by a variety of conservative, Christian democrat and centre-right parties.

It is argued by some commentators that it is no longer possible to detect a left–right dividing line with respect to the role of the state in society, especially after the collapse of communism in Eastern Europe. For example: 'The old certainties, in which the left–right dichotomy was largely based around attitudes towards the state, are gone.'[1] This view, including its more grand version, 'The End of History',[2] in which Francis Fukuyama took the view that ideological debate came to an end with the triumph of 'liberal democracy' after the fall of communism, says that all debate about the relative merits of the state and the market have come to an end and there is some form of 'liberal consensus' about what is the rightful role of the state and the limits to government actions. This position claimed that the similarities would outweigh the differences between political parties, which would converge on a consensus.

The financial crisis of 2008 marked, at least, a gap in the argument: if the state was to keep out of the legitimate sphere of the private sector, it would not have rescued, and in many cases taken into public ownership, failed banks. If the state had been properly pursuing its consensually agreed policies of economic regulation, the banks would not have collapsed in the first place. While the banks were to be returned to private ownership as soon as possible, the old dichotomy of 'minimal state' and 'interventionist state' was put under stress by the banking crisis. The subsequent fiscal crisis and the correction of the deficit allowed an argument about the speed of correction, but not about the need for a (more) balanced budget.

We will see in Chapter 3 that the size of the state, at least measured by the proportion of national product channelled through it, is subject to variation. These variations are partly a product of the scale of economic growth – growth generates increased revenue if tax rates are held steady – and partly a result of political preference, and willingness to tax and spend at particular levels.

At its extreme, the definition of the difference in attitude is that there is a choice between collectivism as a value exercised through state institutions, public services and regulation and individualism exercised through the market and individual choices. The collectivists try to solve problems such as the need for healthcare or the prevalence of unemployment through state intervention of one sort or another.

There are many forms that collectivism can take, such as mutually-owned banks, the pooling of risk by the purchase of insurance or membership of civil society organisations. State provision is only one option for the collectivisation of risk. There are those who argue that collectivism is a form of 'social contract', through which the state will provide security and a range of benefits in exchange for adherence to the law and a commitment to pay taxes. Historically, such a contract has become more explicit at times of crisis, whether economic or military. In Britain there was never a completely explicit 'deal' such as those agreed in some other European countries, although the establishment of the institutions of the British welfare state post-World War Two, such as the National Health Service, the National Assistance Act and the Education Act, was done in a spirit of explicit bargaining about benefits, financing and the co-operation of the organised workers with regard to pay and conditions of work.

Individualists would argue that in principle almost everything the state does, from compensation to the unemployed, to healthcare and education, could be provided either through the market, or through non-state collective actions. In practice many people, including Members of Parliament, would prefer these forms of provision to state-provided, tax-funded insurance and services. From this view, the state should adopt a minimal necessary set of functions and the minimum possible cost to the tax payer. Proponents of such a view refer back to the writings of Hayek[3] who believed that the market and private arrangements were not only economically superior to state provision, but also morally superior. Margaret Thatcher, Prime Minister from 1979 to 1990, represented this view.

While institutions were created and legislation passed immediately after World War Two, many of the elements of the welfare state were in place for working-class people before the war, including a state social security system, means tested access to secondary education and a national health insurance scheme. What happened in the period from the mid-1940s was that these benefits and services became universal. This meant that contributions were no longer voluntary and that the middle classes gained access to services now provided by the state, which they had previously funded from savings or insurance. To ensure universality, services were largely controlled by the central government rather than left to local institutions and organisations.

There may have been general agreement that the welfare state was a good idea, especially from those who benefited from it, which included most of the population. There is no doubt that the returning soldiers and others who had lived through the war were keen for a form of state and welfare provision which would prevent a return to the deprivation of the Depression. However, the welfare state was not without its opponents. Howard Glennerster[4] has shown that there has always been a right-wing group in the Conservative Party opposed to universal benefits and tax-funded services. The Conservative administration elected in 1951 reduced income tax, cut education spending, introduced prescription charges in the NHS and reduced NHS staffing levels. Differences of opinion about the right scale and scope of the state have persisted both between and within parties ever since. The Conservative governments led by Margaret Thatcher proclaimed that they wanted to reduce the scale and scope of the state. The Labour governments elected from 1997 set about from 2000 growing the scale of the state, not by adding new services but by spending more on education, the health service, the criminal justice system and on social security. As within the Conservative party there have always been divergent views on the preferred scale of the state, so the Labour Party has contained different views. One of the symbolic changes to Labour policy that marked its 'modernisation' was its rejection of its founding belief in nationalisation.

After the end of the Labour run of governments it was difficult to determine whether the argument, or the majority, has swung over to the 'small state' position. The spending cuts announced in the last Labour budget of March 2010 and the first Coalition budget of June 2010 were broadly similar in their plan to reduce the deficit, albeit the Coalition's plan was to reduce the deficit more quickly. There were clearly members of the Coalition government whose preference was for a smaller state, whatever the state of the public finances, but it was not possible to distinguish financial expediency from principle in the spending and taxation decisions.

THE THIRD WAY

When Tony Blair, Gordon Brown and Peter Mandelson led the 'modernisation' of the Labour Party, they sought to distance themselves and the party from its previous positions on the desirability of public ownership and to some degree on the boundary between the public and the private sectors. Not wishing to present the change as simply a swing to the right, they began to speak of a 'Third Way', and had their sound-bite phrase backed up by respectable academics, especially Anthony Giddens, the sociologist.[5]

In 1998 Prime Minister Tony Blair published a Fabian pamphlet called *The Third Way: New Politics for the New Century*. Social Democrats in Europe and the then Democratic President of the USA proclaimed that they represented a new type of politics, leaving behind old definitions of left and right. This was not the old Third Way between capitalism and communism but a new Third Way. As Blair explained: 'The Third Way is not an attempt to split the difference between right and left. It is about traditional values in a changed world. And it draws vitality from uniting the two great streams of left-of-centre thought – democratic socialism and liberalism.'

What this meant in practice was that policies could be picked from a fairly narrow menu without the prejudice of principles. If a market solution looks acceptable, then it is based on the good parts of liberal individualism. If public spending is required, for example to reduce child poverty, then the decision is based on the socially responsible parts of social democracy.

Mr. Blair continued:

> My politics are rooted in a belief that we can only realise ourselves as individuals in a thriving civil society, comprising strong families and civic institutions buttressed by intelligent government… In recent decades, responsibility and duty were the preserve of the right. They are no longer, and it was a mistake for them ever to become so.

The idea that public services and benefits, as supported by the old Left, were responsible for a decline in individual responsibility and duty is broadly similar to the Conservative Party's line that council estates create unemployment and crime. It certainly has the same results in practice in the social security system and the attitude to the management and ownership of public housing.

THE BIG SOCIETY

David Cameron carried on with much the same strand of political thought, although rebranded with a new label, the 'Big Society'. The idea was included in the Conservative Party manifesto[6] for the 2010 general election:

> The size, scope and role of government in the UK has reached a point where it is now inhibiting, not advancing, the progressive aims of reducing poverty, fighting inequality, and increasing general well-being. We can't go on pretending that government has all the answers. Our alternative to big government is the Big Society: a society with much higher levels of personal, professional, civic and corporate responsibility; a society where people come together to solve problems and improve life for themselves and their communities; a society where the leading force for progress is social responsibility, not state control. The Big Society runs consistently through our policy programme. Our plans to reform public services, mend our broken society, and rebuild trust in politics are all part of our Big Society agenda. These plans involve redistributing power from the state to society; from the centre to local communities, giving people

the opportunity to take more control over their lives…. Our public service reform programme will enable social enterprises, charities and voluntary groups to play a leading role in delivering public services and tackling deep-rooted social problems. We will strengthen and support social enterprises to help deliver our public service reforms by creating a Big Society Bank,7 funded from unclaimed bank assets, to provide new finance for neighbourhood groups, charities, social enterprises and other nongovernmental bodies... (p. 37)

In a speech in March 2010, David Cameron claimed that the Big Society idea was central to the party's political offer:

Throughout the past four and a half years, I have consistently argued for, and developed policies to bring about, a shift from state to society in tackling our most stubborn social problems. Big society – that's not just two words. It is a guiding philosophy – a society where the leading force for progress is social responsibility, not state control. It includes a whole set of unifying approaches – breaking state monopolies, allowing charities, social enterprises and companies to provide public services, devolving power down to neighbourhoods, making government more accountable. And it's the thread that runs consistently through our whole policy programme – our plans to reform public services, mend our broken society, and rebuild trust in politics.

In practice, the Big Society idea was not very prominent in the 2010 election campaign and David Cameron had to spend a lot of time explaining and defending it after the election. It was a difficult task during a period when the public sector budget was being cut, including subsidies, grants and contracts for the voluntary sector: promoting the voluntary sector as a viable alternative to state provision seemed to be a central part of the Big Society idea. 'Big Society' was offered as a principle to support cuts in state-run services, transfer of service provision from the state to other providers, transfer of powers from local authorities to 'communities', denigrate the integrity, motives and performance of public servants and to distance government from the institutions of the state.

Some commentators have found it difficult to distinguish the differences between the 'Third Way' and the 'Big Society'. Samuel Brittan, writing in October 2010 in *Financial World*, said:

When I hear about 'the Big Society' I have some difficulty in remembering whether it comes from Tony Blair or David Cameron. This is not entirely unfair. Cameron was a professed admirer of the former Labour Prime Minister and tried to borrow some of his methods to revitalise the Conservatives. But in truth of course Blair called his approach 'The Third Way'.8 The similarity between the two ideas lies mostly in what they are against: monolithic state organisations; a monopoly of service provision by state-owned organisations and state employees; uniform services; top-down approaches to planning and service delivery. The practical agreement between the Labour and Conservative parties' policies extended to the use of competition between providers for the right to deliver public services, including promoting private sector providers in healthcare; both parties have their ways of detaching individual institutions, especially schools and hospitals, from direct hierarchical governance; both emphasise individual choice as part of the process of delivering public services.

A CENTRALISED OR DECENTRALISED STATE?

Another set of differences is about the degree to which the state should be centralised or decentralised. Constitutional change to allow degrees of autonomy for Scotland, Wales and Northern Ireland was vigorously pursued by the Labour governments from 1997. The process has resulted in significant differences in institutions and policies in each of the countries of the United Kingdom, and in different parties in power. In England the Coalition government proclaimed itself in favour of what it called 'localism', by which it meant the expansion of autonomy from government control of local authorities in England. In practice this did not extend to fiscal autonomy, to the relaxation of 'ring-fenced' budgets for particular services or relaxation of central policy controls.

In both Scotland and Wales, there are explicit agreements between government and local authorities, including agreed service targets expressed as outcomes. Local authorities are subject to central financial constraints in both countries. In Northern Ireland, partly because of repeated suspensions, the central administration has yet to develop mature autonomy. The proposal to extend political devolution to the English regions through regional parliaments was abandoned after the first candidate was rejected in a local referendum.

The Coalition government weakened the regional government presence as part of its cost-cutting from 2010. England as a whole has no equivalent to the elected bodies and relatively autonomous government arrangements of the other countries, nor does there seem to be any political will to create any English institutions.

There seemed to be a consensus among the parties at Westminster for a combination of devolution to Scotland, Wales and Northern Ireland but not to England, and for a comparatively centralised state machinery, both within England and the other nations, with regard to local government. Then the Coalition published its 'Localism' Bill in December 2010, which seemed to suggest the government was in favour of much greater decentralisation. The Bill covered housing as well as local government issues and the local government clauses included:

- giving councils a general power of competence
- allowing councils to choose to return to the committee system of governance and allowing for referenda for elected mayors in certain authorities

- abolishing the Standards Board regime and the model code of conduct, and introducing local accountability and a criminal offence of deliberate failure to declare a personal interest in a matter
- giving residents the power to instigate local referenda on any local issue and the power to veto excessive council tax increases
- allowing councils more discretion over business rate relief
- providing new powers to help save local facilities and services threatened with closure, and giving voluntary and community groups the right to challenge local authorities over their services.

On the face of it the Bill seemed to mark a break with previous centralised policies. Advocates of local autonomy had for many years been arguing for a general competence power to enable local authorities to do things without the permission of central government.

However, a report by the House of Commons Communities and Local Government Committee expressed some scepticism about the real shift in power from the centre. Some witnesses who gave evidence thought that the Bill was simply a way of transferring responsibility for the cuts in expenditure to divert attention from the government. In any case the rhetoric surrounding the Bill was not just about the relationship between central and local government, but also about devolution beyond local government to the 'community', as part of the Big Society idea. The committee was doubtful about the prospect:

> The Government must be wary of assuming that decentralisation will reduce public sector costs in the short or medium term. It should not be quick to declare localism a failed experiment if efficiency savings do not instantly materialise. Indeed, the chances of localism transforming the way the country is governed may be hampered at the outset by a lack of resources to prime the pump by building community capacity. Localism is a goal worth pursuing no matter what the fiscal circumstances, but realism is needed about how fundamental change will be achieved without resources to support it.[9]

It is too early to assess the full extent of real decentralisation, but the signs are that the government will keep its grip on what happens locally. In addition to the functions overseen by the Department of Communities and Local Government, other departments' programmes, especially the Department for Work and Pensions policies and services for unemployed people, remain firmly centrally planned and controlled, and delivered locally through centrally-managed contracts.

POLITICS AND MANAGEMENT: VALUES

Detailed choices about management arrangements also reflect political values. In Part Two we discuss the different control mechanisms that are used in the public sector, which are underpinned by attitudes to trust, to professionalism and to the motivation of people who work in the public sector. The Labour governments adopted what has been termed a 'managerialist' attitude to public sector work. All parts of the public sector were subjected to targets, measurement, incentives and inspection and audits, in an attempt by government to control individual behaviours across the public sector. In addition, many services were subject to competition, through which both price and quality of services would be checked against alternative suppliers. This twin approach, top-down control on the one hand and competition on the other, reveals a low-trust attitude to the people employed in public institutions.

The Coalition had two major elements of policy towards the public sector: the fiscal policy, reversing Labour's growth in spending; and structural changes, introducing a Thatcher-style set of neo-liberal proposals introducing privatisation and competition, in a more radical way even than the Blair–Brown governments had planned. The first of these was the proposed reorganisation of the National Health Service. As we saw in the first chapter, for the NHS, reorganisation is a permanent state, the paint barely dry on the new signs before they are painted over again with new institutions and new arrangements. The 2011 plan was radical in the sense that it introduced the idea that 'any willing provider' would be allowed to bid for healthcare contracts which would be regulated by 'normal' European competition law: open to any European company to bid; regulated by a body with the same functions as those operating in power and water. In other words, the provision of healthcare was to be treated like any other regulated market, albeit funded by government expenditure.

This approach, of opening up competition to all comers, was also planned for the rest of the public sector. In February 2011, David Cameron made a series of speeches in which he called for the introduction of more competition, and giving companies an automatic right to bid for public service delivery contracts. This was billed as an effort to stop the public sector monopoly on service provision (a monopoly which had been broken down already in 1980 by the Thatcher administration). The speeches trailed the release of a White paper, 'Open Public Services'. This White Paper blamed continuing inequalities in educational attainment, health outcomes and life expectancy on the centralised approach to public service provision. It proposed five principles for the changes it proposed:

- 'Wherever possible we will increase choice.
- Public services should be decentralised to the lowest appropriate level.
- Public services should be open to a range of providers.
- We will ensure fair access to public services.
- Public services should be accountable to users and to taxpayers.'[10]

In practical proposals, the White Paper mostly extended previous policies of the Labour governments with calls for more choice of service provider, more competition, equity of access to services, decentralised management and accountability through publication of data. Where there were new ideas, they consisted of the extension of 'payment by results' in service contracting (while making caveats about how new providers were to fund their entry into a payment-by-results market), the encouragement of mutual organisations to take over public

services under contract, the extension of personal budgets to the health sector, a~
tion of a right to make an offer to provide public services, the 'Community Right t~

Some of the ideas seemed to be designed to take care of services that wo~ because of the budget cuts: the 'Community Right to Buy' 'will enable loc~ community organisations to have a fair chance to bid to take over land and buildings that ar~ important to them, such as their village shop or last remaining pub, their community centre, children's centre or library' (p. 25). All of these proposals were put out for consultation.

The role of the central state in this decentralised system was defined in much the same way as before: setting standards, licensing and registering providers, regulation and financing the services.

The Coalition government's programme contained a commitment to enable alternative forms of ownership, including mutuals, to provide public services. The commitment had mostly been made in the Conservative Party manifesto for the 2010 election:

> We value the work of those employed in our public services, and a Conservative government will work with them to deliver higher productivity and better value for money for taxpayers. We will raise public sector productivity by increasing diversity of provision, extending payment by results and giving more power to consumers. Giving public sector workers ownership of the services they deliver is a powerful way to drive efficiency, so we will support co-operatives and mutualisation as a way of transferring public assets and revenue streams to public sector. We will encourage (workers) … to come together to form employee-led co-operatives and bid to take over the services they run. This will empower millions of public sector workers to become their own boss and help them to deliver better services – the most significant shift in power from the state to working people since the sale of council houses in the 1980s.[11]

CONCLUSION: THE END OF CONSENSUS?

We will see in Chapter 3 that the deficit was not entirely caused by the financial crisis and the subsequent loss of tax revenues, because the Labour Government had not implemented its policy of maintaining a balanced budget 'over the economic cycle'. The trend to growth in public spending from 1999 to 2008 indicates a willingness to spend on healthcare and education, and on the civil service and welfare programmes to pursue objectives about public service standards and the volume and quality of healthcare and education.

It is difficult to distinguish the Coalition's policies that are designed to reduce the deficit and those that represent a thoroughly different view of the role, scale, functions and organising principles of the public sector. In times of balanced budgets, a decision to cut 20–25% from departments' spending plans would have been seen as ideologically-driven, more extreme even than the efforts to roll back the state by the 1979 government: with a deficit to be managed and cut, the reductions in spending could be seen as pragmatic rather than political.

Perhaps there never was a consensus about the scale and scope of the state, and there is still a divide between the main English parties about the issue. Certainly the SNP has different ideas about state intervention in the economy, and the role of fiscal policy in exiting recession. After all, it seems that the end of the left–right divide has yet to happen.

Further reading

Tim Bale, *The Conservative Party from Thatcher to Cameron* (Cambridge: Polity Press, 2011).
Matt Cole, *Political Parties in Britain* (Edinburgh: Edinburgh University Press, 2011).
James Mitchell, Lynne Bennie, and Rob Johns, *The Scottish National Party: Transition to Power* (Oxford: Oxford University Press, 2011).
Andrew Rawnsley, *The End of the Party* (London: Vintage, 2010). The years of Labour party in government.
Alan Sandry, *Plaid Cymru: an Ideological Analysis* (Cardiff: Welsh Academic Press, 2011). An analysis of the range of ideologies in the Welsh nationalist party, in addition to its nationalism.

DISCUSSION POINTS

- What are the ideological roots of policy differences towards the public sector?
- Do individualism and collectivism mean different policies towards the role and scope of the state?
- Are markets the best way to manage the provision of public services?

NOTES

1 Simon Griffiths (2009) 'The Public Services under Gordon Brown: Same reforms, less money', *Policy Studies*, 30, 1: 53–67, p. 56.
2 Francis Fukuyama, *The End of History and the Last Man* (London: Penguin, 1992).
3 Friedrich Hayek, *The Road to Serfdom* (London: Routledge, 1944).
4 Howard Glennerster, *British Social Policy Since 1945* (Oxford: Blackwell, 1995).
5 Antony Giddens, *Third Way: The Renewal of Social Democracy* (Cambridge: Polity Press, 1998).
6 'Invitation to Join the Government of Britain: The Conservative Manifesto', 2010.
7 The 'Big Society Bank' was an idea recycled from the previous government to tap the funds left unclaimed in unused bank accounts.
8 www. samuelbrittan.co.uk/
9 House of Commons Communities and Local Government Committee, 'Localism', third report session 2010–12, p. 32.
10 Ibid., p. 6.
11 Conservative Party Manisfesto 2010, p. 27.

CHAPTER 3
Public Spending

SUMMARY

This chapter is about the 'envelope' of total public spending. Macro-economic policy is made up of monetary and fiscal policy instruments and is both about maintaining growth and stability and about finding the resources for public services and transfers. It looks at the history of public spending from the 1960s and how spending varies with the economic cycle. There is then a description of how the money is spent, on different policy areas, and where the money comes from.

   It then discusses the differences in opinions about how fiscal policy can affect the economy and whether fiscal policy can influence the economic cycle, and goes on to describe how policy was played out between 1997 and 2010, a period that included both a large growth in the volume of spending on public services and the economic crisis from 2008.

LEARNING POINTS

- The economic cycle has a major impact on the amount of taxes collected and on fiscal policy.
- The big areas of growth in public spending in the past decade have been health, education and social protection.
- Income tax and national insurance account for 45% of government revenues.
- Public expenditure per head is higher in Scotland, Wales and Northern Ireland than in England.
- The financial crisis of 2008–9 was not the sole cause of the fiscal deficit.

THE MACRO-ECONOMIC POLICY CONTEXT

While government spending is directed at all the particular objectives of each programme, the aggregate of spending and of taxation and borrowing is heavily influenced by the macro-economic context. Economic growth generates growth in the tax revenues available, recession automatically reduces the tax available and increases the expenditure on transfer payments. Interest rates set the cost of new government borrowing. The rate of inflation will affect the quantity of public services that can be provided for any given amount of money.

The decisions about how much to spend and how much tax to collect in any given year depend very much on the economic cycle. Even if governments believe that they can affect the peaks and troughs of the cycle through their macro-economic policy, none has yet eliminated the cycle. Economic cycles do not generally correspond with electoral cycles. Traditionally, governments aim to make the electorate feel happy before general elections by not taxing them too hard and by spending generously, so budgets tend to be more balanced at the beginning of a term of office than at the end. If this particular cycle is out of synchronisation with the economic cycle, deficits at the end of the term of office may be bigger than they would otherwise have been.

Macro-economic policy has two main policy instruments: monetary policy is about the supply of money in the economy and the interest rates payable on borrowing; fiscal policy is concerned with the overall level of spending and taxation. Money supply is a product of how much money government puts into the economy and how much credit the banks supply. Bank regulation, especially control over the ratio of deposits to loans, is a major instrument of monetary policy. The setting of interest rates is the other important element: in the UK, Bank of England rates are set by the independent Monetary Policy Committee using an inflation rate target as its sole objective. This process allows the government to set the inflation target while delegating the interest rate decision. Whether the committee decision on base rates influences all interest rates depends on how the market reacts to its decisions. Banks and other lenders have to take a view on the premium they will be able to charge above the base rate for different types of loans.

Here we are mainly concerned with fiscal policy, since decisions about the overall level of spending are translated through the budget and medium-term expenditure planning process into the amount of cash available for public services and for transfers. At the highest level, the decision is about how to balance government revenue and government expenditures. A simple rule for government to follow would be always to have a balanced budget: when recession comes and tax revenues fall, then spending would fall in proportion; when growth happens, more tax is collected and spending can expand. Apart from a brief excursion in the 1980s the UK government has never adopted this rule. It has been generally accepted that deficits would occur during recessions and, hopefully, high growth would generate enough tax revenues to pay off some of the borrowings incurred during the recessions.

In the long run, taking one cycle with the next, the policy has generally been either to balance income and expenditure, or to run a small, sustainable deficit that is paid for through growth and inflation.

FISCAL POLICY AND THE ECONOMIC CYCLES

We can now look at the level of public spending over the past four decades. Figure 3.1 shows Total Managed Expenditure from 1964–5 to 2008–09 in real terms.[1]

While showing a steady growth over the period, Figure 3.1 also reveals three periods of accelerated public spending. One leads up to the peak in 1975–76, a growth which led to a deficit that resulted in intervention by the International Monetary Fund which demanded expenditure reductions in return for support. This fiscal crisis occurred under a Labour administration and left a long shadow on the Labour Party, which had to try for many years to regain financial credibility. The second acceleration was the period from 1992 to a peak in 1997, when the government led by John Major was replaced by a Labour administration under Tony Blair. A period of consolidation until 2001 was followed by another acceleration, representing a 50% real terms increase in spending over ten years.

What does this pattern of aggregate spending tell us about fiscal policy? We need to know the impact of the economic cycles over this period. One way of measuring the economic cycle is to estimate the 'output gap', or the difference between the actual output in any given

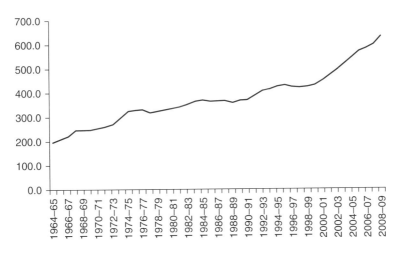

Figure 3.1   Total Managed Expenditure, 1964–65 to 2008–09, £bn at 2008–9 prices

Source: HM Treasury, Public Finances Databank

year and the capacity for output in the economy. In recession years, the output gap is large and negative; in boom years, the economy may be producing at above its trend level, or its apparent potential, producing inflation. Figure 3.2 shows estimates of the output gap from 1976 to 2009. It illustrates that there were low points in 1981, 1992 and 2009, with high points at 1989 and 2000. If you combine the two series, you will see the level of borrowing and debt fluctuates mostly with the stage of the cycle. Figure 3.3 shows the level of net borrowing and the current budget surplus or deficit from 1981.[2]

While there are fluctuations in the rate of growth of spending, the amount of the deficit is largely a result of the fluctuations in economic activity and therefore the call on funds for unemployment and other benefits and the amount of tax collected from incomes, profits and sales.

That is not to say that the level of deficit or surplus is only a function of the level of economic activity: it is also a result of the decisions governments make about spending and taxation. The judgement is partly about forecasting economic growth: spending decisions are made on the basis of future levels of economic growth and therefore tax revenue growth. If forecasts turn out to be optimistic, and growth is less than forecast, the deficit will be higher than anticipated. If the opposite is true, the lucky Chancellor of the Exchequer raises more tax than anticipated and surpluses may occur. As we will see, this happened between

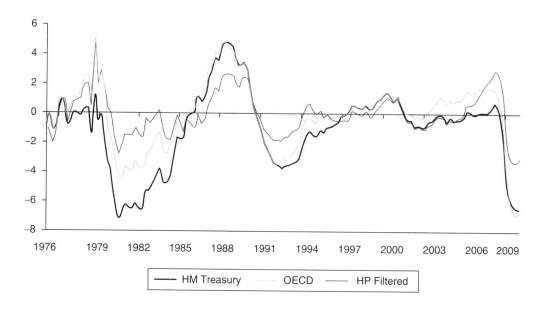

Figure 3.2   The Output Gap 1976–2009

Source: HM Treasury, Public Finances Databank

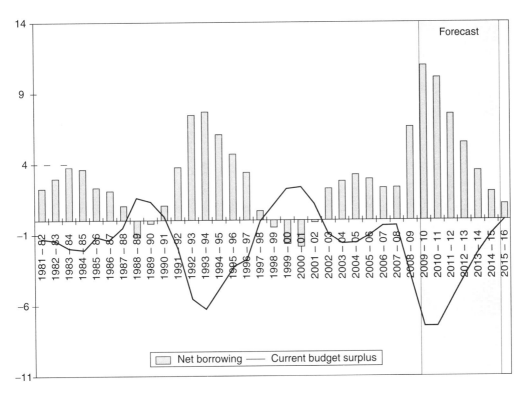

Figure 3.3 Budget surpluses and net borrowing 1981–2015/6

Source: HM Treasury, Public Finances Databank

1999 and 2001, with unanticipated 3% per annum growth creating a current account surplus of £23 billion in 2000–2001. In a period of recession, one policy option is to run a deficit in the hope and expectation that the multiplier effect of the extra spending will stimulate economic growth.

WHAT IS THE MONEY SPENT ON?

Having looked at what has been happening to the total of public spending we now ask the question: what was the money spent on? If we look back over two decades we can see which sectors have grown the most and where the large volumes of spending are. Figure 3.4 shows public expenditure on services, in real terms indexed to 2008–09 price levels in the years 1989–90, 1999–00 and 2009–10.[3]

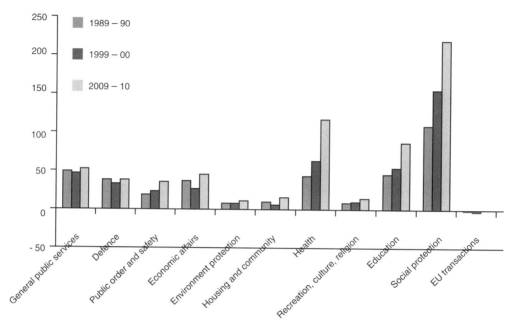

Figure 3.4 Public expenditure on services by function in real terms 1989–90, 1999–00 and 2009–10, £bn

Figure 3.4 shows that the largest two categories, Health and Social Protection, have also been the fastest growing sectors. A breakdown of the social protection expenditures is given in Figure 3.5.

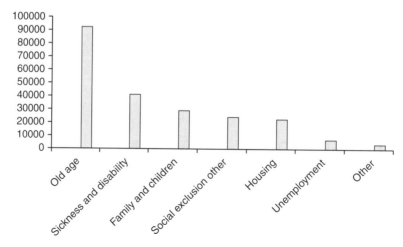

Figure 3.5 Breakdown of Social Protection expenditure 2009–10, £bn current prices (Total = £128,377bn)

Source: Budget 2010.

One distinction worth making is between 'discretionary' and 'non-discretionary' expenditure. Some categories of expenditure are more discretionary than others. Social protection payments are discretionary in the long term but non-discretionary in the short term – once the eligibility criteria have been set and the rates of payment laid down, the government simply has to pay up whatever benefits are legislated for: the state pension is paid to everyone who reaches pensionable age and is entitled within the pension rules. Jobseeker's Allowance will vary with the numbers of people out of work; housing benefit paid will rise and fall according to the incomes of those entitled to it. In the long term, eligibility criteria and generosity of benefits can be varied. Other expenditures are more discretionary: recreation, culture and religion spending is a matter of taste and preference; defence spending is a function of the assessment of threats and ambitions in foreign policy; above a basic level of provision, education expenditure can be varied.

WHERE DOES THE MONEY COME FROM?

Figure 3.6, which is taken from the June 2010 budget, gives the breakdown of government receipts.

Apart from council tax and business rates, all other sources of revenue are directly affected by the business cycle, depending on the volume of economic activity. In any one-year budget period, the level of revenues is a forecast whose accuracy depends on the quality of the economic projections. The taxes imposed and their rates are a matter of political choice. One choice is between progressive taxes, whose impact is proportionately larger on individuals and companies with the highest incomes, and 'flatter' taxes such as

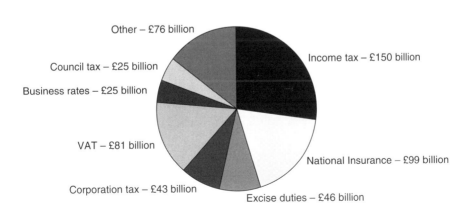

Total receipts: £548 billion

Other – £76 billion
Income tax – £150 billion
Council tax – £25 billion
Business rates – £25 billion
VAT – £81 billion
National Insurance – £99 billion
Corporation tax – £43 billion
Excise duties – £46 billion

Figure 3.6   Government receipts 2010–11

Source: Office for Budget Responsibility, 2010–11 estimates

Value Added Tax. Income Tax, National Insurance and Corporation Tax are all relatively progressive and make up 53% of tax revenues.

PUBLIC SPENDING IN THE DEVOLVED ADMINISTRATIONS

Decisions about the total of public expenditure in Scotland, Wales and Northern Ireland are made in London, using a formula[4] to split departmental expenditure between the countries, with adjustments for differences among the countries, including population density. Once the totals are allocated, there is discretion in the devolved Assemblies, Parliaments, Government and Executive to reallocate the funds among functions according to local priorities. The devolved administrations do not set local tax levels. The application of the formula has resulted in variations in spending per head among the devolved administrations and England. These differences for 2009–10 are shown in Table 3.1.[5]

All three devolved administrations spend more per head than the UK average. How the expenditure decisions are made within the administrations and governments will be addressed in Chapter 5, Managing Public Finances. The important point here is that the devolved administrations do not operate their own fiscal policy, separate from that of the UK government. The Scottish Parliament had not, at the time of writing, used its discretionary power to vary taxes in Scotland. The devolved administrations' budgets consist only of the expenditure side of the equation, in choices about where to spend the allocated moneys.

WHY IS THE LEVEL OF PUBLIC SPENDING IMPORTANT?

The level of public spending and the proportion of the GDP that is collected in tax and spent on transfers and services is a matter of political debate. While contemporary politics lacks the clarity of the distinction between 'left' and 'right' of earlier periods, there are still differences between politicians in their attitudes to taxation and public spending.

The first major difference concerns the question whether the aggregate of public spending and taxation should be a certain proportion of GDP: public spending as a percentage of GDP varies across the world, and some politicians take an ideological position about 'big government'. Some take a moral position that 'we' should be allowed to decide what to do with our money, rather than governments deciding. Others argue that the market is the only

Table 3.1 UK expenditure per head, by function and country 2009–10, £m

	General public services	Defence	Public order and safety	Economic affairs	Environment protection	Housing and community	Health	Rec., culture, religion	Education	Social protection	Total exp. on services
England	121	1	517	604	176	237	1,896	121	1,398	3,487	8,559
Scotland	235	2	541	1,038	246	369	2,066	229	1,511	3,845	10,083
Wales	263	1	541	743	179	188	1,956	198	1,430	4,097	9,597
Northern Ireland	252	0	749	951	137	674	1,881	224	1,531	4,263	10,662
UK	141	1	527	657	181	258	1,913	137	1,413	3,569	8,798

way to allocate resources efficiently and that governments will always make sub-optimal resource allocation decisions. Hence, the larger the relative size of the public sector, the less efficient will be the allocation of resources in the economy as a whole.

In addition to these arguments, there is a view that as states compete for inward investment in a world in which capital flows are free and volatile, the level of taxation is an important competitive factor. High levels of profit tax for companies and income tax for their managers will frighten off investment, as national governments conduct a negative auction to attract investors.

The second major policy debate is whether fiscal policy can be used successfully to mitigate the economic cycle, with a tight fiscal policy used to reduce inflation at the boom end of the cycle and loose fiscal policy with deficits permitted at the bottom of the cycle. Advocates of the use of fiscal policy in this way have been labelled 'Keynesians' after J.M. Keynes, whose *General Theory of Employment, Interest, and Money*[6] challenged the 'classical' economists' analysis that general equilibrium would prevail and that all fluctuations would be smoothed by the free market. Published in 1936, after the Great Depression, the 'General Theory' put forward the idea that people's consumption and savings habits could lead to imbalance between aggregate demand and aggregate supply and by inhibiting investment might prolong the bottom of the cycle. Public works at the bottom were one way of injecting aggregate demand at this point, which would reflate the economy, assuming that the recipients of the payments for the public works spent a proportion of their earnings.

One objection to this practice is the difficulty of knowing where the economy is on the cycle at any time: once the bottom has been identified, it may already have passed and stimulus will cause inflation. If the top of the boom has already passed, tightening fiscal policy may slow the rate of economic growth. There is a further argument about the scale of public spending, which is that public spending 'crowds out' private investment, especially when government borrowing pushes up interest rates, making private investment less profitable. Incidentally Keynes himself recognised this point: 'The method of financing the policy and the increased working cash, required by the increased employment and the associated rise of prices, may have the effect of increasing the rate of interest and so retarding investment in other directions...' (*General Theory*, p. 119).

Those who do not subscribe to the idea that the business cycle can be mitigated by fiscal policy advocate balanced budgets. A variant of this position is that the determinant of the level of price changes is the volume of the money supply, and that the only effective instrument of macro-economic policy is the control of the growth of the money supply, in line with the growth in output. Conservative governments have espoused this idea, but only briefly tried to implement it.

Labour governments after 1997 started their period of office with a tight fiscal policy, resulting in a budget surplus on current account between 1997 and 2001. As we shall see in the next section, this surplus turned into a deficit after 2001 and the deficit grew during the period up to the 2008 crisis.

THE FISCAL CRISIS OF 2008 AND ITS AFTERMATH

The financial crisis from 2008 produced a big drop in aggregate demand as well as big fiscal deficits for governments: most governments decided to try to mitigate the recession with fiscal stimulus and in many cases with a monetary stimulus (mainly governments buying back their own debt with cash). Figure 3.3 showed the UK government's fiscal stimulus in 2008 and 2009. The policy was not without controversy, in the United Kingdom and elsewhere.

The macro-economic context changed dramatically in 2008. As economic activity went into a steep decline, tax revenues fell sharply and the budget deficit rose to 7% of GDP, while net debt rose to over 60% of GDP. It is important to understand how the public finances arrived so quickly at such a bad position: can the collapse of the fiscal position be attributed solely to the world economic crisis or how much can be attributed to fiscal policy (decisions about spending and taxation)?

In the first two financial years, the Labour government implemented the spending plans of the outgoing government, with surpluses on current account and a reduction in the level of outstanding debt. In 2000, the plans changed to a strategy of growth in spending, financed by increased tax revenues generated by economic growth. The government decided to spend more on public services, especially on health[7] and education, and to increase the

Table 3.2   From deficit to surplus to deficit 1997–2009

1997	5-year deficit reduction plan. Borrowing falls by 2% of GDP	**2003**	Deficit for 2002–03 £11.7bn, forecast for 2003–04 £21.3bn
1998	Fiscal tightening of 1% of GDP for 1998–99	**2004**	Deficit forecast for 2004–05 £10.5bn
1999	Current account surplus of £4bn for 1998–99, projected £11bn surplus for 1999–00	**2006**	Deficit forecast for 2005–06 £11.4bn
2000	Announces 2.5% per annum growth in current spending in the following 3 years. Net investment to grow from 0.9% of GDP to 1.8%	**2007**	Deficit forecast for 2006–07 £9.5bn. Spending review forecasts current spending to grow 1.9% per year, net investment to be 2¼% of GDP
2001	Economy grew by 3% in 2000, budget surplus for 2000–01 estimated at £23bn. NHS spending to rise 7% per year to 2007–08	**2008**	Pre-budget report forecasts negative growth. Fiscal stimulus by cutting VAT from 17.5% to 15%, £3bn of capital spend brought forward. 'Golden rule' suspended
2002	Tax receipts for 2001–02 £7.6bn lower than forecast	**2009**	Budget forecasts GDP to shrink 3.5% in 2009. Fiscal stimulus of 0.5% of GDP. Net borrowing £175bn, deficit 9% of GDP

generosity of transfer payments, especially those transfers that targeted child poverty, which was an important priority. At the same time, the government's fiscal policy – sometimes referred to as the 'fiscal stance' – was based on two rules: the 'golden rule' which stated that over an economic cycle government would borrow only to invest and not for current spending; and the 'sustainable investment rule' which stated that public sector net debt as a proportion of GDP should be held at a stable and 'prudent' level. The growth in spending was to be financed out of taxation which in turn was to increase in volume because of high levels of economic growth. The sustainable investment rule was defined as maintaining the level of net public debt at or below 40% of GDP. In 1996–97 the level of net debt was 42.5% of GDP and it was reduced to 29.7% at its lowest point in 2001–02.

From 2002 the planned expansion of public spending, with no borrowing over the economic cycle for current expenditure, was sent off course by a shortfall in taxes below their forecast level. In each subsequent year there was a deficit on current account, and spending grew faster than revenues. This did not represent a Keynesian-style intervention, rather a commitment to increase the volume and quality of public services that was not matched by the growth in revenues. Once the recession came, with negative growth in the economy from 2008, fiscal stimulus was applied to head off the downturn. The stimulus-driven deficit was added to the pre-existing deficit, and the 'golden rule' of no borrowing for current spending over a whole cycle was suspended.[8]

The impact of these changes on the annual change in net borrowing is shown in Figure 3.7.[9]

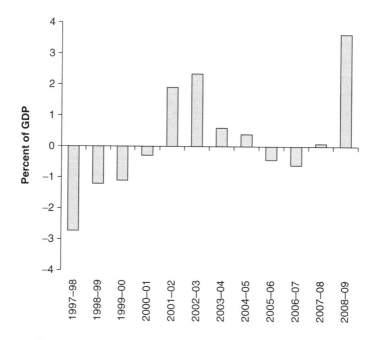

Figure 3.7   Annual change in net borrowing as a % of GDP

Source: Alan Budd, *NIER* No. 212: p. 37

The net change in borrowing of nearly 4% of GDP is mainly the result of the drop in tax revenues because of the swift shrinking of the economy, along with a continuation of the planned growth in public spending. Figure 3.8 shows the change in revenues and spending (excluding the spending on bank rescues). It shows that receipts not only failed to keep up with spending but actually went into decline. It also shows that the level of spending exceeded revenues in all years after 2001.

The Labour government produced its last budget in March 2010. After Labour lost the election in May 2010, the coalition between the Conservatives and the Liberal Democrats took office and produced its own budget in June. This budget proposed to reduce the deficit faster than the March one. The proposed deficit and outstanding debt of the two budgets are reproduced in Table 3.3.

The Labour budget of March 2010 proposed to reduce the deficit to 4.2% of GDP by 2014/15, while the June Coalition budget proposed a reduction to 2.2% by that year. There are agreed targets for both of these numbers in the Stability and Growth Pact, signed in 1997 by member countries of the Euro zone and others to create macro-economic stability in Europe. The targets are a deficit of not more than 3% of GDP and outstanding debt of not more than 60% of GDP. Almost all members of the Euro zone broke these targets

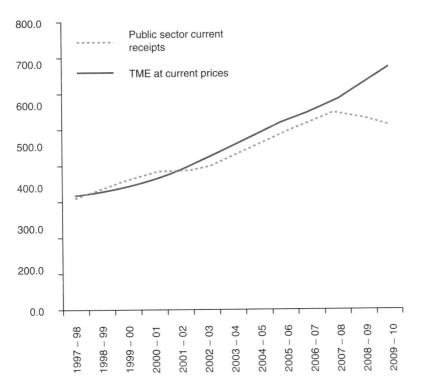

Figure 3.8   Total managed expenditure and current receipts, 1997–8 to 2009–10, £bn

Source: HM Treasury, Public Finances Databank

Table 3.3 Deficit and debt projections (% of GDP), March and June 2010

	08–09	09–10	10–11	11–12	12–13	13–14	14–15	15–16
Deficit, March 2010 budget	6.7	12.2	11.2	8.6	6.9	5.3	4.2	
Deficit, June 2010 budget	6.8	11.3	10.1	7.6	5.6	3.6	2.2	1.2
Debt, March 2010 budget	55.5	71.4	80.5	86.0	88.7	88.7	89.2	88.7
Debt, June 2010 budget	55.8	71.2	78.9	83.6	85.5	84.9	83.1	80.4

during the crisis, and we can see from Table 3.3 that the UK government also did, by a large margin in 2009–10. While the outgoing government planned still to exceed the GSP deficit target in 2014–15, the incoming government's plan was to undershoot it. Neither budget was based on a belief that the debt target could be met. The June 2010 budget proposed a Total Managed Expenditure of £737.5bn in 2014/15, a figure that was revised upwards by £2bn in the Spending Review of October 2010. This was presented as a cut in spending in real terms, with inflation running at over 3% per annum by 2011. In cash terms it represented an increase in spending, up from £696.8bn in 2010–11.

CONCLUSIONS

We have seen that fiscal policy consists of a combination of policy about the economy and policy about how much money to spend on public services. The amount of money available from taxation is limited by the amount of economic activity and the taxes and tax rates set by governments. The fiscal crisis at the end of the last decade was caused by a combination of ambitious spending plans and a decline in economic performance.

Further reading

Alan Budd, 'Fiscal policy under Labour', *National Institute Economic Review*, No. 212, April 2010. An assessment of the fiscal stance, its implementation and the reasons for the deficit.

Rowena Crawford, Carl Emmerson and Gemma Tetlow, 'A survey of public spending in the UK', *Institute of Fiscal Studies Briefing Note BN 43*, June 2010. A detailed description of and commentary on UK public spending and its trends.

QUESTIONS FOR DISCUSSION

- To what extent is the level of public expenditure influenced by the economic cycle?
- If a government wants to restore balance between expenditure and income, what are the main policy instruments at its disposal, and what are the constraints on its actions?

NOTES

1   Source: HM Treasury, Public Finances Databank, accessed 2010.

2   Ibid.

3   Ibid.

4   This is known as the 'Barnett Formula'.

5   Source: *Public Expenditure Statistical Analysis, 2010*, HM Treasury, CM 7890, table 9.15, p. 132.

6   London: Macmillan, 1936.

7   In January 2000 the Prime Minister, Tony Blair, made a public announcement that the government intended to increase public spending on health to match the EU average as a % of GDP by 2003–4.

8   Alan Budd wrote an assessment of the Labour government's fiscal policy in the *National Institute Economic Review* in 2010: see Further reading.

9   Ibid., p. 37.

CHAPTER 4
Social Policies and Management

SUMMARY

This chapter finds common threads in the development of social policies. It finds tendencies to move away from universal, standard benefits and services to means-tested and targeted ones, from a monopoly of state provision of many services to a 'mixed economy'. A theme in management has been a tension between successive governments' desire to control policy from the 'top' while devolving accountability and management responsibility. It concludes that targeting of benefits has probably been a major reason for a very high economic activity rate, that provision of residential care for adults has been almost totally privatised as a result of the mixed economy policy, while schools are still predominantly state run and, at secondary level, comprehensive. School performance seems to have improved in the early years of performance controls, but has tapered off more recently. The judicial system has been reorganised and given large quantities of extra resources, but outcomes, apart from crimes reported to the British Crime Survey, have not improved. The NHS has been subject to persistent changes in structure and management methods, a process which the Coalition has decided to continue with another reorganisation. Housing policy has been to privatise provision, to such an extent that local authority housing is now less than 9% of the housing stock.

LEARNING POINTS

- Different policy instruments have been used in different social policies and the choice of instrument has changed over time.
- There have been trends affecting all social policy areas, including a move from universalism to selectivity, from monopoly supply to a mixed economy, and in some sectors, large scale privatisation.

CHOICE OF POLICY INSTRUMENT

When governments decide that a problem requires a policy response, they have to choose a set of policy instruments to alleviate or solve the problem. The department, local authority, agency or quango then has the task of implementing the policy through the instruments chosen. Different instruments require different management arrangements, skills, staff, and systems and so on. Occasionally, a government will decide to switch instruments, requiring the implementing institution to profoundly change what it does.

Policy instruments include laws requiring or banning certain behaviours; the provision of services, either directly or under contract; the payment of a subsidy, either to a provider or to the consumer of a service; the collection of a tax that is designed to affect people's consumption patterns; the creation of rights for citizens with the concomitant obligation on an institution to enable those rights to be claimed; the creation of obligations from citizens; education and exhortation designed to persuade people to change their behaviours.

Whether revisiting an old policy problem or facing up to a new one, governments have to weigh the likely impact of each type of instrument, its cost, the ease with which it can be implemented, the political acceptability of the chosen instrument and its fit with political ideology.

As we look at the major areas of social policy, from income support, to housing, social care and education, we should remember that each policy is implemented through a particular set of chosen instruments and that others were available when the policy was designed or evolved, and that the instruments chosen may change.

For example, the history of housing policy consists of a series of changes in policy instrument. The 1950s definition of the problem was that there was a shortage of supply of housing, relative to the number of households. The main solutions were a building programme, mainly by local authorities, paid for largely by taxation, with a continuing subsidy of the supply side. Later, owner occupation was encouraged by tax relief on interest payments on housing debt, a subsidy to the demand-side for owner occupiers who paid income tax. The subsidy for public housing was replaced over time by a demand-side subsidy, housing benefit, and the subsidy for owner occupation was gradually phased out, first by not index-linking the limits and then by abolishing the subsidy altogether.

Another example is pre-school child care and nursery provision. A policy of state-provided nurseries funded by government was once the main policy towards the policy problem of entertaining, educating, socialising and caring for children before they are old enough for primary school. This instrument was switched to a demand-side subsidy, a voucher for pre-school childcare. This switch required the creation of a network of private providers, a system of licensing and inspection and the virtual demise of the old management problem of directly managing nursery schools.

Social care for adults has also been subject to a change in policy instrument. Care homes for older people provided by local authorities with their own premises, and directly employed staff ('home helps') helping older people to cope in their own homes, used to be the predominant policy instruments for care for older people. The Community Care policy switched the provision of both services to private providers by changing the subsidy from the supply side to the demand side, with a means-tested entitlement to a certain volume of care, at a predetermined price, to be purchased in the community care market. The policy used the idea of an entitlement, with access determined by an assessment and rationing process to replace assessment and direct provision.

For other policy problems, there are numerous policy instruments in use simultaneously. Once the misuse of illegal drugs was defined as a priority for policy action, many instruments were used. Prohibition, the use of the law to determine individuals' behaviours, was clearly insufficient. One instrument chosen was subsidy for drug rehabilitation by private and voluntary sector providers; another was education and exhortation ('just say no' campaigns); another was the provision of various services such as needle exchanges to reduce the harm to the individual from drug misuse. Policy towards the harm done by tobacco consumption has a different set of instruments: taxation of tobacco products is used as a financial deterrent; rehabilitation is offered directly by the NHS for people who want to stop tobacco misuse; education and exhortation are paid for by government; regulation of the advertising and display of tobacco products aims to keep tobacco out of public view.

These examples show that the choice of instrument, and the policy switch from one instrument to another, required agility on the part of implementing agencies: the switch from subsidy of the supply side to subsidy of the demand side required a change of skills for housing authorities; the creation of a community care market required social-services managers to acquire market-making skills, both as commissioners and providers of care; people in the anti-drugs services need to be able to switch from abstinence-creation to harm reduction.

TRENDS IN POLICY AND MANAGEMENT

The United Kingdom's 'welfare state', and its choice of policy instruments, are the product of a mixture of influences over a long period. With origins in the Liberal governments of 1906–14, which introduced an unemployment insurance scheme and mutual health insurance societies, the health and unemployment insurance systems were consolidated at the end of the Second World War, providing a universal, free healthcare system, a universal state pension and unemployment benefits. Since then, there have been periods during which fiscal necessity, sometimes combined with ideology, has affected the generosity of pensions and benefits, and periods during which governments have expanded social welfare provision. The healthcare system has seen steady growth in spending in most periods.

In comparison with other countries, the UK system looks less generous than those of northern Europe, especially with regard to unemployment and other social security payments, but more generous than the United States system. National spending on healthcare was until recently lower than the European average and much lower than the combined private and public spending in the US. We saw in Chapter 3 that the later years of the Labour governments brought a policy of bringing health spending up to the European average. With regard to benefits for unemployed people, the UK system, with its emphasis on 'welfare-to-work', looks more like the USA and less like northern Europe. The provision of a state pension is a European trait, but the level of state pension is, like unemployment benefit, less generous than those of the UK's European neighbours. The other characteristic that stands out is the reliance on tax-based rather than insurance-based benefits. While there is a National Insurance scheme, in practice national insurance contributions are mixed up with other tax revenues in the national budget and many benefits, especially healthcare, are not contingent on having made contributions to the scheme.

While the welfare state has, with a few exceptions, developed as a series of universal benefits, there have been some common tendencies in policy towards it, pursued with varying degrees of enthusiasm by successive governments. Looking back to the post-war origins of the welfare state institutions, with a single National Health Service, nationally-managed pension and unemployment benefits schemes, a relatively uniform education system and educational entitlements, it is surprising how little has changed despite many ideas about how it should change: well over a million employees in the NHS, a central bureaucracy running or regulating most services, and central funding through national taxation are all characteristics that would have been recognisable to the founders in the 1940s.

That is not to say that there have not been changes. One important development has been the gradual move from universal and uniform benefits to means-testing and conditional access. Examples include housing, where public housing entitlement has always been based on a needs assessment but the subsidy payable was originally spent on 'bricks and mortar' rather than to the tenant, so that all tenants benefited from subsidised accommodation. Now, housing benefit is a subsidy to tenants who need it and the housing accounts balance. Another is the Jobseeker's Allowance, a payment to unemployed people. While previous versions were a universal entitlement, people claiming benefits now have to demonstrate a willingness to work or undergo education or training. Similarly, access to residential care for elderly people was traditionally a right, subject to a means test. Now, it is subject to an assessment of need, and access is rationed.

Another tendency is towards mixed provision of services, by private and other independent service providers, rather than by state-owned and state-run organisations. The two biggest examples are housing and care homes. As well as selling public housing to tenants, governments have pushed through the transfer of management and ownership of publicly provided housing to a variety of management organisations, some established solely for the purpose. We will see that care homes for elderly and other people in need are now in a large majority run by the independent sector. Other examples include contracting for street cleaning and garbage collection, outsourcing back-office functions, selling and leasing back building in various sectors. When transfer to the independent sector has not proved possible, less monolithic ownership and governance forms have been established: further education colleges, for example, were separated from local authorities and made into independent corporate entities; the Coalition government created 'free schools' in 2011, independent of their constituent local authorities; governance arrangements for NHS Trusts were invented to make them more independent. All of these arrangements were attempts to break up the apparently monolithic hierarchical organisations in these sectors.

Linked to this tendency is a recurring theme of giving people choices, especially choice of service provider. One example is the abolition of school catchment areas so that parents and pupils could choose their schools. There is some choice of service and service provider in the community care regime, once people have passed the need and eligibility tests. 'Direct payments', under which people assessed as being eligible for care can receive cash to buy their own care, had grown slowly to around 13% of the social care budget by 2010, with the Coalition promising to extend the approach to 1 million people by 2013. Choice of health-care providers was introduced slowly, 'choose and book' finally coming into force for sec-ondary healthcare treatment in December 2005. Under this scheme patients were offered a choice of hospital, rather than being allocated one by their family doctor. This direction is further emphasised by 'practice-based commissioning' through which an increasing volume of healthcare will be commissioned locally by general medical practitioners, ostensibly with and on behalf of 'their' patients. This idea was started by the Labour government and taken up in slightly different form, with consortia of GPs, by the Coalition.

Another common theme has been the tension between governments' desire to control everything from the top and their inadequate capacity to do so satisfactorily in any detail. While governance arrangements have been designed to enhance local accountability and give control over detail to individual institutions, Ministers and civil servants have issued a torrent of circulars, guidance and advice that threaten to disable front-line management. In the mid-2000s, for example, there was a public concern about the standard of food served in schools. By 2005 there were 30 pages of guidance about lunch and a further 30 pages of guidance about non-lunch food in schools.

In principle, the model has generally been that the policy and overall priorities should be set by government: priority areas for health improvement, such as cardio, cancer and mental health; priority targets for education, such as scores by pupils at various stages in their school career; overall policy on house building. These priorities and targets were incor-porated into a formal target system, which we will see in more detail in Chapter 6. At the same time, managers were to be given more control over budgets, employment of staff, and management of resources to enable them better to meet the central targets. Government was to set out its desired 'outcomes', while managers could get on and manage the 'inputs'. It has not worked out as simply as that, as Ministers and civil servants were unable to resist getting involved in the details of day-to-day management.

Finally, policy has been managed through the funding mechanisms: we will see how the performance contracting system operated in Chapter 6 and how it became an important element of the relationship between policy and management. Funding based on an assessment of quality, as well as on volume of activity, has been applied to some degree in school education, in the universities, in local authority capital spending allocations. This use of budget allocations to 'buy' results has implications for management: if managers choose to respond to the incentives, they must steer their organisations towards achieving the targets set for them.

INCOME MAINTENANCE

The Labour governments planned to change the welfare system from one which simply paid out benefits to one which created incentives and opportunities for people to work and disincentives to staying on benefits – what has been called a 'work-focused benefits regime'. As well as trying to create a system that encouraged and helped unemployed people into jobs, there was a commitment to ending child poverty and to creating more equal life chances. Gordon Brown's period of office as Chancellor of the Exchequer coincided with the development of these policies and many commentators have discerned his input to their creation. The policy instruments included attempts to reduce the 'poverty trap' whereby the loss of benefits created incentives not to move from benefits to work because of the small (or negative) difference in net income that such a move would make. This included the establishment of a minimum wage for the first time in 1999, the creation of 'working families tax credits' as well as child tax credits which, along with the child benefit, all made it more worthwhile to go to work for people with children. At the same time, subsidised child care provisions made working more financially worthwhile for parents. The 'New Deal' also created benefits penalties for people who did not actively seek work. Some of these policy instruments were inherited from previous governments, such as the Conservatives' 'Family Credit' from 1986. 'Jobseeker's Allowance', Labour's benefit for unemployed people, was paid for a shorter period and harder to qualify for than previous unemployment benefits.

   To illustrate the scale of the National Insurance benefits, the numbers of people in receipt of the main benefits in the UK in 2010 were as shown in Table 4.1.[1] The Child Tax Credit went, in 2010, to 5.8 million families (7.8 million were entitled to the universal Child Benefit).

   Stephen Driver of the London School of Economics published an assessment of the welfare programme.[2] In the decade from 1997, the number of people in work increased

Table 4.1   Recipients of main benefits, UK, 2010

Retirement/State pension	12,417,000
Employment and support allowance	1,038,000
Survivors pensions	103,000
Industrial injuries	262,000

by 2.7 million, creating an economic activity rate of 75% of the working age population, one of the highest in Europe. Employment among single parents increased from 46% to 57%. How much of the employments effects can be attributed to the welfare policy and how much to economic growth over the period has not been successfully evaluated. One aspect of unemployment that seems to be intractable is the number of people on permanent incapacity benefit, a problem that was made a priority by the Coalition government from 2010, who instituted a new programme of assessments for people on incapacity benefits.

The social security system is both a safety net for people in temporary difficulties and a system devised to encourage or force people to go to work. For managers and workers in the system, this expresses itself as a dilemma: good customer service demands that people are helped to receive their entitlements while unemployed claimants are encouraged to look for work.

There are conflicting expectations from the benefits system. Ministers expect certain things – an efficient delivery of service, especially to those people considered 'deserving', such as genuinely disabled people, widows and pensioners, while making benefits difficult to obtain by the 'undeserving', who might be differently defined by different ministers: single and never married parents, fit unemployed people, new age travellers. Service management is difficult if such distinctions have to be made at the point of service delivery. In practice, staff have commonly dealt differently with different classes of claimant, although managers have encouraged them to deal equally with everyone.

Senior management in Jobcentre Plus encourage good customer service, through middle management initiative, the development of innovative solutions, the establishment of telephone help-lines and better designed forms. In addition, the creation of the unified job-seeking and benefits service (a reversion to a previous model) provided an opportunity to design and provide a whole new set of premises, created to enhance customer service.

COMMUNITY CARE

Policies towards care for elderly people who need help with everyday life, adults with mental health problems or learning difficulties and people with drug and alcohol problems have developed in largely the same direction over the last three decades: service provision is based on an assessment of need and search for service provision within cash-limited budgets; the provision of services, whether in people's own homes or in residential accommodation, is separated out organisationally from the process of assessing and buying services; there is a 'mixed economy' of services, with directly publicly provided services in a steady decline as a proportion of the total provision. The example of residential services in England, shown in Figure 4.1, illustrates this last point.

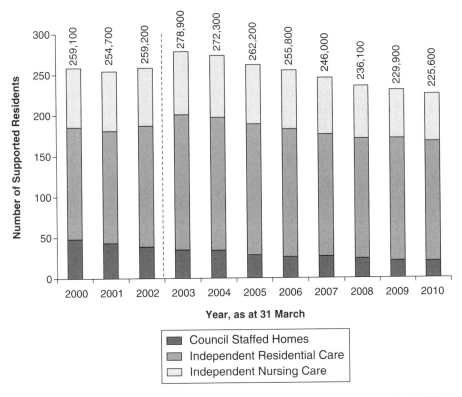

Figure 4.1   Number of supported residents by type of accommodation in England 2000–2010

Source: NHS Information Centre/Government Statistical Service (2011) *Community Care Statistics* 2009–10, Fig. 5.1

Figure 4.1 shows a steady decline in the number of people in residential care since 2003, and the continuing crowding out of the public sector provision by independent nursing and residential care, the public provision representing less than 10% of the total. The category 'independent nursing care' refers to medical care provided. The distinction between medical and social care in England and Wales is an administrative one: social care is financed out of the social services budget and is subject to a means test to decide whether the person being cared for pays or the local authority does. All medical care, including nursing care, is provided through the Health Service and is always free at the point of 'delivery'. In Scotland both sorts of care are free; in Northern Ireland medical and social care are provided through an integrated system.

In addition to residential care, there has been an increase in the use of home care to enable people to stay in their own homes, a service that has also been subject to privatisation through contracting. In both cases, the management tasks in the public sector consist of first rationing (assessing eligibility) and then buying the service.

EDUCATION

Schools

There has not been much difference in policy among the main parties with regard to school education. Policy has included a desire to make schools more 'self-managing', with increasing autonomy for Boards of Governors and school leadership teams to run their own budgets, hire teachers, set the remuneration for heads and manage individual performance. At the same time there has been a centralisation of overall policy with a national curriculum setting what is taught in schools and the publication, in England and Scotland, of performance league tables designed both to name and shame poor performers while praising good performers and offering information for parents as they choose schools. These policies of simultaneous centralisation of the curriculum and decentralisation of management left the education authorities squeezed into a diminished role.

In the case of those secondary schools that opted to become Academies, which they could from 2000, local authorities had no further role in their management. The first Academies were opened in 2002: they were schools, normally located in deprived areas, started on the site of a school that was previously performing badly. The Academy process required a sponsor willing to invest some cash (a relatively small, single payment of about £1 million, contributing to the start-up costs which ranged from £18 to £37 million) and take part in the management of the school. The sponsors included churches (both the Catholic Church and the Church of England), a football club, two City livery companies and a collection of rich individuals. In addition to Academies, the Labour government invented the 'Trust' school, similar in all respects except sponsorship to the Academies. These were set up by the 2006 Education and Inspections Act.

The Coalition government continued the idea of school autonomy by introducing in 2010 what it branded 'free schools'. These were almost identical to Trust schools, especially with regard to the feature that no down-payment was required, and parents could form a group to establish the school.

As well as trying to make schools more autonomous, a theme of education policy for the last 30 years has been to provide parents and pupils with more choice of school, especially at secondary level. In order to exercise this choice, people must live in an area where there is spare capacity within travelling distance.

The state schools provide a very large majority of school places in the United Kingdom. Table 4.2 shows that the private schools have 621,000 places, out of a total of 9,691,000, which represents 6.4%, a figure which has only grown from 6.1% in 1970. Table 4.2 also shows that the consistent attempts to create different types of school, such as grammar schools and Academies, had by 2008/9 only applied to 12% of school places, with comprehensive schools accounting for 82% of places.[3]

Table 4.2   School pupils by type of school: UK, thousands

	1970/71	1980/81	1990/91	2000/01	2008/09
Public sector schools					
Nursery	50	89	105	152	150
Primary	5,902	5,171	4,955	5,298	4,869
State-funded secondary schools					
of which, admissions policy					
Comprehensive	1,313	3,730	2,925	3,340	3,243
Grammar	673	149	156	205	221
Modern	1,164	233	94	112	142
City technology colleges	.	.	8	17	3
Academies	.	.	.	.	122
Not applicable	403	434	298	260	197
All public sector schools	9,507	9,806	8,541	9,384	8,948
Non-maintained schools	621	619	606	609	621
All special schools	103	148	114	113	107
Pupil referral units	.	.	.	10	16
All schools	10,230	10,572	9,260	10,116	9,691

Source: *Social Trends* 40 (2010), Table 3.7

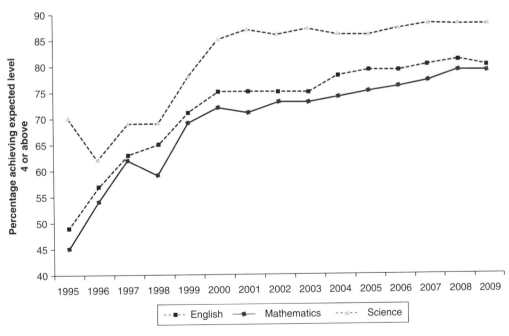

Figure 4.2   Percentage of pupils achieving the expected level (4 or above) in Key Stage 2 tests 1995–2009

A third theme of education policy has been an attempt to improve standards in the state schools. National testing at 'Key Stages' has been used to try to push the standards up. Figure 4.2 shows an example, the attainment of level 4 at Key Stage 4. The levels of attainment are set nationally and measured for every child in England. What Figure 4.2 shows is that early efforts to push up standards produced positive results, followed by diminishing returns but steady, slow improvement.[4]

Post-school education

An important aim of the Labour governments was to increase the participation rate in post-school education. Table 4.3 shows the scale of the expansion.[5]

As in the case of schools, there was also a process of increasing the autonomy of further education colleges from local authority control, by making them independent legal entities with their own Boards of Governors and powers to manage their own affairs, including finances.

As part of the fiscal corrections the Coalition government decided to switch a proportion of the funding of education from a subsidy to a supplier, to a loan to the consumer, the student, while at the same time changing the rules about how many students could be admitted to an institution. This was an attempt to 'make the money follow the student' and cause institutions to compete against each other. The maximum fee level was set at £9,000 per annum, with the expectation that different universities would charge different fees, competing for students on price as well as on quality and other attractions. In the event

Table 4.3   Students in further and higher education, by type of course and sex: UK, thousands

	Men				Women			
	1980/81	1990/91	2000/01	2008/09	1980/81	1990/91	2000/01	2008/09
Higher education								
Undergraduate								
Full-time	277	345	510	593	196	319	612	735
Part-time	176	148	224	262	71	106	320	42
Postgraduate								
Full-time	41	50	82	137	21	34	31	132
Part-time	32	46	118	114	13	33	123	160
All higher education	526	588	934	1,106	301	491	1,126	1,451

Source: Social Trends 41 (2011), Education and Training, p. 17

most Universities chose to set their fees at the upper limit, or close to it, so the competition that ensued from the 2012 academic year was mostly on quality, although some universities chose to compete on price.

As far as management is concerned, the Universities have always been subject to quality inspections and to a funding regime that rewards research achievement. The Universities have been in competition for funds, through the process of assessing their research output.[6] The managerial response to this has been to try to attract researchers with high scores, competing with higher pay for the high achievers, a process that has been compared with the competition for football players.

CRIMINAL JUSTICE

Criminal justice policy was a prominent feature in Labour's election campaigns, and in Labour's targets for the achievement of outcomes. The slogan was that the government would be 'tough on crime and tough on the causes of crime'. One main policy instrument was legislation: in the first seven years, the government put through fifty Acts of Parliament relating to criminal justice.

Along with other services, expenditure on the criminal justice system was increased substantially by the Labour governments, raising the proportion of GDP spent on criminal justice to over 2.5%, the highest rate of all OECD member countries. The extra spending was concentrated on policing, with an increase in police numbers, in civilian support to enable the police to spend more time on crime-related duties, as well as Police Community Support Officers, and on the Crown Courts and the Probation Service.

The third policy instrument was the use of managerial methods to increase the effectiveness of the justice system – high-level targets were set for the police, the speed with which the courts dealt with cases, the reconviction rates of convicted criminals. Targets were also set for the levels of crime, as measured by the British Crime Survey, for the number of people using illegal drugs, for the number of organised crime gangs disrupted.

These targets were to be pursued through an increasingly centralised management of the police forces, the courts and the prison and probation services. Figures 4.3[7] and 4.4[8] show the organisations involved in the criminal justice system. The Ministry of Justice was created in 2007, its functions taken out of the Home Office. The National Offender Management Service was created in 2004 by combining the Prison and Probation services and eventually putting them both under a single line of command. Figure 4.4 shows the hierarchy of the Ministry of Justice presiding over the Court Service and the National Offender Management Service.

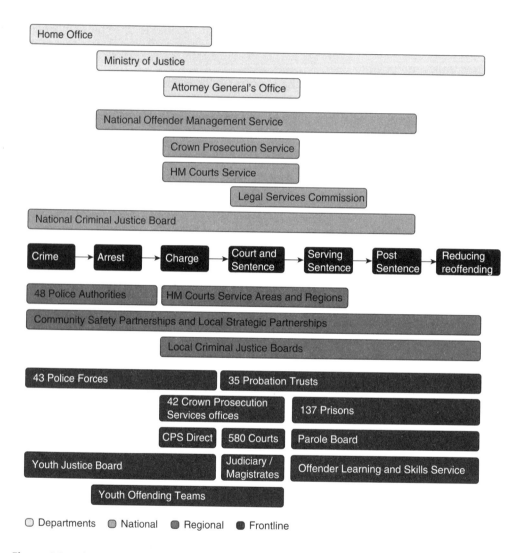

Figure 4.3   The organisations in the criminal justice system, England and Wales

Source: National Audit Office (2010), p. 8

The overall aim of criminal justice policy was to reduce the level of crime. Looking at this overall target, the British Crime Survey data for personal and household crime in England and Wales are shown in Table 4.4.

Table 4.4 shows a downward trend until 2007–08, followed by a slight upturn. The decrease in crimes reported to the survey between 1995 and 2007–08 was 47%. This head-line figure has been used to claim the success of the crime policies.

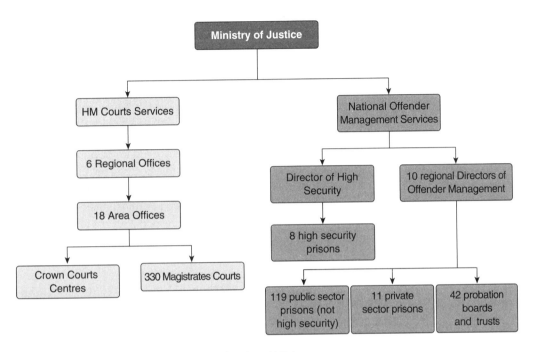

Figure 4.4   The Ministry of Justice, England and Wales

Source: National Audit Office (2010), p. 12

Table 4.4   British Crime Survey offences 1983–2008/09 (Home Office)

England & Wales	Millions		
	All household crime	All personal crime	All BCS crime
1983	7.7	4.2	11.9
1987	9.0	4.4	13.4
1991	10.4	4.7	15.1
1995	12.4	6.9	19.4
1999	9.4	5.6	15.0
2003/04	7.2	4.5	11.7
2007/08	6.5	3.8	10.2
2008/09	6.8	3.9	10.7

Source: *Social Trends* 40 (2010), Table 9.2

An evaluation[9] of the first ten years of criminal justice policy under Labour assessed its success. One reservation about the use of the British Crime Survey to claim success is the narrow range of crime captured by the BCS: it excludes domestic violence, rape, homicide, crimes against retail premises and white collar crime including fraud. A Home Office study quoted by the evaluation estimated that the BCS captures less than 25% of crimes committed, of which it estimated 60 million in 2000. The second reservation concerned the question of attribution of the reductions to changes in criminal justice policy: much of the reduction in the volume of crime was reduction in vehicle crime and burglary, most of which can be attributed to better security of cars and homes than to actions by the criminal justice system. The third reservation concerned the trends: the government published targets in 2004 which were less ambitious than the trends already evident from its first term of office; the downward trend could well have happened regardless of the impact of criminal justice policies.

Three main aspects of the way crime was managed concerned the government: the 'justice gap', meaning the proportion of offences committed that resulted in a conviction or caution; the re-offending rate, measured by the number of convicted criminals who were reconvicted after their sentence; the prevalence of 'anti-social behaviour', or low-level behaviours that caused nuisance to people but did not necessarily constitute crimes.

The Labour manifesto of 1997 spoke of the justice gap, complaining that at that point fewer than one in fifty crimes resulted in a conviction. One policy aim was to close that gap. An analysis by the Centre for Crime and Justice Studies in 2011[10] showed that almost all of the improvement in this area was achieved by an increase in the use of summary, out-of-court sanctions such as 'Penalty Notices for Disorder', of which 176,200 were issued in 2008. Eleven such sanctions were created by the Labour governments, including Anti-Social Behaviour Orders, Terrorist Control Orders, Serious Crime Prevention Orders, Drinking Ban Orders, etc.

Table 4.5, Criminal justice trends 1998–2010, gives some statistics for the trends in spending, staffing and activity in the criminal justice system in England and Wales. Reflecting the general increase in spending that we saw in Chapter 3, the table shows an 80% increase in probation staff (most of which was not in qualified probation officer numbers), close to 50% real terms increase in police expenditure and a 10% increase in police officer numbers. Over the same period the numbers of people sentenced stayed the same, at around 1.4 million convictions, while the prison population rose by 26%. The table also shows a statistic not contained in the BCS data, the number of homicides, which increased by 24% over the period.

The second main objective was reducing the reoffending rate, seen as a measure of the effectiveness of the prison and probation services in 'reforming' sentenced criminals. The definition and measurement of reoffending is a technical matter in the field of criminology, but here we can look at some raw statistics that show a moderate success in this area. Figure 4.5 shows reconviction rates for adults and juveniles. Of course reconviction rate is not the same as reoffending rate: it measures those who were caught reoffending and convicted, not those who committed further crimes.[11]

Table 4.5 Criminal justice trends 1998–2010, England and Wales

	1998	1999	2000	2001	2002	2003	2004	2005	2006	2007	2008	2009	2010	% change 1998–2008
Probation staff	8,267	9,054	9,462	10,702	11,615	15,251	15,890	17,234	18,247	15,386	14,991			81
Prison Service employees	41,196	43,088	43,854	44,085	45,419	47,224	48,607	48,418	48,331	49,293				20 (98–07)
Police officers	126,814	126,096	124,170	125,682	129,603	133,366	139,200	141,230	141,381	140,514	140,230	142,151	142,132	11
Police spending (real terms, £m)	9,828	10,099	10,593	11,258	11,485	12,186	13,353	14,112	14,577	14,600	14,546			48
Average prison population	65,298	64,771	64,602	66,301	70,778	73,038	74,657	75,979	78,127	80,216	82,572	83,559		26
Numbers of people sentenced	1,407,998	1,424,349	1,348,494	1,419,608	1,489,827	1,547,352	1,482,453	1,420,571	1,414,742	1,362,064	1,405,938			0 (99–08)
Number of homicides	607	642	672	765	795	943	771	780	711	716	753	651		24

Source: Rebecca Roberts (2011), 'Justice, harm and official statistics', in Centre for Crime and Justice Studies (2011), (ed. Arianna Silvestri) *Lessons for the Coalition: an end of term report on New Labour and criminal justice*, London: Hadley Trust

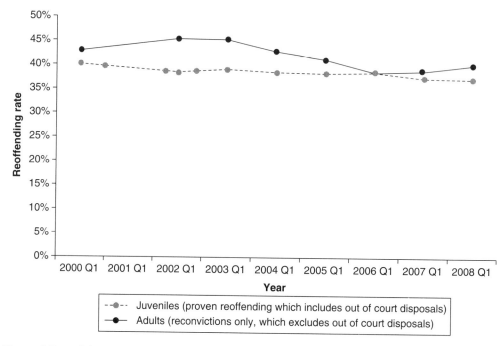

Figure 4.5   Adult reconviction rates and juvenile proven reoffending rates 2000–2008

Source: *Justice Statistics Bulletin* (November 2010), p. 2

The third main objective, to curb anti-social behaviour, was supposed to be achieved through issuing Anti-Social Behaviour Orders. These orders had a peak of implementation in 2005, and declined in use thereafter. In total 1,800 were issued up to 2009, as shown in Table 4.6.

Table 4.6   ASBOs issued 2004–2009

2004	2005	2006	2007	2008	2009
3,479	4,122	2,705	2,299	2,027	1,671

HEALTH POLICY: THE NATIONAL HEALTH SERVICE

Since it was founded in 1948 the National Health Service has been subject to many reviews and reorganisations. From the beginning, there have been debates about how local the management of the service should be, how politically accountable, whether it is a national service and how reasonably equitable national standards might be achieved in all geographical areas. The role of doctors in the service has similarly always been controversial, as has the nature of the contractual relationship between the NHS and the various medical professions. Structural changes have been frequent, including the creation and destruction of a wide variety of organisations at sub-national levels, sometimes for small areas, sometimes for large areas, sometimes with two tiers of administration between the Department of Health and the service providers, sometimes with indirectly elected boards and sometimes with appointed boards. In this section we will look in some detail at the succession of policies towards the NHS, to show that most feasible permutations of changes to the hierarchy, market arrangements, centralisation and decentralisation have been tried at one time or another.

The Conservative governments of the 1980s and 1990s made two main changes. They divided the service into a set of 'purchasers' and a set of 'providers' of health services and started a set of controls to give the Secretary of State for Health and the National Health Service Executive considerable control over what happens in most parts of the NHS. Previous reorganisations and interventions failed either to equalise access to health facilities or to bring doctors under political control. The second main change was to introduce explicit objectives about the incidence of ill health, rather than the volume of treatment to be provided for people who are ill. Throughout the subsequent reforms, these two principles have been maintained: an internal 'market', soon extended to an external market for some services; and the use of health outcomes as overall goals for the organisation. It should have come as no surprise when the Coalition government announced its very own version of NHS changes that these two principles were preserved.

Markets and competition

Ever since the White Paper *Working for Patients*, 1989, established a different form of financial management in the service, a guiding principle has been that budgets would not be allocated to people providing services, rather to another set of people who would specify what they wanted the providers to do. These people would, initially, be the district health authorities and the larger GP practices. The new arrangement meant that service providers, such as hospitals, would not have a plan for the year and a budget, but rather a set of contracts for the year with agreed prices. Where there was only one large contract with the local health district, the arrangement was very much like a budget and a plan. Where there was a variety of purchasers and many providers in competition, the new arrangement had some characteristics of a market and a set of contracts.

In these latter cases managers and medical professionals were put into competition with each other. In the previous system the volume of work which a hospital did was determined by how much budget it received, how many patients were referred to it and how efficient it was. The budget was based mainly on historical patterns, with some adjustment from 'over-provided' areas. Referral patterns were mainly historical, based on where people lived and which general practitioners knew which hospital doctors. Efficiency was set by how well managers were managing, how good the facilities were and how hard the medical staff worked. In the new system, the idea was that hospitals would compete on price and/or the quality of work. Most contracts were large 'block' contracts which contained not only an allocation of funds but also a specification of what the providers were expected to do for the money. Efficiency was slightly more easy to measure, because procedures would have their unit costs defined. At the same time, purchasers would ask for an efficiency improvement each year, expressed as a reduction in the unit prices, achieved by individuals doing more work, by speeding up the throughput of patients (sending them home sooner) or by paying people less.

Another big change was to transfer a proportion of the health budget to GP fundholders, who could purchase services for their patients from hospitals or other providers of their choice. As the amount spent by GP fundholders grew, their influence on hospitals increased. While there is evidence that costs were not reduced as a result of this, the change did alter the relationship between general practitioners and their traditionally more senior hospital colleagues.

The only difference between this, 1989, revision and the 2011 Bill was that in 2011 the decisions were allocated to consortia of GPs and other practitioners including surgeons, a variant on GP commissioning by individual practices. Meanwhile various other tiers of health authority had been established, including Primary Care Trusts.

Outcome targets

In 1992, the government published a White Paper, *The Health of the Nation,* which set out targets for improvements in health in five 'key areas': coronary heart disease and stroke, cancers, mental illness, HIV/AIDS and sexual health, and accidents. Twenty-seven specific targets were also declared. Some referred to incidence of diseases such as the proportion of people with coronary heart disease or lung cancer. Some were causes (proportion of people smoking or obese) and some were outcomes (accidents and suicides). The paper recognised that the targets were achievable through a variety of preventive measures and that their achievement required the collaboration of a range of organisations.

The idea was that regional health authorities should adopt their own targets to contribute towards the achievement of the national ones. Each year, progress towards the targets was monitored and published. While the achievement of the targets was not within the competence of any single body within the NHS, it did provide a focus for efforts to prevent the main avoidable causes of death and disease. It especially provided a way of making primary healthcare more important than hospitals in improving health standards as well as helping with collaborative efforts.

What is radical about these targets is that they are not concerned with the activities of any organisation, but rather the effect of organisations working together to achieve a particular result. As we shall see in Chapter 6, it is only when results are measured or assessed that management can be fully turned towards achieving what people need.

Standards, not competition: the NHS Plan

The Labour government's policy towards the NHS contained some continuities with the past and some changes. What did not change was the struggle to maintain some central control through a system of target setting and managerial mechanisms and incentives. The old power battles between professionals, managers and politicians continued in an atmosphere of crisis and problems. Reducing the size of waiting lists and the time spent waiting for treatment were specific manifesto commitments by the Labour Party, and the government were not satisfied that the inherited arrangements were adequate to allow it to fulfil its promises. The internal market was dismantled and new institutional arrangements established. As the NHS Plan (2000) said:

> Competition between hospitals was a weak lever for improvement, because most areas were only served by one or two local general hospitals. Other methods of raising standards were ignored. The market ethos undermined teamwork between professionals and organisations vital to patient-centred care. And it hampered planning across the NHS as a whole, leading to cuts in nurse training and a stalled hospital building programme.[12]

The new arrangements replaced the market with an attempt at centralisation in which the 'centre' would 'set standards, monitor performance, put in place a proper system of inspection, provide back-up to assist the modernisation of the service and, where necessary, correct failure' (para 6.6). Underneath the NHS Executive and its regional offices were the Health Authorities which, together with the local authorities, were responsible for setting the health targets for their area. NHS Trusts, including Primary Care Trusts, ran services, whether in hospitals or in the community. Services were commissioned by Primary Care Groups which made 'commissioning plans' but did not organise competitions or market mechanisms as they commissioned care from the Trusts and, in certain cases, from the private and voluntary sectors. This replaced the system of GP fundholding. The other organisational innovation was the establishment of the National Institute for Clinical Excellence whose job is to set national guidelines for prescribing and treatment. Its principle is 'evidence-based treatment' which is interpreted as treatment based on nationally collected evidence about 'what works'. These changes reflected the 1997 White Paper *The New NHS*.[13] While the internal market and competition were abandoned, the changes did not reverse the decision to separate the functions of commissioning and providing services, with budgets allocated to the commissioners. This was one of the most significant of the previous changes as it aimed to change the balance of power away from the service providers. The power shift was not as great as it might seem because the service commissioners are dependent on the providers for the services they fund, unless there is spare capacity and competitors within reasonable distance.

The changes were not enough to solve the political problem that the NHS was causing the government, expressed in the size of and time spent on waiting lists and in a general feeling of crisis and under-investment. The main new solution was to commit more money and aim to increase the amount spent on healthcare to a proportion of the national product closer to the European average. The problem of the backlog of hospital and clinic building and maintenance was to be solved through extensive use of the Private Finance Initiative. Neither of these measures could produce immediate results. Healthcare professionals have long training periods, and instant staff increases can be achieved only by importing qualified staff, a solution that was tried. A lasting solution to a shortage of staff could only come from growing the medical schools and other training and paying staff enough to keep them in the service and in the United Kingdom. The building programme got underway but not without controversy, as we shall see in Chapter 13, because of the additional costs involved in providing a profit for the PFI partners.

Apart from the financial solutions, the institutional arrangements replaced the market but continued with a series of targets, national standards, service frameworks and a system of inspection and monitoring with attached incentives. The Commission for Health Improvement was expanded and all parts of the NHS were classified as green, yellow, or red, with organisations achieving green status having easier access to cash for investment and a light touch inspection. While initially a very centralised system, the ambition was eventually to devolve performance management to Health Authorities, provided that they achieved 'green' status.

The new arrangements, as with so many other changes, were announced as 'modernisation' and indeed one of the new bodies was called the Modernisation Agency, whose job was to help service providers to redesign their service access arrangements. The 2000 White Paper *Modernising the NHS*, claimed that the organisational form and management methods were rooted in their 1946 origins, despite the extensive reorganisations and system changes that were put in place during the previous twenty years, with planning, targets, general management, the internal market, the switch of budgets from providers to commissioners. It was as if 'modernisation' was an absolute term in the sense that organisations and services are either modern or not. For practitioners, it was just another set of institutional arrangements in a long series of attempts at change.

The King's Fund believed that the NHS Plan marked a fundamental change in the nature of the NHS:

The NHS Plan signalled significant reform. The Government has set out a new vision of the NHS where instead of being a monolithic structure that both commissions and provides care, is to be a set of rights to treatment, at specified and assured standards, from a widening base of diverse suppliers, public and private... This is an NHS that Aneurin Bevan, its Labour founder, would struggle to recognise.[14]

Primary Care Trusts as budget holders and 'payment by results'

Shifting the Balance of Power, the 2001 White Paper, created Primary Care Trusts that took on the function of the health authorities as the conduit for about 80% of the NHS budget. Above them 28 Strategic Health Authorities[15] were to act as the agents of the Department of Health in controlling the PCTs. After these structural changes were made, in 2004 the process of giving patients choice of healthcare provider was started. By the beginning of 2006 the NHS had introduced 'Choose and Book', a part of the ICT (information and communication technology) system under which patients, with their general practitioners, get to choose among four or more providers for their secondary healthcare. Meanwhile a new funding regime was introduced, called 'Payment by Results'. This was not an accurate title, since the new system introduced payment not by results, but by the volume of activity at a nationally agreed tariff. The tariff is based on average costs, modified slightly to take account of local circumstances. The idea behind the change in the payment system was that since service providers get paid according to their level of activity, they have incentive to do more work. Purchasers faced with choices at fixed prices can choose where to get treatment on the criteria of convenience and quality, subject to adequate information about these.

Patricia Hewitt, Secretary of State for Health, said that the new arrangements were not a market, especially because they did not involve price competition:

I do not believe that we are turning the NHS into a market, and nor do I think that we should. Indeed, it would be a pretty odd kind of market where the user cannot pay and the providers cannot compete on price.

Yes, we are giving patients and users more choice. Yes, we are giving providers more freedom to innovate and, where it is appropriate, to compete against each other. And where we mean 'competition', we should say so, instead of pretending that 'contestability' is something different. Yes, money will follow the patient. But why should choice, innovation, competition and financial discipline be confined to private markets? Why should the use of the private sector, when it gives us new hospitals, when it benefits patients and the public, have to mean 'privatisation'?

What we are creating – not only in health and social care, but in education and many other public goods – are not markets, but modern public services. And I believe we do ourselves a disservice when we use the jargon of markets, instead of coming back to our values, the values of public service, and the goals we seek to achieve on behalf of all those we represent.[16]

At the same time as the new funding arrangements were introduced, there were two other major changes to the NHS in England. There was yet another White Paper (*Our Health, Our Care, Our Say*) that paved the way for more contracting out for PCTs and encouraged private and 'social enterprise' bodies to take the provision of healthcare away from the PCTs. At the same time, yet another reorganisation was proposed, reducing the number of Strategic Health Authorities and PCTs and making them coterminous with the local authority tier responsible for adult care services. These changes were introduced just as the levels of pay in the NHS were restructured and increased under another initiative, 'Agenda for Change'. This was a job evaluation solution to the problem of equal pay for equivalent work in the NHS, especially the disparity between men's and women's pay for equivalent work. It also allowed a general increase in pay for most staff in occupations that were to expand in numbers.

During fiscal year 2005–6 the financial system became unstable, as some Trusts overspent their budgets, up to a total of about £1 billion,[17] while others underspent, to a total of about £300 million. The net effect of the two was a deficit in the NHS budget as a whole of just less than 1%. The old problem of hospitals stopping work to save costs towards the end of the financial year was back: the 'payment by results' regime made it necessary for the 'failures' to stop work, or reduce costs. Early evaluation of the scheme suggested that there was not much impact on the volume of work that could be attributed to the new arrangements.[18] In fact, 'Non-elective activity increased at a significantly higher rate for NHS trusts that were not operating under payment by results... than for foundation trusts [that were].'[19]

The quest for greater autonomy for managers had resulted in the establishment of 'NHS Foundation Trusts', a scheme under which NHS Trusts could opt to become 'public benefit corporations', with locally selected Boards and a more independent management regime. A pamphlet about the scheme claimed that the trusts were central to its management strategy:

> NHS Foundation Trusts will be at the cutting edge of the Government's commitment to devolution and decentralisation in the public services. They will not be subject to direction from Whitehall. Local managers and staff working with local people – rather than remote civil servants – will have the freedom to innovate and develop services tailored to the particular needs of their local communities.[20]

The Coalition's Health and Social Care Bill

The Coalition inherited a system that had many features of which it approved: a market, use of the private sector to provide services, decentralisation and devolution of power. While it extended the use of competition and gave a changed role to the regulator, one of the major characteristics of its reforms was that it was yet another structural reorganisation, this time doing away with the PCTs and the Strategic Health Authorities, transferring the budgets back to the GPs, where they had been before the PCTs were created.

The Health and Social Care Bill introduced by the Coalition government in 2011 was another variant on the theme of internal markets, external provision when appropriate and the split between the service providers and the commissioners. This time, competition was reintroduced in a more extreme form, with freedom to compete offered to the private sector and new entrants, under European competition regulations, and a newly named regulator, to be called 'Monitor':

> The main duty of Monitor in exercising its functions is to protect and promote the interests of people who use health care services –
>
> (a) by promoting competition where appropriate, and
> (b) through regulation where necessary.[21]

Whereas, as we have seen, the Labour governments had pulled back from full-scale competition, because of its effects on predictability of provider budgets and the transaction costs involved in the market, the Coalition was prepared to pursue the policy of competition and unfettered entry of providers. But the changes they introduced were a matter of degree (and reversion to a system of fundholding that had been tried before), and not of principle.

HOUSING

Housing policy in the United Kingdom has many strands, and since the distant days of the Ministry of Housing and Local Government, responsibility for housing policy has been spread around several departments. In the immediate post-war period, replacement of houses lost by bombing, plus redevelopment and expansion, was done in large part by local authorities, whose house-building efforts exceeded those of the private sector. Figure 4.6 shows the historical pattern of building in the UK by tenure.

Figure 4.6 shows a peak production of dwellings of over 400,000 per year in the mid-1960s, a figure never met since. It also shows a decline in local authority new house construction since the mid-1970s, replaced mostly by the private sector and in much smaller numbers by other 'social landlords', the housing associations. The distribution of new building among the tenures continued: by 2009, local authorities built 850 homes, social landlords 31,860, and the private sector 139,270.[22]

Council housing, as a major tenure, was eroded by council house sales in the 1980s, when around 2 million council dwellings were sold to their tenants, and by the transfer of large

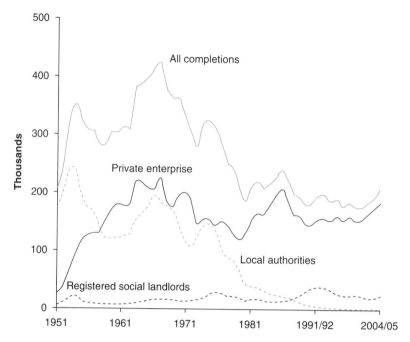

Figure 4.6   Housebuilding, completions by sector, United Kingdom 1951–2004/5

amounts of council housing to housing associations. The distribution of housing tenures to 2009 is shown in Table 4.7.

Table 4.7 shows that of the 27 million dwellings in the UK, local authorities and social landlords have about 2.5 million each, there are around 3 million private rented dwellings, and the rest, around 70%, are owner-occupied. These proportions are consistent across the UK, except that Scotland has a slightly smaller proportion of owner occupation, at 65%.

The instruments of housing policy are many, and may not always be consistent with each other. For the owner-occupied sector, policy instruments include bank regulation, which influences how much money banks can lend for house purchasing, the choice of whether to allow tax relief on interest payments for housing, planning policies towards new house building. For private renting, there have been periods of rent control, planning regulations about the subdivision of housing into flats and rooms for letting, and tax arrangements for landlords.

Policy towards the public sector is concerned with subsidy, whether to the construction of social housing or towards rents for tenants, the definition of eligibility criteria for subsidy and entitlement to social housing, rules about rent levels and rules about how social housing construction is financed. During the local authority house building boom, policy was largely implemented and mostly decided at local level. The transfer of council housing to social landlords effectively nationalised housing policy, including policy on allowable rents. The institution the Housing Corporation was used to channel the flow of public

Table 4.7 UK Housing by Tenure, thousands of dwellings

	owner occupied	privately rented or with a job	housing associations	local authorities	All dwellings
2005	18,138	3,117	2,140	2,800	26,197
2006	18,106	3,404	2,205	2,704	26,419
2007	18,161	3,607	2,303	2,584	26,656
2008	18,117	3,939	2,440	2,415	26,911
2009	17,991	4,231	2,531	2,356	27,108
2010	17,846	4,502	2,591	2,325	27,264

Source: Department of Communities and Local Government, *Housing Statistics 2010, Table 101*

funds to housing associations. The Corporation was split in 2008 into a housing regulator (the Tenant Services Authority) and a funder, the Housing and Communities Agency. As far as subsidy is concerned, 50% of the income of social landlords comes in the form of housing benefit payments, the majority paid directly to them; in the case of housing association benefits, 90% is directly paid.[23] Total housing benefit for 2009–10 was £20 billion. For capital expenditure by housing associations, roughly half comes from government and half is raised on the markets (slightly less from the markets in Scotland).

Owner occupation as a tenure has been the preferred option for government since the 1980s, as the trend shows. The policy issue now is, how can or should housing be made available for those who cannot afford to buy? Total house building is running (pre the current recession) at about 200,000 dwellings per year, with new household formation and net immigration adding about 260,000[24] households per year. The shortfall of new building to household growth, even if building recovers to pre-recession levels, indicates an increasing pressure on prices, therefore continuing difficulties for first-time buyers to enter the property market. The alternative for these people, especially if they are in work, is the private rented sector.

The social housing sector has been largely allocated to people not in work, whether beyond retirement, economically inactive, unable to work for health reasons or unemployed. According to Shelter, the housing charity, 31% of social housing tenants are retired and 29% otherwise economically inactive; the median income of social housing tenants is less than half the median income of people in all tenures. Allocation policies have clearly created a housing tenure for the less economically active and poorer members of society. If these policies continue, the sector needs to be able to keep up with the needs of the groups to which this housing is targeted.

Housing subsidy ('Local Housing Allowance') is also available to private tenants, calculated on the difference between income and an 'allowable rent'. One of the Coalition's early policies was to reduce the amount of the 'allowable rent' by imposing a cap of £500 per week in order to reduce the Local Housing Allowance element of the Housing Benefit bill. This was running at the £20 billion figure mentioned earlier. The effect was to move recipients of HB from high rent areas: it was estimated (London *Evening Standard*, 01.06.11) that 90% of private tenants in receipt of HB in the London borough of Kensington and Chelsea would be forced to leave the borough.

CONCLUSIONS

Changes in the way in which social policy has been pursued have altered the way that the public sector is managed: in some cases managers have had to become more competitive (we will see how in more detail in Chapter 11). We have seen structural changes in the NHS, housing, the benefits system and the criminal justice system. In education, policy has been designed to improve performance with a combination of national standards and more managerial autonomy for schools. Market-type solutions and the introduction of competition have been central to provision of social care, management within the health service, and are increasingly used to generate competition between schools and universities. Housing provision has been largely privatised and left to the market, with a residual, though still significant, role for the public and 'third' sectors.

Further reading

Pete Alcock, *Social Policy in Britain* (London: Palgrave Macmillan, 2008). A history of the development of social policy.
Ken Blakemore and Edwin Griggs, *Social policy: an Introduction* (Milton Keynes: Open University Press, 2007).

DISCUSSION POINTS

- How do the changes in the way social policy is implemented impact on managers in the public sector?
- What is the role of the private sector in implementing social policy?
- How does the choice of policy instrument affect the effectiveness of social policy?

NOTES

1 Source: Paul Spicker, *How Social Security Works,* Bristol: Policy Press, 2011.
2 Stephen Driver, 'Work to be Done? Welfare Reform from Blair to Brown', *Policy Studies*, 30, 1, 2009, pp. 69–84.

3 Source: *Social Trends* 40, 2010, Table 3.3.

4 Source: National Curriculum Assessments at Key Stage 2, England, 2009, Department for Children, Schools and Families, and National Statistics, 2009.

5 Source: *Social Trends* 40, 2010, Table 3.7.

6 The Research Excellence Framework, previously called the Research Assessment Exercise, is an elaborate process of peer review by which departments are ranked according to volume of their output, its quality and its impact.

7 National Audit Office, 'Criminal Justice System: landscape review', 2010, p. 8.

8 Source: Ibid., p. 12.

9 Enver Solomon, Chris Eades, Richard Garside, Max Rutherford, *Ten Years of Criminal Justice Under Labour: an independent audit*, Centre for Crime and Justice Studies, Kings College London, published by the *Sunday Times* and the Hadley Trust, 2007.

10 Centre for Crime and Justice Studies (ed. Arianna Silvestri) (2011) *Lessons for the Coalition: an end of term report on New Labour and criminal justice*, London: Hadley Trust.

11 Source: *Compendium of Reoffending Statistics and Analysis*: Executive Summary, Ministry of Justice Statistics Bulletin, November 2010, p. 2.

12 Department of Health (2000) *NHS Plan, a plan for investment, a plan for reform,* para. 6.3.

13 Department of Health (1997) *The New NHS, modern, dependable*, Cm 3807.

14 King's Fund (2005) *An Independent Audit of the NHS Under Labour (1997–2005),* London: King's Fund, p. 11.

15 In England – we saw in Chapter 1 that there is a different structure in each country in the UK.

16 Speech, 13 December 2005.

17 Causes of the overspend are not clear, at the time of writing. Pay rises for NHS employees under Agenda for Change, in excess of predicted salary budgets, probably accounted for 60% of the overspends.

18 Audit Commission, *Early Lessons from Payment by Results* (London: Audit Commission, 2005).

19 Ibid., p. 15.

20 Department of Health, *Short Guide to NHS Foundation Trusts*, 2003, p. 4.

21 Health and Social Care Act 2011, para 53.

22 Department of Communities and Local Government (2011) *House Building Statistics 2010*, Table 209.

23 These figures are from Peter King, *Understanding Housing Finance*, second edition (London: Routledge, 2009).

24 Department of Communities and Local Government (2010) *Housing and Planning Statistics: National Statistics, 2010.* Estimates added for Scotland, Wales and Northern Ireland.

PART TWO

2A

Directly managed services

2B

Outsourced and privatised services

INTRODUCTION

Markets, bureaucracies, clans and networks

The many choices of modes of governance can usefully be reduced to four basic options, markets, bureaucracies, clans and networks.* The history of public management in the UK may be seen as a process of changing the balance among the four modes.

The 'clan' metaphor refers to governance through shared values and through high levels of trust operated among members of a 'clan' who recognise each other. While referring in general to a pre-modern period in which clan allegiance was the dominant way in which people related to each other, within the clan and between it and non-members, the notion of governance through high trust and shared values can be applied to organisations that are self-regulating. Professions, for example, such as medicine and law, inculcate professional values among their members as part of the training and induction processes. They then uphold those values by peer pressure and by essentially internal moral codes and disciplinary procedures. By extension, the 'clan' mode might be a way of running any organisation in which there is a set of shared values.

The 'bureaucracy'† can be seen as a 'modern' mode of governance, replacing loyalty to an inside group with adherence to orders from above in an organised way, whereby people are recruited to positions because they have the requisite skills and occupy those positions in the hierarchy to carry out tasks specified by the organisation. The difference between the bureaucracy and the clan is that behaviours are defined and enforced by the organisation in a bureaucracy, and by the profession or other group in the clan. In principle, if a hospital is managed in clan mode, the organisation does not have to concern itself with the details of the medical staff's behaviour, which will be regulated by their professional ethics and skills. If a hospital is run as a bureaucracy, behaviours, standards and performance are set by a management hierarchy, not the professions.

The market is different. In a market the key relationship is between the customer and the organisation: if the organisation wants to create and keep a customer, its members have to produce something of value and sell it at an acceptable price. Behaviour is regulated by customers' choices: if the organisation fails to do what its customers want, it ceases to exist, and such a risk exerts discipline on the members. To stick to our hospital example, if the medical staff of a private hospital do not perform procedures that people want to buy at a price they are willing to pay, the hospital will close.

The origins of the modes of governance of the welfare state are to be found in both clans and bureaucracies: self-regulating professions, especially in medicine and education, owed as much loyalty to their professions as to the organisations that employed them, or in the case of many doctors, contracted with them. Outside the 'welfare state'-type fields, highway engineers, railway engineers, lawyers, judges, military officers have had varying degrees of professional competence and professional ethics to inform and direct their work. The attempts to bring the professions under political control can be seen as imposing bureaucratic ways of working on a clan system.

The use of markets came later: imposing competitive tendering, introducing private providers of services, and the creation of internal markets are ways of replacing the clan culture and the bureaucratic culture. If these mechanisms are used in conjunction with individual choice by the consumers of public services, the switch is complete.

But the privatisations, introduced as part of this process and for other reasons, did not create competitive markets: water, power, long distance transport by rail are all at best imperfect markets and at worst monopolies, at least at the level of the individual consumer. The market produces market failures, which have to be corrected by regulation, itself a form of bureaucratic intervention.

The fourth mode, the network, requires the user or consumer of services to use a network of providers and suppliers to generate a bundle of services: rather than approach an organisation, the consumer is faced with a variety of suppliers of parts of a service and has to access the network to create their own value. Pushing the idea of free choice by a variety of suppliers to its limit, the implication is that the organisations themselves cease to exist in previously recognised modes of governance and become a network of contracts, sub-contracts, alliances, partnerships and individual operators. Successful surgeon X hires herself out to the highest bidder with the best operating theatre, for periods determined by the volume of sales. A group of highly skilled teachers rent a school from an entrepreneur and sell education. A consortium of general practitioners purchase services from a variety of healthcare providers on behalf of 'their' patients, who in turn can choose which GP to use.

These four modes of governance form a useful heuristic framework for understanding the many attempts to control, reform, change and improve public services and the arrangements for delivering them. In a sense, anything pre-modern or professionally based was seen by all reformers as inferior to a hierarchical arrangement. Both Conservative and Labour administrative ideology favoured markets over hierarchies. More recently, the idea of fragmentation and networks within a market structure has been seen as preferable to more conventional markets. To complicate the issue further, there have also been preferences about ownership; various forms of privatisation have been used to remove services and assets from public ownership and control. Private ownership is not the same as rule by markets: private monopolies or oligopolies can be created, especially where the technology of the sector favours a small number of suppliers. The ownership choice itself is not simply between public and private – not-for-profits, mutuals, charities, social enterprises can all provide public services. This has sometimes been defined as the 'Third Sector' between public and private.

So we have 12 possible combinations of governance and ownership, shown in Figure Intro to part 2.1.

The combination of clan control with elements of hierarchical bureaucracy (especially in the allocation and control of finance) and public ownership represents the post-war 'welfare state'. From the beginning there was tension, especially in the health service, between the clans of the medical professions and the bureaucracy represented by the Ministry of Health. The imposition of rules, standards, instructions, protocols, targets on the professions is all part of the attempt to move from clan to bureaucracy.

Markets are an alternative to bureaucracy, to be used when there is 'organisational failure', or the bureaucracy fails to control the professionals in ways that satisfy the politicians. Markets can also be used to tame the clans, substituting market discipline for self-regulation.

The network, a fragmented system in which the individual is forced to devise their own network with themselves at the centre, is ideologically attractive for politicians who favour individualism over collectivism, markets over planning and hierarchy, and self-reliance over solidarity.

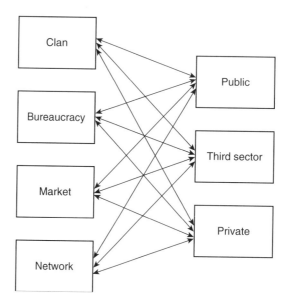

Figure Intro to Part 2.1 Governance and ownership

Source: author

Political ideology also produces preferences for ownership: the founders of the welfare state created publicly owned institutions, not just in public services but also in extractive and manufacturing sectors, as part of the post-war reconstruction effort. Within the Labour party there have always been those who would have preferred to maintain public ownership of as much as possible: the 'modernisers' have been partly defined by their willingness to transfer ownership to private capital. The Conservatives have never, even from the beginning of the welfare state, favoured public ownership.

The Third Sector is a compromise: even neo-liberal ideologues will accept mutuality or charitable status as preferable to public ownership, if pure private ownership is not possible. In the following chapters we will see in some detail how the government has tried to influence, control, shape the public services using various combinations of governance and ownership mechanisms.

Chapters 5 and 6 are concerned with financial management and performance management. Here the methods used are mostly the development of hierarchical relationships, but with 'contractual' forms that emulate one version of how market relationships operate: a series of performance contracts whereby performance is offered in exchange for budget. Chapter 7 is about the use of information and communication technology, initially as part of the control mechanism within the hierarchical framework, but later in an effort to create networks. Chapter 8 looks at the dual role of people as citizens with rights and obligations and as consumers with consumer rights. The dilemma of citizenship rights and obligations rooted in the constitution and in politics and consumer rights derived from market orientation is at the heart of the relationship between individuals and public services: citizenship rights are essentially collective and exercised through the political process, while consumer rights are individual.

Chapter 9, on audit and inspection, is a story about a move from essentially clan-type relationships through which professionals help each other within a framework of mutually understood values and standards, to a hierarchical and bureaucratic inspection process, where standards and targets are produced by the organisation, not the profession.

Chapter 10 is about repairing the fragmentation that comes from replacing an integrated bureaucracy with a fragmented market-based approach. The performance management system described in Chapter 6 produced a narrow focus among managers, looking to achieve individual performance targets, rather than thinking holistically about citizens and their needs and preferences.

Part Two is concerned with managing those parts of the public services that have been moved from public to private or Third Sector ownership, by control systems that either are markets, or require managers to behave as if they were operating in a market environment. Chapter 11 sets up the framework of management through markets, by enforced competition, by creating or reinforcing markets for labour and capital, and the consequences of the market approach. Chapter 12 looks in more detail at the central mechanism of the market approach: the contract.

Chapter 13 is about a specific form of relationship between the public and the private sectors, the Public–Private Partnership, which has been used to provide serviced buildings and infrastructure and in some cases, such as prisons, all-inclusive services.

The last chapter, 14, is about how public services are managed when they are completely privatised, but there is still some notion of the public interest that governments feel the need to define and protect: the use of regulation. Regulation is like inspection without the ownership rights.

Notes

* The title of a seminal article by William Ouchi, 'Markets, bureaucracies and clans', *Administrative Science Quarterly*, *25*, 1, March 1980, pp. 129–141.
† As defined by Max Weber.

PART 2A Directly managed services

CHAPTER 5
Managing Public Finance

INTRODUCTION

Financial management and performance management are strongly linked. The split between financial management in this chapter and performance management in the next is inevitably not absolute. The chapter starts with a look back to the origins of some of the processes now in use and finds that the basic idea of 'programme budgeting' dates back to the 1970s, while the emphasis on measuring and managing unit costs of outputs goes back to the 1990s. The national budget process is then described, especially the lengthening of the process to include reports before the budget is made and the use of periodic 'spending reviews' as a prelude to annual budget decisions. It shows recent budgets and defines the differences between Departmental Expenditure Limits (the costs of running departments) and the Annual Managed Expenditure (funds that flow through departments). It then looks at how budgets are made in the devolved administrations and in local government in England and in the NHS. The chapter concludes with an analysis of how budget cuts can be made, the most pressing requirement for financial management in the foreseeable future.

LEARNING POINTS

- The classification of the budget enables plans to be made according to how predictable and controllable expenditure is in the different categories.
- The budget process is almost entirely 'top-down', with money cascading from the Treasury, even in local authorities and the NHS.
- Cutting spending, in the hierarchical approach used for budgeting in the UK, involves arbitrary cuts at the top and implementation much further down the chain.

A BRIEF HISTORY OF FINANCIAL MANAGEMENT IN GOVERNMENT

The budget process has been refined and reformed over a long period. Parallel with changes to the way the Civil Service is organised and managed, the financial planning and financial control processes have also been changed over the years. Without delving too far back into history we can see that the evolution of the financial planning and control systems has had consistent ambitions. The first is to make a direct link between the process of policy-making and the process of resource allocation: if budgets are constantly rolled forward, adjusted for inflation, then policy will never be reflected in the budgets. Secondly, there has been an ambition to define, measure and control costs. Hence, rather than allocating funds to categories such as salaries, running costs, buildings, etc., there has long been an ambition to know how much services cost. This ambition required some definition and measurement of 'outputs', rather than inputs. Once outputs are defined and their unit costs measured, steps can be taken to improve efficiency, or reduce unit costs.

These three objectives run through fifty-plus years of reform to the financial system. The Plowden Report,[1] published in 1961, resulted in a series of regular reviews of public spending and changes to the accounting system. The report recommended that regular reviews be carried out of the whole of public expenditure, to avoid piecemeal planning. A Public Expenditure Survey Committee (PESC), consisting of the Principal Finance Officers of each department, was set up in 1961 to look at the relationship between policies and spending and to look across all areas of spending. PESC continued in operation until 1998. In 1970, after the Fulton Committee[2] report, a formal process called Programme Analysis and Review introduced a version of programme budgeting through which resources were allocated to programmes according to priorities: in other words that policy choice was to be central to the budget process. Another change implemented as a result of Fulton was the establishment of cost centres with defined costs and objectives – 'management by objectives'[3] had arrived in government, and has been there ever since.

The third ambition, improving efficiency, was given impetus in 1979 by the incoming Conservative government, under Margaret Thatcher, through a series of 'efficiency scrutinies', organised by Derek Rayner of Marks and Spencer through a new institution, the Efficiency Unit. These scrutinies examined unit costs and proposed ways to reduce them; 266 reviews were completed and annual savings of £600m were claimed as a result.

The search for efficiency improvements was made more formal in the Financial Management Initiative, launched in 1982. Cost centres, with objectives and output measures, together with systems of accountability for resources used, were established across all departments by 1984. The next step in the process was to split the Civil Service into the cost centres responsible for service delivery, on the one hand, and the policy-making departments on the other. Derek Rayner's successor at the head of the Efficiency Unit, Sir Robin Ibbs, initiated this development in 1988. Departments' service delivery functions were split off into Executive Agencies, each responsible for a fairly narrow range of services. Through a system of Framework Documents, financial planning could now be fully focused on outputs: the departments in effect 'bought' outputs, or services, from the Agencies. Unit costs, volume of services and some measures of service quality could now be specified alongside financial allocations. Once the programme was largely complete, about 75% of civil servants were working in Executive Agencies.

The three objectives of the reforms of financial management, linking spending to policy, establishing cost centres and identifying and controlling unit costs, were the main concerns of all refinements to the system for the subsequent 20 years. While later reforms were often presented as innovations, the basic framework was in place by 1990. The main innovation after 1990 has been the attempt to go beyond outputs as the main unit of control, and concentrate on 'outcomes' or the results of spending. This aspect of financial management, the focus on outcome performance, is one of the subjects of Chapter 6.

BUDGETING AT NATIONAL LEVEL

We saw in Chapter 3 that the fiscal stance, the choice of how much money to spend and how much to raise, sets the control total for public spending – while there are bids from departments in a bargaining process, the total is set in advance. There could be alternative ways of making budgets, based on some agreed assessment of need and building up from the costs of meeting those needs, but that is not how the UK system is organised.

Since 1998 part of government expenditure has been forecast for three years. That expenditure which is most subject to cyclical fluctuation is subject to an annual budget. So expenditure on items that are based on an entitlement, such as Jobseeker's Allowance, are forecast each year and are classified as 'Annually Managed Expenditure' (AME), which consists essentially of money that flows through departments, rather than costs incurred by them. Costs of running departments and providing services are classified as Departmental Expenditure Limits (DEL) (as shown in Table 5.1 below) and are forecast for three years at a time. Added together, these two amounts are called Total Managed Expenditure (TME). So, TME = AME + DEL + capital expenditure. The purpose of this distinction is to enable departments to plan their running costs over a period of longer than one year.

Another feature of the planning process is that since 2003–4 budgets have been produced on a full 'Resource Accounting and Budgeting' basis (RAB). RAB budgeting and accounting means that expenditures are recognised when they are incurred, not when the cash is spent. Capital expenditure is budgeted each year according to capital depreciation and capital charges, rather than interest and principal repayment in that year. The idea of this is that choices can be made about how to resource services with no bias towards either capital or revenue expenditure: the choice can be made according to the relative resources used.

Since 1999–2000 there has been end-of-year flexibility in budgets, which is an attempt to end the previous potentially wasteful process by which departments spent all their remaining allocation in the last months of the year, in order not to lose those amounts from next year's budget.

Within the overall 'envelope' of TME, there is an iterative process of discussion between the Treasury and the spending departments about the size of individual budgets. As we saw in Chapter 3, priorities during the expansionary period of the Labour governments were set by the Prime Minister with an emphasis on health and education services growing at a faster rate than the average. One element of the process that departments face is the periodic Expenditure Review by which departments have to defend their programme and its expenditure against other priorities. In the mid-1990s the review was labelled the Fundamental Expenditure Review; Labour called them 'Comprehensive Expenditure Reviews' and carried them out every second year from 1998, except for the last one which was delayed from 2006 to 2007. The next Review was done in October 2010 and the title of the published report was simply 'Spending Review'. The idea of the spending reviews is to ask fundamental questions about the need for the expenditure, the justification for the service to be a government function, together with questions about how the service should be provided.

The other element of the process, which was introduced by the Labour administration, was a pre-budget report in the autumn (generally November) before the budget was announced in the spring. The pre-budget report contains economic forecasts, medium-term fiscal forecasts, and sets out the policy framework within which the details of the forthcoming budget will be produced.

At times of reductions in the size of the envelope another institution plays a prominent role in the budget negotiation. The Public Expenditure Committee (PEX) consists of senior cabinet members who, in some years, conduct bilateral negotiations with individual Ministers to drive their budgets down. In the 2010 process, ministers were invited to join the Committee once they had made their own settlement with it.

The budget that is announced in a speech to the House of Commons each April consists of two main elements: a statement of macro-economic policy (sometimes called 'strategy') and a statement of the government's spending and taxation plans for the forthcoming year, and usually the two years after that. The decisions announced are about the changes in tax rates, and the plans for public expenditure. As an example of the spending decisions, Table 5.1 is a summary of the expenditures announced in the June 2010 budget.

Table 5.1   June 2010 Budget, Departmental Expenditure Limits

	Departmental Expenditure Limits £billion		
	Outturn 2008–09	Estimate 2009–2010	Plans 2010–2011
Resource DEL			
Education	46.8	49.6	50.9
Health	90.3	97.6	101.5
of which: NHS England	88.8	96.0	99.5
Transport	5.8	7.0	6.4
CLG Communities	4.1	4.3	3.8
CLG Local Government	24.7	25.5	26.0
Business, Innovation and Skills	17.9	19.2	19.2
Home Office	9.2	9.5	9.4
Justice	9.2	9.6	9.1
Law Officers' Departments	0.7	0.7	0.7
Defence	32.6	35.2	36.0
Foreign and Commonwealth Office	2.0	2.2	2.0
International Development	4.8	5.3	6.1
Energy and Climate Change	0.3	1.2	1.2
Environment, Food and Rural Affairs	2.4	2.5	2.4
Culture, Media and Sport	1.5	1.6	1.5
Work and Pensions	7.9	9.1	8.8
Scotland	24.1	25.1	25.7
Wales	12.8	13.6	13.9
Northern Ireland Executive	7.9	8.8	8.6
Northern Ireland Office	1.2	1.1	1.2
Chancellor's Departments	4.5	4.5	4.1
Cabinet Office	2.0	2.2	2.3
Independent Bodies	0.8	0.8	1.0
Modernisation Funding	0.0	0.0	0.2
Reserve	0.0	0.0	0.6
Allowance for shortfall	0.0	−1.4	0.0
Total resource DEL	**313.5**	**334.3**	**342.7**
Capital DEL			
Education	5.5	7.5	6.7
Health	4.4	5.4	4.9
of which: NHS England	4.2	5.2	4.7
Transport	7.3	8.3	7.2
CLG Communities	7.1	9.2	6.2
CLG Local Government	0.1	0.2	0.0
Business, Innovation and Skills	2.1	3.0	2.0
Home Office	0.8	1.0	0.8
Justice	0.9	0.9	0.6

(Continued)

Table 5.1   (Continued)

	Departmental Expenditure Limits £billion		
	Outturn 2008–09	Estimate 2009–2010	Plans 2010–2011
Law Officers' Departments	0.0	0.0	0.0
Defence	9.0	9.2	10.1
Foreign and Commonwealth Office	0.2	0.2	0.2
International Development	0.9	1.3	1.6
Energy and Climate Change	1.7	1.9	1.9
Environment, Food and Rural Affairs	0.6	0.7	0.5
Culture, Media and Sport	0.8	0.6	0.5
Work and Pensions	0.1	0.3	0.2
Scotland	3.3	3.9	3.2
Wales	1.6	1.9	1.7
Northern Ireland Executive	1.2	1.2	1.1
Northern Ireland Office	0.1	0.1	0.1
Chancellor's Departments	0.3	0.4	0.3
Cabinet Office	0.4	0.5	0.3
Independent Bodies	0.0	0.0	0.1
Reserve	0.0	0.0	1.5
Allowance for shortfall	0.0	−1.2	0.0
Total capital DH	**48.5**	**56.6**	**51.6**
Depreciation	11.6	13.3	14.3
Total Departmental Expenditure Limits	**350.4**	**378.0**	**380.0**

Source: HM Treasury, Budget June 2010

In addition to the decisions for the forthcoming year, Budget 2010 also contained forecasts of the totals of TME, AME and DEL, as well as investment for the next four years. These are shown in Table 5.2.

Table 5.2 shows AME expressed in 'resource' terms, which means using 'resource accounting', or accruals. The DEL is estimated as 'implied' by the AME; in other words, this is what it will cost to run the departments with that level of AME. Capital investment is not included in the TME figure. This budget was published in June 2010, and provides the three-year spending envelope for the years covered by the Spending Review 2010, which was published in October.

Table 5.2   Forecasts of Total Managed Expenditure 2010–11 to 2015–16

| Outturn | Estimate | | | Forecasts | | | |
	2008–09	2009–10	2010–11	2011–12	2012–13	2013–14	2014–15	2015–16
CURRENT EXPENDITURE								
Resource Annually Managed Expenditure	251.3	265.8	294.6	308.0	323.1	337.4	355.0	371.4
Implied Resource Departmental Expenditure Limits	313.5	334.8	342 .7	343.1	341.4	341.2	337.7	340.0
Public sector current expenditure	**564.7**	**600.6**	**637.3**	**651.1**	**664.5**	**678.6**	**692.7**	**711.4**
CAPITAL EXPENDITURE								
Capital Annually Managed Expenditure	16.6	12.1	7.8	7.3	6.9	6.3	6.2	5.2
Implied Capital Departmental Expenditure Limits	48.5	56.6	51.6	41.4	39.6	37.0	38.7	40.8
Public sector gross investment	65.1	68.7	59.5	48.7	46.5	43.3	44.9	46.1
Less public sector depreciation	−18.7	−19.7	−20.6	−21.6	−22.5	−23.4	−24.3	−25.2
Public sector net investment	46.4	49.0	38.9	27.2	24.0	19.9	20.6	20.9
TOTAL MANAGED EXPENDITURE	**629.8**	**669.3**	**696.8**	**699.8**	**711.0**	**722.0**	**737.5**	**757.5**
Spending Envelope for Spending Review 2010					639.6	644.7	649.3	658.7
Of which: Resource spending envelope					591.6	598.9	606.7	614.5
Capital spending envelope					48.0	45.8	42.6	44.1

Source: HM Treasury, Budget June 2010

The Spending Review

In one form or another, Spending Reviews have been conducted since 1992. The incoming government of 2010 inherited the Review from 2007 and decided that it needed a budget with immediate effect one month after coming to office in May. It therefore needed to produce its own Spending Review, which it embarked upon immediately after the budget – a reversal of the more 'normal' process of the review setting the parameters for the subsequent budgets. The review was preceded by a 'Framework',[4] which established the objectives for the review, and the questions to be asked of departments (p. 8):

> Departments will be asked to prioritise their main programmes against tough criteria on ensuring value for money of public spending:

- Is the activity essential to meet Government priorities?
- Does the Government need to fund this activity?
- Does the activity provide substantial economic value?
- Can the activity be targeted to those most in need?
- How can the activity be provided at lower cost?
- How can the activity be provided more effectively?
- Can the activity be provided by a non-state provider or by citizens, wholly or in partnership?
- Can non-state providers be paid to carry out the activity according to the results they achieve?
- Can local bodies as opposed to central government provide the activity?

Most of these questions were very familiar to departments who had been asked very similar questions at every review since 1992. Two questions were slightly different: those concerning 'non-state providers'. 'Can the activity be provided … by citizens' was part of the Big Society idea. It is not entirely clear what it means – it could mean: 'Can people do things for themselves and each other that used to be done by government?' The following question, 'Can non-state providers be paid … according to the results they achieve?', is a reference to outcome-based contracting, a technique that has been tried to a limited extent in services such as job-search and drug rehabilitation. There are few answers to these two questions in the published Review.

The Review itself[5] announced plans for changes to the NHS and to the way schools are managed, but was used mainly to make adjustments to the 2010 budget (the net effect of which was an increase of £2.3bn in planned spending to 2014–5 from £737.5bn to £739.8bn) and set out the departmental settlements for the forthcoming four years. In doing this, it provided a medium-term expenditure forecast. Table 5.3 shows planned DELs.

The Review also contained plans for AME and capital spending. Perhaps because the general election produced a new government that wanted to change the spending plans for the whole of the Parliament, the DELs cover the next four years, unlike the 2007 Review which covered three.

From these extracts from the 2010 Budget and Spending Review, the demarcation between the two elements is not as clear in practice as in principle: the purpose of the review was originally conceived as taking a deep and long-term look at spending and options, and the

Table 5.3   Expenditure review 2010

Baseline[2]	£ billion					Per cent
		Plans				Cumulative real growth
	2010–11	2011–12	2012–13	2013–14	2014–15	
Departmental Programme and Administration Budgets						
Education	50.8	51.2	52.1	52.9	53.9	−3.4
NHS (Health)	98.7	101.5	104.0	106.9	109.8	1.3
Transport	5.1	5.3	5.0	5.0	4.4	−21
CLQ Communities	2.2	2.0	1.7	1.6	1.2	−51
CLG Local Government 5	28.5	26.1	24.4	24.2	22.9	−27
Business, Innovation and Skills	16.7	16.5	15.6	14.7	13.7	−25
Home Office	9.3	8.9	8.5	8.I	7.8	−23
Justice	8.3	8.1	7.7	7.4	7.0	−23
Law Officers' Departments	0.7	0.6	0.6	0.6	0.6	−24
Defence	24.3	24.9	25.2	24.9	24.7	−7.5
Foreign and Commonwealth Office	1.4	1.5	1.5	1.4	1.2	−24
International Development	6.3	6.7	7.2	9 .4	9.4	37
Energy and Climate Change	1.2	1.5	1.4	1.3	1 .0	−18
Environment, Food and Rural Affairs	2.3	2.2	2.1	2.0	1.8	−29
Culture, Media and Sport	1.4	1.4	1.3	1.2	1.1	−24
Olympics	–	0.1	0.6	0.0	–	–
Work and Pensions	6.8	7.6	7.4	7.4	7.6	2.3
Scotland	24.8	24.8	25.1	25.3	25.4	−6.8
Wales	13.3	13.3	13.3	13.5	13.5	−7.5
Northern Ireland	9.3	9.4	9.4	9.5	9.5	−6.9
HM Revenue and Customs	3.5	3.5	3.4	3.4	3.2	−15
HM Treasury	0.2	0.2	0.2	0.2	0.1	−33
Cabinet Office	0.3	0.4	0.3	0.2	0.4	28
Single Intelligence Account 11	1.7	1.7	1.7	1.7	1.8	−7.3
Small and Independent Bodies	1.8	1.8	1.6	1.5	1.4	−27
Reserve	2.0	2.3	2.4	2.5	2.5	–
Special Reserve	3.4	3.2	3.1	3.0	2.8	–
Green Investment Bank	–	–	–	1.0	–	–
Total	**326.6**	**326.7**	**326.9**	**330.9**	**328.9**	**−8.3**
Memo:						
Central government contributions to local government	29.7	27.5	26.3	25.5	24.2	−26
Local government spending	51.8	49.8	49.5	49.5	49.1	−14

(Continued)

Table 5.3   (Continued)

| Baseline[2] | £ billion | | | | | Per cent |
| | Plans | | | | | Cumulative real growth |
	2010–11	2011–12	2012–13	2013–14	2014–15	
Central government contributions to police	9.7	9.3	8.8	8.7	8.5	−20
Police spending (including precept)	12.9	12.6	12.2	12.1	12.1	−1 4
Regional Growth Fund	–	0.5	0.5	0.4	–	–

Source: HM Treasury, *Spending Review 2010*, Cm 7942, p. 10

Budget as being the detailed proposals on both tax and spending for the forthcoming year, with a forecast for three. In practice, the Budget has four-year forecasts and the Spending Review has allocations of DEL. The main difference between the two is that the Budget contains the fiscal policy decisions, whereas the Spending Review is only concerned with expenditure.

As to the detailed content of the Spending Review, Table 5.3 Departmental Expenditure Limits shows the contribution that the expenditure cuts were to make to the correction of the deficit. Overall and over the full period, there was a cut in cash terms of 8.3% (in resource Departmental Expenditure Limits excluding depreciation). What this was to mean in real terms would depend on the rate of inflation of the costs involved in these budgets. Along with the Spending Review, the government announced a pay freeze for public sector workers earning over £25,000 per year for two years, restricting the inflation of the pay bill. The biggest percentage cut was to be in central government contributions to local government spending at 26%. As we saw in Chapter 3, local government spending is to a large extent hypothecated, or 'ear-marked', restricting the local authorities' room to manoeuvre in making cuts. A disproportionate impact was made on very visible services such as care of the elderly, library services, etc. The other big cut was in policing, with a 20% cut in government contribution and a 14% cut in total spending, which more than cancelled the previous government's increases in police spending. Other, smaller budgets were to get very big percentage cuts, including transport, business, innovation and skills, food and rural affairs, culture, media and sport. The only expenditures with a cash increase (but probably a real-terms reduction) were health, international development, work and pensions (benefits were inevitably to increase) and a 28% increase in Cabinet Office expenditures.

Finance in the devolved administrations

You will see lines in Table 5.3 for Scotland, Wales and Northern Ireland. Apart from a small amount of revenue from rates in Northern Ireland, council tax in Scotland and Wales and the as yet unused power of the Scottish government to raise an additional income tax, public expenditure in the devolved administrations is financed through the central tax system, with allocations by formula to Scotland, Wales and Northern Ireland.

Within the three devolved administrations, the central budget task is to divide the resources up among the departments, local authorities and other public bodies.

Public spending in Scotland consists of the disbursement of the funds allocated by the UK government, direct spending in Scotland by the UK government, and spending by the 32 Scottish local authorities and public corporations. As in the UK process, spending is divided into DEL and AME, with multi-year plans for the former. The largest category of spending by the UK government in Scotland is social security, managed by the Department of Work and Pensions. Scottish local government spending is financed through government funding (Aggregate External Finance) and locally raised council tax. As in the rest of the UK the non-domestic rate (a property tax on business) is pooled and redistributed.

Table 5.4   2011 Budget Scotland

2011–12 Draft Budget	DEL resource £m	DEL capital £m	DEL total £m	AME & other £m	Total £m
The First Minister	234.6	20.5	255.1	–	255.1
Finance and Sustainable Growth	1,364.5	854.7	2,219.2	3,230.4	5,449.6
Health and Wellbeing – Health	11,014.4	744.0	11,758.4	100.0	11,858.4
Education and Lifelong Learning	2,319.0	162.1	2,481.1	102.5	2,583.6
Justice	1,196.6	70.9	1,267.5	–	1,267.5
Rural Affairs and the Environment	489.8	49.6	539.4	–	539.4
Administration	228.5	7.5	236.0	–	236.0
Crown Office and Procurator Fiscal	105.5	2.7	108.2	–	108.2
Local Government	8,354.7	691.8	9,046.5	2,179.5	11,226.0
Scottish Government	25,307.6	2,603.8	27,911.4	5,612.4	33,523.8
Scottish Parliament and Audit	93.1	2.8	95.9	–	95.9
Total Scotland	25,400.7	2,606.6	28,007.3	5,612.4	33,619.7

Source: Budget Scotland 2011

Table 5.5   Budget, First Minister, Scotland

	2010–11 Budget £m	2011–12 Draft Budget £m
Europe and External Affairs	16.7	16.1
Culture and Gaelic	194.2	174.9
Corporate and Central Budgets	9.5	8.2
Historic Scotland	49.3	47.0
National Archives of Scotland	10.1	8.9
Total office of the First Minister *of which:*	**279.8**	**255.1**
DEL Resource	251.5	234.6
DEL Capital	28.3	20.5
AME		

Source: Budget Scotland 2011

The summary of Scotland's 2011 Budget is shown in Table 5.4. The definitions of DEL, AME and resource are the same as those used in the UK budget. About one-third of the budget consists of the grants to local authorities, and another third is spent on health. The Scottish budget is then broken down within each line. For example the 'First Minister' budget breakdown is shown in Table 5.5. In turn, each line in the second level is broken down to a third level. All of these budget headings are concerned with programmes, not categories of expenditure. The Health budget is broken down in two ways: by programme and by geographical area.

Local government funding is distributed through two elements: a formula and an agreement (the Single Outcome Agreement) between the government and the local authorities on the aims of the spending. The Single Outcome Agreement is discussed in Chapter 6. The Budget shows both the current and capital spending by local authorities, by function. Table 5.6 shows the revenue budgets.

Northern Ireland's Executive makes a budget to spend the funds distributed by the UK government, plus local rates, at Regional and District level, plus borrowing and European Union funding. The Northern Ireland budget, including AME and DEL, is shown for 2010–11 in Table 5.7.

The budget for public expenditure in Wales is allocated according to ministerial responsibilities or Main Expenditure Groups. A summary of the 2011 budget is shown in Table 5.8. In Wales, 'accrued income' (all sources, other than taxation) is budgeted separately. The Wales budget is approved by the National Assembly for Wales. The budget process in Wales is set out in Box 5.1. The process is relatively quick, reflecting the fact that many major decisions have already been taken before the budget leaves London.

Table 5.6   Revenue budgets of local authorities, Scotland

	2010–11 Budget £m
Education	4,803.2
Social Work	2,844.1
Police	968.4
Fire	275.6
Roads and Transport	494.2
Environmental Services	695.0
Planning and Development Services	320.5
Culture and Related Services	634.1
Emergency Planning	5.0
District Courts	0.5
Administration of Housing and Council Tax Benefits	28.0
Private Sector Housing Renewal	21.5
Housing Benefits	1.8
Non-Housing Revenue Account Housing	42.6
Homelessness	73.5
Housing Support Services	273.9
Welfare Services	4.1
Licensing	1.8
Elections	10.1
General Grants, Bequests and Donations	9.5
Registration of Births, Marriages and Deaths	7.9
Local Tax Collection (including Non-Domestic Rates)	40.4
Council Tax and Non-Domestic Lands Valuation	32.8
Non-Road Lighting	11.5
Corporate and Democratic Core	188.3
Statutory Repayment of Debt	1,021.5
Equal Pay/Single Status (prior year cost provision only)	14.7
Other Miscellaneous Services	40.3
Non-Distributed Costs	71.9
Total Budgeted 2010–11 Net Revenue Expenditure	**12,936.7**

Source: Budget Scotland 2011

Table 5.7   Northern Ireland, Total Planned Allocations 2010–11

	2010–11	
	Current Expenditure £m	Capital Investment £m
Agriculture and Rural Development	269.0	−170.9
Culture, Arts and Leisure	142.4	79.9
Education	2,765.9	201. l
Employment and Learning	833.1	237.3
Enterprise, Trade and Investment	229.8	78.2
Finance and Personnel	526.1	16.0
Health, Social Services and Public Safety	5,354.8	218.2
Environment	135.7	182.6
Regional Development	2,508.0	459.9
Social Development	5,314.1	287.0
Office of the First Minister and Deputy First Minister	88.9	17.3
Northern Ireland Assembly	47.6	0.3
Other Departments	21.3	0.4
Total Allocations	**18,236.5**	**1,607.3**

Source: *NI Budget 2010,* Northern Ireland government website: www.northernireland.gov.uk

Table 5.8   Wales Draft Budget 2011–12

Summary of Resource and Capital Requirements
Welsh Ministers

Ambit	Resources (£000)	Accruing Resources (£000)
Health and Social Services	5,059,584	964,399
Social Justice and Local Government	3,514,629	30
Economy and Transport	921,487	278,013
Children, Education, Lifelong Learning and Skills	2,021,731	69,348
Environment, Sustainability and Housing	606,034	74,010
Rural Affairs	136,556	343,591
Heritage	146,634	5,980
Public Services and Performance	63,382	220
Central Services and Administration	347,320	8,500
Total Resources Requested and Accrued Income relating to Welsh Ministers	**12,817,357**	**1,744,091**

Source: Welsh Government, Cardiff

Box 5.1   How does the budget process work?[6]

Budget process in Wales

Each year, Wales receives a budget allocation from the UK Government. The Welsh Assembly Government develops plans on how to spend the budget. These plans are presented in the draft Budget which is laid before the National Assembly, scrutinised by Committees and debated in Plenary, before being formally approved by the Assembly.

Key dates

The budget planning process began earlier this year but the timeline below outlines some of the main dates in the budget planning process between November and February.

17th November

The Welsh Assembly Government publishes its Draft Budget. The Draft Budget sets out how available resources will be distributed between Ministerial portfolios and spending programme areas.

November– January

Assembly scrutiny of the Welsh Assembly Government's Draft Budget.

18th January

The National Assembly for Wales will debate the Draft Budget.

1st February

Final Budget laid before the National Assembly for Wales.

8th February

The National Assembly for Wales will debate the Final Budget.

Local government in England

We have seen that the allocations to local government in Scotland, Wales and Northern Ireland are placed and managed within the devolved administrations. In England the process is managed by the Department for Communities and Local Government. Local authorities' revenues consist of:

- Revenue support grants, both block grants and specific grants
- Fees and charges

- Council tax
- A share of the national non-domestic rate
- For capital spending: capital grants, borrowing, capital receipts, current revenue used for capital spending.

The proportion of local authority revenue that comes from central government, including the non-domestic rates, is about 95%. The grants are calculated using a formula for each of seven major service blocks: Children's Services, Adults' Personal Social Services, Police, Fire and Rescue, Highway Maintenance, Environmental, Protective and Cultural Services, Capital Financing. The formulae are based on the size of the relevant population adjusted for poverty, population density and other factors reflecting different costs. Once the grants arrive with the local authorities, about half are then available for the authority to decide which services they should in practice be spent on; the other half are tied to particular services, such as 'dedicated schools grant' and the police grant. There is also an adjustment for the relative size of the council tax base.[7]

Because of the financial controls through the use of 'hypothecated' grants that may only be used for their defined purpose, and the use of 'capping' of the amount that the Council Tax can raise, local authorities' budget processes are tightly constrained.

As an example of a local authority budget, Figure 5.1 shows Birmingham City Council's revenues for 2010–11, while Figure 5.2 shows what the Birmingham City Council spend the money on. Only 9% of the revenue derives from the Council Tax, while another 12%

Where the Money Comes From

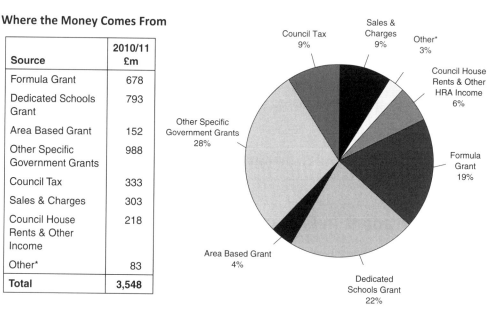

Source	2010/11 £m
Formula Grant	678
Dedicated Schools Grant	793
Area Based Grant	152
Other Specific Government Grants	988
Council Tax	333
Sales & Charges	303
Council House Rents & Other Income	218
Other*	83
Total	**3,548**

Figure 5.1   Birmingham City Council revenues 2010–11

*Other includes: Rents £45m; Other Grants & Contributions £34m; Transfer from Collection Fund £3m; Application of Corporate Resources and Temporary Use of Corporate Reserves £1m

comes from fees and charges and 'other' revenue, mostly interest on positive cash flow. Council house rents are paid into the Housing Revenue Account, which is run at a balance, income being from rents and expenditure the cost of maintaining and financing the housing and collecting the rents. At local authority level, therefore, decisions about revenue are largely outside the control of those making the budget.

When we turn to the expenditure side of the budget, we see that a large part of the budget is controlled from outside. The Schools budget is hypothecated and is simply transferred to schools, again using a formula. Housing Revenue Account has to balance, 'Benefits' is equivalent to central government's AME, in that it consists of funds that flow through the authority. That leaves 62% to be spent with local discretion, subject to some statutory constraints.

One implication of this degree of outside control is that when there are general budget cuts, they will fall on those parts of the budget that are not set out in the specific grants. So schools budgets will be protected, while, for example, adult community care or help for young people and families are not protected and will take a disproportionate cut.

In itself, domination by central funding of the local authorities' revenues does not necessarily imply total central control over what the authorities do, but a combination of specific grants and central controls over what services are delivered and how they are managed reduce local authorities to agents of central government.

Having established that central government exercises a great deal of control over the local authorities, when the cuts were imposed to the grants available to local authorities

Where the Money is Spent

Service Area	2010/11 £m
Schools	840
Children, Young People & Families	686
Benefits	528
Audits & Communities	380
Housing Revenue Account	218
Transport & Regeneration	181
Local Services & Community Safety	165
Constituencies	119
Other Services	431
Total	3,548

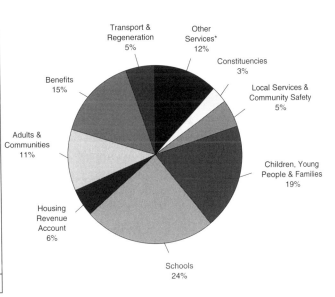

Figure 5.2 Birmingham City Council expenditure 2010–11

from 2009 on, it was the councils that had to make the hard choices about what to cut. The control is asymmetric in growth and decline: much of the growth was accompanied by an increase in hypothecated funds, while many of the reductions are discretionary.

THE NATIONAL HEALTH SERVICE

Financial planning in the NHS centres on the division between 'purchaser' and 'provider' functions. Figure 5.3 shows how in England the funds flow down from the top.[8] Of the £99.8 billion, £68.5 billion flows to NHS bodies, of which £60 billion was spent by the Primary Care Trusts. Dentistry was financed separately, along with funds for the Strategic Health Authorities and training. The figure also shows the (relatively) small centrally-managed budgets and the Health Department funding for personal social services.

For the hospitals and other service providers, the financial management process starts with the signing of contracts with the PCTs for work for the forthcoming year, sometimes more than one year. With 'payment by results' the actual flow of funds depends on the volume of work performed by each provider.

THE ART OF CUTTING BUDGETS

After the long period of Labour governments' expansion of public spending, public sector managers had to re-learn the old arts of cutting spending once the Coalition government announced its spending plans in October 2010, following the reductions announced in the last Labour budget. For younger managers it was a lost art, having been trained throughout a period where budgeting was largely a matter of choosing the priorities for growth.

The first decision when facing a budget reduction is whether it is possible to make a level, proportionate cut across all services, or whether there needs to be discretion. A small budget reduction might well be achieved by asking all departments for a uniform percentage cut in spending. It is then up to managers fairly far down the hierarchy to find efficiency savings, lose staff through 'natural wastage'[9] and hope that their co-workers will cover the gap. Bigger cuts require more deliberate actions by the top management. In 2011, local authorities and government departments were required to make substantial cuts that could not be achieved by such relatively easy, across-the-board arithmetic.

Once a large cut has to be made, strategic decisions have to be taken. Announcing the local authority funding settlement that resulted from the Spending Review of October 2010, Eric Pickles, the Secretary of State for Communities and Local Government, set out how

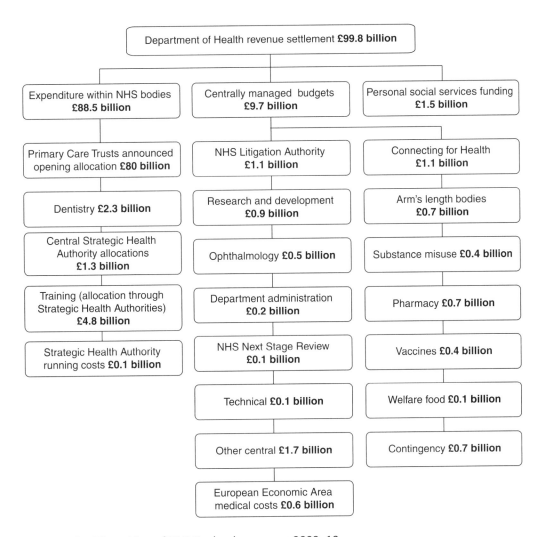

Figure 5.3 Disposition of NHS England resources 2009–10

Source: National Audit Office 2011

the government thought that local authorities should make the necessary cuts, of 7.25% in real terms for each of the subsequent four years:

> … the onus is very much on councils themselves to make the most of this unprecedented freedom and flexibility to focus all efforts and resources on protecting hardworking families, vulnerable people, and frontline services. That must mean:

- fundamentally re-examining every aspect of the way that councils work;
- eliminating all traces of waste by becoming more transparent and improving procurement practice;
- maximising efficiency and productivity, drawing on the lessons of the LGA-led productivity programme;
- sharing departments, officers and back office services between different local authorities; and
- bringing excessive senior pay under control.

The emphasis must be on creativity and innovation. Councils must really put every aspect of service delivery under the microscope, focusing on early intervention and drawing on the significant expertise, reach and resources in the voluntary and community sector.'[10]

There is no mention here of the fundamental choices to be made about cuts in services. When services have to be cut there are four main ways:

1   An even cut in the volume of inputs: a school can be run with fewer staff; a social services department can lose some social workers
2   A cut in the volume of outputs or services for all users: libraries can reduce opening hours and the purchase of books; schools can cut extra-curricular activities and non-core curriculum subjects such as extra foreign languages or music
3   A change in the numbers of people eligible for services: fewer adults can receive social care; fewer patients will be able to undergo elective surgery
4   Abolition of some services: advice bureaux can be closed down, play facilities closed, subsidies to voluntary organisations abolished.

It is clear from these options that service providers, whether in health or local authorities or government departments, are faced with some cuts that are harder to justify than others: the core curriculum must be preserved, so peripherals such as music are cut: emergency healthcare is less easy to cut than elective surgery. All services are on a spectrum of discretion: some are well defined by statute and must be provided, others are more discretionary. So when a government announces a 7.25% cut in local government funding, the cut necessarily falls unevenly within local authorities as they protect the statutory core.

In addition to cutting services, managers try to cut the overhead costs: the 'back office' services mentioned in Pickles' letter. The same principles apply to cutting overheads as cutting direct services: they can be asked to make uniform, even cuts by increasing productivity; they can be asked to change the people for whom they provide services; they can be asked to perform fewer tasks. A variant is to share back-office staff: local authorities started sharing Chief Executives (for example the London boroughs of Camden and Islington) and other functions in advance of the 2010 cuts.

For central government, the choice on overheads was to make a (mostly) even cut in administrative budgets across the board. Some were expected to make additional cuts, above the average 34%. The administrative budget cuts announced in the 2010 Spending Review are shown in Table 5.9.

These evenly distributed but unspecified cuts in administrative budgets added up to a 34% reduction in cash terms over the period 2011–2014/15. These cuts have clearly not

Table 5.9   Administrative Spending Cuts, Central Government

	£ million					Per cent
	Baseline		Plans			Cumulative real growth
Administration Budgets	2010–11	2011–12	2012–13	2013–14	2014–15	
Education	508	466	432	401	372	−33
NHS	5,074	4,500	4,000	3,715	3,715	−33
Transport	295	272	252	233	216	−33
CLG Communities	452	399	360	323	289	−42
Business, Innovation and Skills	918	838	687	641	609	−40
Home Office	731	650	598	562	538	−33
Justice	704	655	606	561	517	−33
Law Officers' Departments	69	64	61	57	51	−33
Defence	2,183	2,025	1,877	1,736	1,598	−33
Foreign and Commonwealth Office	248	229	212	196	182	−33
International Development	128	121	112	103	94	−33
Energy and Climate Change	236	218	202	187	174	−33
Environment, Food and Rural Affairs	652	601	555	515	478	−33
Culture, Media and Sport	180	166	151	129	116	−41
Work and Pensions	1,541	1,483	1,290	1,166	1,105	−35
HM Revenue and Customs	1,025	945	875	812	754	−33
HM Treasury	158	153	148	133	117	−33
Cabinet Office	177	163	151	140	130	−33
Single Intelligence Account	82	82	74	62	61	−33
Small departments	404	375	350	315	300	−33
Total administration budgets	**15,765**	**14,404**	**12,993**	**11,986**	**11,415**	**−34**

Source: Spending Review 2010, HM Treasury

been arrived at through a process of analysis of the priorities and possibilities for cuts: they are imposed by the Treasury and are implemented within departments, whatever the obstacles to their achievement might be.

The other choice to be made, despite the fact that capital and revenue expenditure is supposed to be treated equally under accruals accounting,[11] is between recurrent and capital spending. In the reductions in spending announced in October 2010, £11 billions were in capital budgets, compared with £13 billions in service cuts. Cumulative capital spending cuts were 29% over the four years covered by the Spending Review, up to 2014–15.

During the process of making cuts, the managers and politicians involved in the process will take action to protect their services. This can involve announcing the biggest cuts in the most popular or the most visible services and making a very public statement about the consequences. This is known in the NHS as 'shroud waving', or painting a picture of the worst possible consequences of cuts in an effort to gain public support against those imposing the spending reductions.

The National Audit Office produced a useful guide to spending cuts in 2010,[12] and the stages in the cuts process are shown in Figure 5.4.[13]

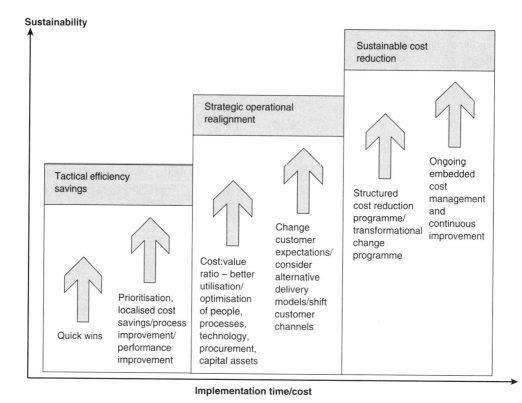

Figure 5.4   Stages of cost reduction

Source: A Short Guide to Structured Cost Reduction, National Audit Office, 2010

The NAO recognises that big cuts are unlikely to be achieved by efficiency savings or changes in the method of delivery of services. The word 'prioritisation' implies de-prioritisation and cancellation of some services, while 'change customer expectations' means 'tell people what they can no longer expect to receive'. The scale of cuts proposed by the Coalition's first Budget and Spending Review imply large real reductions in the volume and quality of public services.

CONCLUSIONS

Budgeting is largely a process of decision-making at central government and Treasury level transmitted downwards to spending departments, the devolved administrations, the local authorities and the NHS. At the top level, budget cuts are simply cuts in expenditures that have to be translated into cuts in services at lower levels. The scale of cuts in recent years means that managers and politicians at local level have to make big decisions about what services to cut, because the cuts are unlikely to be feasible only through more efficient use of resources.

Further reading

Stuart Adam, Carl Emmerson, and Anoushka Kenley, *A Survey of Local Government Finance* (London: Institute of Fiscal Studies, Briefing Note 74, 2007). The intricacies of the grant system.

H.M. Coombs and D.E. Jenkins, *Public Sector Financial Management* (London: Thompson, 2002). Details of the UK public finance and accounting system.

HM Treasury, *Managing Public Money* (London: The Stationery Office, 2007). A description of the process of budgeting and financial control.

QUESTIONS FOR DISCUSSION

- The budget process in the UK has grown up in a period of expansion of the public sector: does it work well for a period of public spending cuts?
- The Coalition government announced that local authorities were to have more financial freedom – in a period of expenditure cuts, how are they likely to use this freedom?

NOTES

1   HM Treasury, *The Control of Public Expenditure (Plowden Report)*, Cmd. 1432 (London: HM Treasury, 1961).
2   *The Civil Service*, Cmnd 3638 (1968), Chairman Lord Fulton. This was the first comprehensive review of the structure and processes, including management, recruitment and training, of the Civil Service since the

Northcote–Trevelyan 'Report on the Organisation of the Permanent Civil Service' advocated a professional and impartial Civil Service in 1854.

3 Peter Drucker, *The Practice of Management* (London: Butterworth-Heinemann, 1955) set out the principles of management by objectives.

4 HM Treasury, *The Spending Review Framework*, Cm 7872, June 2010.

5 HM Treasury, *Spending Review 2010*, Cm 7942, October 2010.

6 Source: Welsh Assembly Government 'Budget Timeline', 2010.

7 For details of the way that the money is distributed in England, all the formulae are published on the Department for Communities and Local Government website. Explanations are available each year in *The Local Government Finance Report (England)*.

8 National Audit Office (2011) *National Health Service Landscape Review*, HC 708, session 2010–11.

9 'Natural wastage' occurs when there is staff turnover and exiting staff are not replaced.

10 Letter to local authorities from Eric Pickles, Secretary of State for Communities and Local Government, 20th October 2010.

11 Under accruals accounting, capital is accounted for as resources used in the year, rather than cash expended. Hence recurrent and capital spending should be treated as equivalents in terms of resources used for decision making purposes.

12 National Audit Office (2010) *A Short Guide to Structured Cost Reduction*.

13 Ibid., p. 3.

CHAPTER 6
Managing Performance

SUMMARY

While the financial management system was partly designed to manage performance, there are also other elements to the performance management system in the United Kingdom. The system has been constructed as if the government were the 'principal' and the departments, NHS, local authorities, etc. were its 'agents' who would only act according to the government's wishes if the incentive and contractual arrangements were designed to provide incentives, rewards and punishments to ensure their compliance. This chapter discusses the framework of these arrangements and how the performance management system was developed to enable the government to concentrate on the outcomes, or results of public sector activities, policies and programmes. Targets, standards and performance measures all cascaded from on high to those delivering the services.

LEARNING POINTS

- Performance management has been based on the idea of the 'principal–agent' problem.
- The system was designed to be continuous from a series of high-level goals, through organisational targets to individual targets for public sector workers.

WHY MEASURE AND MANAGE PERFORMANCE?

Accountability

Public sector organisations are in principle accountable to the public for three things: that money has been spent as agreed and in accordance with procedures; that resources have been used efficiently; that resources have been used to achieve the intended result. At the same time politicians are supposed to be accountable for the policy decisions they make while holding the management of the organisations to account for their actions. Government has been increasingly willing to make explicit, measurable promises.

Accountability for these promises requires ways of measuring performance. Accounting for how money has been spent is relatively simple, despite the mysteries of accountancy.

Whether resources have been used efficiently is a question which requires some measure of the output or value of services provided, which can then be compared with the cost of provision. Here the problems of measurement begin: how to measure the outputs of schools, hospitals, prisons and so on?

The third question, did the service achieve what it was supposed to, requires an assessment of what works best in the particular service, or indeed what works at all. Here the relationship between management and professionals or experts is important. One aspect of the specialised occupations in public services is that people claim to know what works and what does not, without necessarily being able to explain or demonstrate it. When politicians, through their managers, take control of public services away from the professionals, they need evidence of what policies and services produce the desired results and a system of measurement and monitoring to make sure that people are doing what they are told and achieving what the government wants them to.

Promises and targets

The Labour governments were brave enough to make specific electoral promises, using targets whose achievement could be verified in areas such as class sizes in primary schools, or waiting lists for medical treatment. They also published targets that were less easy to pin down to policy or service delivery, such as the incidence of cancer and the rate of teenage pregnancy. They took the work of the previous governments on target setting through the Citizen's Charter initiative and, in the first term, made 'Service First' an important part of their toolkit for delivering measurable improvements in public services. The government's critics from the Left dismissed this attempt as 'managerialism', using methods derived from management rather than politics to run state services. Rather than electoral accountability through local government and parliamentary elections, it chose the methods of 'management by objectives' to make and monitor promises.

As John Bourne, then Auditor and Comptroller General, put it:

One solution seemed to be the introduction of 'management by objectives'. Instead of believing the bureaucratic mantra that if the right staff were recruited, their duties specified and co-ordinated in successive hierarchical layers then results would be automatically achieved, it came to be argued that the right way forward would be to set specific objectives for organisations as a whole, disaggregated for the various lower levels of the organisation, and cascaded down to objectives for each member of staff to achieve in a specified period of time.[1]

There is no doubt that the government had a belief that management methods could improve the standard of public services. Specific targets were set for the level of attainment in literacy and numeracy in schools, backed by a measurement system and given priority through the introduction of literacy and numeracy hours in schools. The same was true of the campaign to reduce the numbers on waiting lists for surgery: simple targets made a priority and given resources can usually be achieved. The question is whether the overall standard of services can be improved by using multiple targets, some of which may conflict with each other. For example, waiting lists may be reduced by offering shorter hospital stays resulting in more re-admissions, or may be achieved by exceeding budgets. Literacy and numeracy may be improved at the expense of physical fitness. Targets concentrate managers' and professionals' efforts on those items that politicians specify as important.

Having made such explicit promises to the electorate, the government then faced the problem of how to make a contract with the managers and employees of the public services that would allow the government to achieve the targets and therefore gain and retain public support. While the Labour governments continued to use markets, strengthened the inspection and monitoring agencies and took powers to punish poor performers and replace their management, in some cases by private companies, the main control mechanism was a series of internal contracts setting out targets, mostly expressed as outputs and outcomes, which have been formalised as Public Service Agreements (PSAs).

As the Audit Commission put it, 'Each department's PSA was in effect its contract with the Treasury: linking increased investment arising from the CSR to improved productivity and outcomes; and with the public: articulating departmental priorities and setting clear targets for improvement over the next three years.'[2]

Implicit in the government's actions is the belief that through targets, publication of results and the threat to managers that they will lose their jobs, and to whole institutions that they would be privatised or replaced in some other way, managers and workers would behave as required by the government. At the same time incentives, often in the form of performance-based pay, were established for those meeting the targets. Sometimes these incentives were at the level of the institution: if they perform well they are rewarded with higher budgets and a 'light touch' inspection regime. What exactly was the problem that government's actions have been designed to solve?

Shirking

A particular problem in public services, and especially those produced by professionals, is that the required behaviour is unobservable: it is unrealistic to have an inspector for every teacher, nurse, doctor and, in any case, how would the inspectors be monitored? The main solution was to produce a set of targets and ways of measuring their achievement and an incentive system to back them up. Individual performance-based pay was introduced to tackle the individual shirking problem. Schools were heavily inspected to tackle the institutional shirking problem and in extreme cases could be put under a regime of 'special measures' or in very extreme cases closed down altogether by being merged with another institution.

Standards

A frustration for politicians and managers trying to run thousands of service delivery operations from Ministries in London, or the Scottish Executive in Edinburgh, is that if only those at the bottom of the performance scale would behave like those higher up the scale, output and quality could be increased at no extra cost. Performance improvement by emulation of the better is one solution to the problem. Closure of the 'plants' (schools, hospitals, prisons, etc.) at the bottom end would, in principle, improve average performance. Even without closures, median performance or top quartile performance can be used as a benchmark for all the units in the service.

Standards go beyond measures of efficiency and include cycle times, courtesy, accessibility and other aspects of quality. All public services have been subjected to quality improvement programmes, the most frequently used being the European Quality Foundation quality model. Since this work was in large part concerned with the quality of interaction between the service and its users, objective measures are not easy to establish: while cycle times and telephone answering times can be measured, the quality of the interaction can only be gauged by asking the customers how they feel. To translate this into a binding contract, resort was made to clauses about the percentage satisfaction level as measured in customer surveys.

A perennial problem with public services is the difficulty in measuring efficiency and improving productivity. Since most of the outputs have no independently measurable value, tracking changes in the cost per unit value of output is hard. One solution in contractual terms is to reduce the overall budget by a fixed amount per year while requesting that output is held constant. Thus, budgets are agreed, then an adjustment is made for 'efficiency savings' or 'productivity improvements', despite the likelihood that the outputs cannot be measured accurately enough to ensure that the volume of production is not reduced proportionately. When budgets were increased, the government was especially concerned that the extra spending should increase the volume of services produced, rather than be absorbed in higher pay and prices.

A 'principal–agent' problem

The problems that the governments have tried to solve through the performance management system are those defined as the 'principal–agent problem'. Originally formulated to explain the relationship between business owners and business managers, the principal–agent relationship is conducted through a series of instructions and attempts to control and measure the behaviour and performance of the agent by the principal. While the language of 'principal–agent' was not explicitly used, the performance system devised was based exactly on such ideas.

The literature[3] on the principal–agent problem predicts that agents will seek ways to act in their own interests, whatever contracts are written and whatever monitoring is put in place. Such opportunities exist when performance control systems are implemented in the public sector. An example is the case of secondary schools whose rewards are derived from their pupils' achievement: the obvious way to improve performance is to select out the potentially poor performers and attract potentially good performers. Such behaviour does nothing for the overall standard of education (the overall aim of the system) but produces the required results for the school. Once this behaviour starts, another contractual solution has to be found: in this case the measures used are not performance by pupils but 'value added' or the gain in performance from whatever starting point.

THE THREE E'S

Both the Treasury and the Audit Commission encouraged the achievement of the 'three E's': economy, efficiency and effectiveness. Economy is about the cost of the inputs used, and making economic use of them. Efficiency is concerned with the cost of producing outputs. Effectiveness is defined as producing results. People concerned with equality of access to services have talked of a fourth 'E', equity, and argued that it should be included in any scheme of performance measurement.

In those parts of the public sector in which there are markets, it could be argued that measures of economy and productive efficiency are taken care of: competition eliminates those producers whose costs are too high or forces them to reduce their costs. There is no need for any independent measurement or analysis of their costs. There may be targets and measurements related to resource use, such as return on capital employed. Where there are no markets, public accountability for the use of resources would require that those given stewardship of public money should demonstrate how well they are spending it. Measurement and reporting of efficiency is an essential part of public accountability, and needs to be independently validated.

The most important aspects of performance management are not technical issues divorced from the real world of politics. Managers operate in a political environment and ignore politics at their peril.

Economy

At its simplest, performance measurement looks at how much money was used up by the organisation over a period. At first sight this might seem trivial and to say nothing about managerial or organisational performance. In practice such measures are given importance by the dominance of the budget process. Budgets are cash limited and in many cases are projected from one year to the next with the expectation of an 'efficiency saving' of a certain percentage of the last year's budget. The notion of the annual efficiency saving relates to a general expectation that productivity, especially labour productivity, increases constantly. Technology changes, improvements in work organisation, enhancement of skill levels all contribute to a trend of improvement in the value of output per worker. Even if outputs cannot be measured, because these processes of improvement are going on in the public sector, it can be expected that productivity will improve every year. Hence budgets can be reduced in real terms without loss of outputs. In those cases where the output either cannot be measured or where the quality varies with cost, what this means in effect is that the main performance target is staying within the budget.

Staying within budget means both not spending too much and not spending too little. The fact that budgets have normally to be used up in a financial year (with some exceptions) means that there is sometimes a need to stop spending in the tenth or eleventh month, while in other cases, there is a rush to ensure that money is spent at those times to ensure that budget targets are met. This necessity overrides other, more sophisticated aspects of performance management. A manager who can demonstrate that the services were effective, the service users were delighted and the other stakeholders were satisfied will not last long if the budget is consistently overspent.

Reporting systems reflect this. Financial management reports of actual expenditure against the projected spend are sent out, usually monthly. While there are variations among sectors and within them, there are two remaining problems even with this most simple measure of performance. The first is that the details of the projected spend are sometimes produced after the year has begun, which means that managers are not sure against which figures they are monitoring the spending. The second is that monitoring systems are still often based on cash outflows in each period. In many services, a decision taken in one month may represent a commitment to spend money for many months or even years. For example, if a social services department assesses a child aged 12 as needing residential care, they undertake a potential commitment to looking after that child in a residential home for four years. A monthly financial report which says that this month £4,000 was spent on the child does not give a picture of the continuing commitment.

Efficiency

In economics there are two definitions of efficiency. Productive efficiency is measured by the average cost of producing goods and services. Allocative efficiency is measured by the extent to which the economic system produces that mix of goods and services which reflects people's preferences as expressed by their consumption decisions. There is an argument that markets promote both types of efficiency. Competition generates the need for producers to reduce their price to that of their competitors. Choice allows consumers to influence producers in their decisions about what to make: if nobody wants what is on offer, producers have to make something else.

For most services, it is possible to devise a measure of volume. Universities can measure the number of hours of student contact the staff have or the hours of staff contact the students have; hospitals can measure the throughput of patients, libraries the numbers of books issued and reference materials referenced, pest control the number of rats captured or cockroaches killed. All that remains to produce a measure of efficiency is to find out how much each one cost, and then make comparisons, either with other producers, or over time.

Such comparisons have to be interpreted with care. The accounting mechanisms used to make the calculations have to be the same: the allocation of overheads, for example, may be made using different methods. The nature of the 'product' may also vary: the fact that Rochdale educates primary pupils for half the cost of doing the same thing in Lambeth may be because the education system is twice as efficient there or because the quality of the education is half as good, or some position in between.

A different consequence of such comparisons might be that those with high costs will concentrate on finding reasons for the differences: council tax is harder to collect in areas where there is a high turnover of population, for example. Such comparisons should be used to raise questions about apparently poor performers, rather than be accepted simply as a certain indicator that one organisation is performing better than another; and the factors affecting the comparative figure should be looked at.

Barzelay[4] argues that the emphasis on measuring and improving efficiency has been a mistake, and that the scientific management approach to performance improvement is based on how manufacturing is managed, where the product is easily defined and measured, whereas public service 'products' are not so easily measured:

> 'Since it excluded the concept of product, reformers' influential conception of efficient government was trouble waiting to happen. It encouraged the notorious bureaucratic focus on inputs to flourish and it permitted more specialised functions to become worlds in themselves. More specifically, an increase in efficiency could be claimed in government whenever spending on inputs was reduced, whereas it was much easier to argue in an industrial setting that cost reduction improved efficiency only when it led to a reduction in the cost per unit of output.'[5]

The other definition of efficiency is whether the organisation produces the range of services which reflects the preferences of citizens or their representatives. At an aggregate level, this is a question of the distribution of resources among the main services: defence, social security, education, health and so on. The notion of Pareto optimality is that there is an allocation of resources which produces the most possible benefits. To move resources from one activity to another would diminish the total of benefits. Classical economists would argue that the market achieves precisely this optimal position: the sum of individual purchasing decisions and the response by producers will produce the best allocation of resources, in this Pareto sense.

However, the question of allocative efficiency poses a different problem. If there are markets in which consumers have a choice of what to buy and from whom, it might be argued that there is an automatic process of matching supply to demand or even need. But what if there is no choice? Political processes of resource allocation substitute for the market. How do we then know whether those choices reflect demand, preferences, or even need?

In practice, allocative efficiency is never measured: there are no mechanisms for measuring whether the result of the resource allocation processes reflects either any individual's set of preferences or any sense of a set of collective preferences. In any case different classes of people have different preferences.

Effectiveness

But what of effectiveness? Given that the success of the allocation process is difficult to measure, is it possible to measure the degree to which those resources which are allocated to services produce the desired results? Progress is being made towards measuring effectiveness in those areas where there is agreement on what a desired outcome is, such as improved health status or acquired knowledge and skills. The issues about measuring effectiveness are partly technical. There are two broad categories of outcome. One is a change in *state*. The purpose of the service might be to improve the quality of a person's health, the durability of a road, the cleanliness of water. While there may be arguments about what to measure, there are numerous examples of how to measure. The second sort of outcome is a change in *behaviour*. The criminal justice system aims to change the offending behaviour of people convicted of crimes. Interventions by social workers are sometimes intended to change the behaviour of parents or children. Such changes may be more difficult to measure than changes in states, although offending rates and rates of abuse can be measured and monitored.

Measuring effectiveness is concerned with finding out what services produce the desired outcomes. The outcomes of services may be different for different stakeholders. As Peter Jackson[6] says:

'Because different stakeholders have different interests in the performance of public sector departments, the stakeholder approach helps to force the question 'whose value for money is being considered?' Value for money will mean different things for different individuals. Often these different perspectives will come into conflict and will need to be resolved. This is the business of politics. Value for money is not a technocratic value-free concept.'

There are many examples of the differences in opinion about what outcomes are desired from services. For example, applicants for planning permission want to be able to carry out their developments, while neighbours may not.

The Labour government was very keen on the idea of specifying outcomes and measuring their achievement. The Introduction to the Public Service Agreements for 1999–2002 said:

> The amount spent or numbers employed are measures of the inputs to a service but they do not show what is being achieved. While the number of new government programmes established or the volume of legislation passed are often critical milestones on the path to achieving change, they are only a means to delivering the real improvements on the ground that this Government wants to see. What really matters is the effectiveness and efficiency of the service the public receives. That is what makes a difference to the quality of people's lives.

> The targets published in this White Paper are therefore of a new kind. As far as possible, they are expressed either in terms of the **end results** that taxpayers' money is intended to deliver – for example, improvements in health and educational achievement and reductions in crime – or **service standards** – for example, smaller class sizes, reduced waiting lists, swifter justice. The Government is therefore setting specific, measurable, achievable, relevant and timed (i.e. SMART) targets, related to outcomes wherever possible. Moreover, as experience of this new approach develops, it hopes to further refine and improve future target-setting.

The contractual basis for performance management

The management of performance in the United Kingdom is based on the idea that there are contracts between the Treasury, or the devolved governments, and the departments, local authorities and other bodies that deliver services. The funds flow in one direction, in exchange for a defined volume of services. The contract is not based on contract law, with the obligations and sanctions implied in proper contracts between two parties, but the idea of a contract is used in the design of the performance system.

A common language has developed, which is shared with many other countries, in which the resources used in producing services are defined as 'inputs', the activities carried out to provide services are defined as 'outputs' and the immediate results of providing those services are called 'outcomes'.

The development of this performance management system has a very long history. While some say that reform of the civil service can be traced back at least to Samuel Pepys' time in charge of the Admiralty in the seventeenth century, we can trace the use of outputs and an interest in performance to the Plowden Committee which reported in 1959 on the public expenditure planning process. The report recommended that regular reviews be carried out of the whole of public expenditure, to avoid piecemeal planning. A Public Expenditure Survey Committee, consisting of the principal finance officers of each department, was set up in 1961 to look at the relationship between policies and spending. Nine years later, after the Fulton Committee report, a formal process called Programme Analysis and Review introduced a version of programme budgeting through which resources were allocated to programmes according to priorities: in other words that policy choice was to be central to the budget process. PSC continued in operation until 1998.

Public Service Agreements

In 1998 the new government conducted its first 'Comprehensive Spending Review'. Like the previous government's process the 'Fundamental Expenditure Review', the idea was to look periodically at the whole of public spending (the plan was to do it every two years), examine the outputs of spending decisions, look across departments and set the framework for budgets for the forthcoming three years. CSRs were conducted in 1998, 2000, 2002, 2004 and 2007. As part of the process, in exchange for the resources allocated to them, departments had to agree with the Treasury a Public Service Agreement, setting out what outputs would be produced with the funds, what outcomes would be achieved, and how services would be reformed and improved over the forthcoming three-year period. These PSAs are high-level documents, setting out overall policy ambitions accompanied by a set of targets for each ambition. While the first round of targets consisted mostly of process and outputs and only 11% of targets were outcomes, by 2000, outcomes were stated in 67% of the targets. The distinction was operationalised by creating another level of plan, below the high-level PSA.

In 2000 and 2002 the PSAs were supplemented by Service Delivery Agreements, setting out more operational proposals and plans about how the departments propose to meet the targets in the PSAs. In principle the PSAs emphasise *outcomes*, while the SDAs emphasised *outputs* and *processes*. Underlying and following on from both these Agreements are documents that are essentially internal to departments, in the form of business plans, which in turn are translated into staff performance and accountability plans. From 2004, SDAs were replaced by Delivery Plans, which served the same function inside the department but were not part of the published agreement.

In principle, at least, all these levels of plan are congruent with each other: individual staff members should know how their performance contributes to the business plan, and how that makes a contribution to the overall outcome targets in the Public Service Agreement.

The hierarchy was set out in a diagram in a 2001 Treasury report[7] and is shown in Figure 6.1.

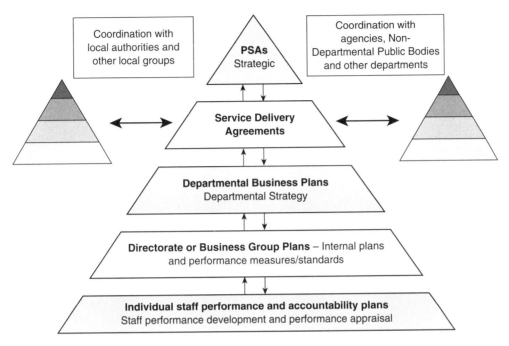

Figure 6.1   The English PSA system

Each PSA had four sections:

1 Vision
2 Measurement
3 Delivery strategy
4 Measurement Annex, setting out data sources, confidence intervals where sampling is involved, baseline data.

The Comprehensive Spending Reviews and their attached Public Service Agreements fitted into the budgeting process. The Treasury produces an annual budget, on an accruals basis – accruals is called 'resource' accounting in the Treasury. In the budget, Departments' running costs are separated from the funds, mostly transfer payments, that pass through the departments. Running costs are called 'Departmental Expenditure Limits', while the funds flowing through are called 'Annually Managed Expenditure': see Tables 5.1, 5.2. The separation is made to distinguish between those items which are under departments' control and those which are mostly a product of the economic cycle and subsidy and transfer policies. The aggregate of the two is called 'Total Managed Expenditure'.

Table 6.1   Pluri-annual financial plans (number of years)

	1998	1999	2000	2001	2002	2003	2004	2005	2006	2007	2008	2009
Fiscal aggregates projection	+0	+2	+3	+3	+3	+3	+5	+5	+5	+5	+5	+5
Total Managed Expenditure projection	+0	+2	+3	+3	+2	+3	+2	+3	+2	+1	+3	+2
Comprehensive Spending Review/ Public Service Agreements	✓		✓		✓		✓			✓		
General election (also 1997, 2010)				✓				✓				

Source: HM Treasury

Contained in the annual budget document are some multi-year projections: a projection is made of the fiscal aggregates (the number of years in this projection has grown to five); and an estimate of Total Managed Expenditure, which is mostly projected over three years, but sometimes only one. The pluri-annual projection periods for fiscal aggregates and Total Managed Expenditure are shown in Table 6.1, along with the dates of the Comprehensive Spending Reviews. Table 6.1 also gives the dates of the CSRs and the general elections.

The Total Managed Expenditure projections vary in length, partly because of the timing of the elections. A new government will have new ideas about both the level and the distribution of spending.

It should be noted that these processes were developed during a period of public spending growth. This has implications for the willingness of departments to participate in a process which ended up with them getting more resources. It also makes evaluation of the impact of the process difficult: results may have improved as much because of the extra resources as from the performance management system.

The process of developing the PSAs progressed from using inputs to using outcomes as the main objects being measured. The NAO review of government performance management shows this in Figure 6.2, the development of outcome measurement.[8]

Performance management in the devolved governments

The performance arrangements in Scotland are centred on the distribution of the allocated spending to departments and to the local authorities. The Government (and previously the Executive) has developed a system of performance management based on outcomes. In Wales there was an agreement between the Assembly and the local authorities, in which

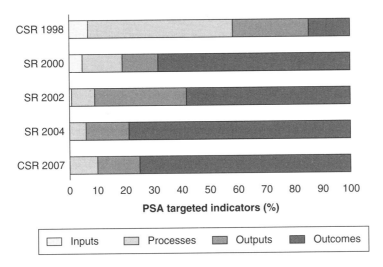

Figure 6.2   The development of outcome measurement

Source: National Audit Office (2010) *Taking the Measure of Government Performance*, HC 284, Session 2010–11

performance is also based on 'outcome agreements'. The 'Single Outcome Agreement', reported each year, is part of the overall agreement between the Scottish government and Scottish local authorities.

Northern Ireland had its own Public Service Agreements, mirroring those of England, but with their own special targets. In Wales, from 2011, there is a set of 'Public Accountability Measures',[9] a list of agreed outcome targets, and the data collection and publication against those targets is managed by the Welsh Local Government Association and Local Government Data Unit.

Local government performance in England

Performance management for local government evolved into a system called Comprehensive Performance Assessment, bringing together from 2002 performance data of all a local authority's departments and functions. This was then extended through the 'One Place' initiative into an assessment of all public services in a geographical area, through a system called 'Comprehensive Area Assessment' (CAA), which was established in 2009. The idea of the CAA was that it would reduce the duplication of inspections, and focus on a small(ish) range of targets with an emphasis on the risk of failure. In an explanatory letter[10] written by all the relevant inspectorates the CAA's approach was:

a single set of national outcomes for local authorities working alone or in partnership, measured through around 200 national indicators,[11] to be determined through the Comprehensive Spending Review; and a single set of up to 35 targets negotiated with each area, plus 18 DfES statutory targets, which will form part of the new Local Area Agreement (the rest of which will comprise local priorities and targets which will not be performance managed by central government). (p. 4)

In addition:

One of the key elements of the CAA is the annual assessment of risks in an area. This reflects a shift away from comprehensive assessments of individual organisations' performance. Evidence of performance and management of the delivery of outcomes will be needed to inform the judgement of risks. However, one of the key features of the shift to risk assessment is the ambition that this should deliver a more forward- than backward-looking judgement. (p. 5)

The Local Area Agreement extended the idea of a contractually-based performance management system to a single agreement for all the public authorities in an area. It was the ultimate in central control of a locality, simplified to only 200 national indicators and 53 centrally set targets. This was the culmination of the centralised control mechanism, offering apparent ubiquitous performance management throughout the land and throughout the public sector.

This whole process was abolished after only one year by the Coalition government.

THE NATIONAL HEALTH SERVICE

Performance management in the NHS has had four main elements:[12]

Targets and national standards These include national targets such as for waiting times and to reduce mortality from cancer and heart disease; National Service Frameworks, which set standards for care of major diseases, such as diabetes; and more detailed national guidance on treatments and drugs issued by the National Institute for Health and Clinical Excellence (NICE).

Inspection and regulation The government has established new regulators of NHS organisations and private-sector providers, and has set new requirements for the regulation of individual professionals.

Published performance information The Department of Health, the regulators and the NHS Information Centre now publish a large amount of data on NHS performance – some aimed at the public, and some aimed at NHS organisations for the purposes of commissioning and service improvement.

Direct intervention from the centre Where care has fallen below national standards, the Secretary of State and the regulators have the power to intervene.

Performance improvement was also pursued, as we have seen, through putting much more money into the NHS, and by a series of modifications to the organisation and the way the parts relate to each other.

The top-down performance management approach is illustrated in Figure 6.3.[13] This shows how the performance regime is operated through the NHS hierarchy: similar to the PSA system, the targets cascade from the Department of Health down through the hierarchy, and are backed up by the regulatory regime.

Health Trusts report their performance using a 'dashboard' – a metaphor about cars commonly used in company performance – setting out their scores against each of the targets. Figure 6.4 shows an example from a health trust from 2010. The scores are grouped into areas of performance, and a colour code is used to indicate green, amber and red for whether they are on or off target, and arrows to indicate the direction of change.

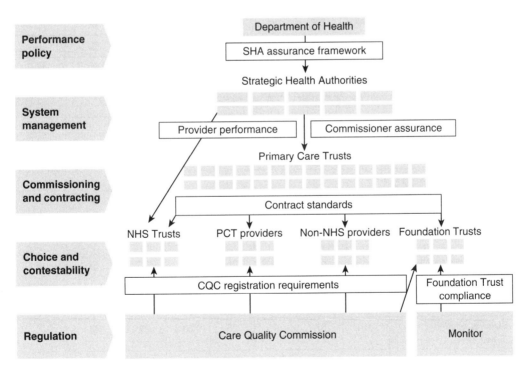

Figure 6.3 Metrics used in NHS performance management from 2008 to 2010

Source: NHS (2008) *Developing the NHS Performance Regime*

KEY INDICATORS								
Finance targets	09–10	Q1	July	August	Sept	Oct	Status	Trend
Statutory break-even duty – headroom	£3.9m	£3.96	£4.30	£3.95	£3.92	£3.71	●	⇨
Cash limit	£7.7m	£9.01	£11.32	£13.04	£11.87	£13.05	◍	⬆
Capital resource limit	£5.4m	£0.78	£1.16	£1.44	£1.97	£2.30	◍	⬆
Public sector payment policy	94%	98%	96%	94%	94%	93%	●	⇨
Financial balance	£0.4m	£0.06	£0.13	£0.05	£0.02	-£0.19	◍	⬇
Cost improvement programme (years 1–2)	£5.2m	£4.80	£4.96	£4.86	£5.01	£4.32	◍	⬇
Bank and agency spend	£10.5m	£2.8	£3.7m	£4.6m	£5.5	£6.29	◍	⬆
Financial risk rating	3	3	3	3	3	3	●	⇨
EBITDA margin	6.64%	6.90%	6.82%	6.24%	6.04%	5.96%	◌	⇨
Monitor targets								
Maintain CRHT	Yes	Yes	Yes	Yes	Yes	Yes	●	⇨
CRHT admissions	96%	96.6%	98.0%	98.7%	97.9%	97.7%	●	⬆
CPA 7-day follow-up	95.6%	96.7%	97.0%	95.8%	96.5%	96.4%	●	●
Delayed transfers of care	6.0%	7.3%	7.3%	7.3%	7.4%	7.8%	◍	⬇
Other national priorities								
MHMDS ethnicity data quality	89%	89%	89%	87%	87%	85%	◍	⇨
MHMDS completeness	97%	97%	96%	97%	97%	97%	●	⇨
Quality and safety measures								
Infections (MRSA and C.Diff)	14	2	0	0	0	0	●	⇨
Complaints received this period	194	64	30	18	25	20	●	⇨
Compliments received this period	585	57	44	25	24	32	●	⬆
SUIs reported this period (Level 5)	109	30	11	10	6	11	●	⇨
SUIs reported this period (Level 4)	213	57	9	25	23	27	●	⇨
Clinical coding (primary)	89%	98%	99%	99%	97%	99%	●	⬆
Clinical coding (secondary)	79%	78%	81%	83%	76%	81%	●	⬆
% of completed HoNOS scores	52%	58%	58%	64%	68%	67%	●	⬆

KEY INDICATORS

Activity measures	09–10	Q1	July	August	Sept	Oct	Status	Trend
Adults with CPA care plans	92%	91%	92%	93%	93%	93%	●	⇨
Adults having received a 12 month CPA review	95%	95%	95%	95%	93%	92%	●	⇨
Emergency readmissions within 28 days (younger)	8.5%	3.9%	3.8%	4.2%	3.8%	4.3%	◌	⇨
Emergency readmissions within 28 days (older)	1.7%	1.2%	1.3%	2.4%	2.6%	2.7%	●	⇨
Length of stay in days (younger)	32	32	32	34	31	31	●	⇨
Length of stay in days (older)	71	72	74	72	74	72	●	⬆
Bed occupancy (younger)	94%	94%	94%	97%	97%	97%	◌	⇨
Bed occupancy (older)	88%	93%	95%	96%	95%	95%	◌	⇨
HR measures								
Sickness rate (%)	4.75%	4.14%	4.55%	3.79%	4.85%	4.23%	●	⬆
Staff turnover (%)	3.65%	3.00%	1.23%	1.13%	0.80%	0.77%	●	⬆
Staff ethnicity	97%	97%	97%	97%	97%	97%	●	⇨
Exception reports								
Caldicott incidents (Level 13–5)	4	3	2	2	0	0	●	⇨
Data Protection Act breaches	40	26	2	5	1	3	●	⇨
Freedom of Information Act breaches	2	0	0	0	1	0	●	⬆

PROJECTS

Project	Progress (2010–2011)	Status	Trend
St. Martins redevelopment	80%	●	⬆
Forensic redevelopment	78%	◌	⇨
Rio	20%	●	⬆
e-Rostering	70%	●	⬆

(Continued)

(Continued)

PROGRESS AGAINST ACTION PLANS & STRATEGIES			
Action plan	**Progress (2010–2011)**	**Status**	**Trend**
Info Gov Toolkit 2009/10 (annual plan)	27%	●	⇨
Equality and diversity (3 yr plan)	65%	●	⇨
Service Line Reporting	60%	●	⬆
Service Line Management	75%	●	⬆

Figure 6.4 An NHS 'dashboard'

EDUCATION

Schools

Published performance 'league tables' for schools were designed both to inform prospective pupils about how the schools they are choosing from perform, and to create motivation for school improvement. Early tables included achievement of the expected attainment levels at the Key Stages, plus the scores in public examinations at GCSE and A level. Once it was argued that the achievement of schools in these tests was at least in part determined outside the school (especially the ability of the pupils when they arrived in schools), an element of 'value-added' was introduced, which measured the difference that the schools made to the actual pupils they teach. Known as 'contextual value added', these measures are designed to give a more accurate assessment of the performance of schools, as contrasted with the performance of their pupils. The logic is explained by the Department for Education:

1   The test and examination results attained by pupils provide important information about the effectiveness of a school – for example, the proportion attaining the equivalent of 5 good GCSEs including English and mathematics at the end of KS4 tells us how many pupils at the school are well prepared for the next stage of their education.

2   When comparing the performance of schools we must also recognise that pupils will have different starting points and that the proportions of pupils at each starting point will vary from school to school. More than half of the variation in attainment at key stage 4 can be explained by prior attainment at key stage 2. Measures of absolute attainment therefore need to be complemented by measures of the progress made by pupils – the value added – from one key stage to another. Value

added (VA) measures, which have been in use for some years now, are thus based on pupils' prior attainment – for example, at GCSE progress is measured from the KS2 tests.

3　Contextual Value Added (CVA) goes further than simply measuring progress based on prior attainment by making adjustments to account for the impact of other factors outside of the school's control which are known to have had an impact on the progress of individual pupils, e.g. levels of deprivation. This means that CVA gives a much fairer statistical measure of the effectiveness of a school and provides a solid basis for comparisons. Nevertheless, no single measure of performance can tell the whole story about a school's effectiveness and CVA must not be viewed in isolation. Attainment data continues to play an important role in painting the full picture of a school's performance.[14]

The definition of 'underachievement', which has serious consequences for schools, does not take account of value added and is defined thus:

less than 35% of pupils at the end of Key Stage 4 (KS4) achieving 5 or more GCSEs A*–C (or equivalents) including English and maths GCSE; and

- below average % of pupils at the end of KS4 making expected progress in English (national median for 2010 = 72%); and
- below average % of pupils at the end of KS4 making expected progress in maths (national median for 2010 = 65%)

However, value added is counted in the assessment of schools' improvement, and a particular level at KS2, in English and maths, is mapped to the achievement of a grade at GCSE – improvements are counted.

The use of league tables based on these measures to praise or 'name and shame' schools has been controversial. For example the Secondary Heads Association criticised the narrow range of targets as distorting schools' attention, and diverting pupils' choice of subjects:

Poorly chosen measures, such as the proportion of an age cohort gaining five A*–C passes at GCSE, create perverse incentives for schools. Resources are often concentrated on pupils at the C/D borderline, sometimes to the detriment of those who could perhaps raise a grade B to an A, or an E to a D. The age relatedness of the performance indicator dictates that many pupils have to be entered for examinations when they are not ready for them. As O'Neill points out, these perverse incentives are real incentives for the schools on which they are imposed. Thus Advanced level students are guided into studying subjects in which higher grades are easier to achieve, contributing to shortages of graduates and teachers in the subjects perceived harder, such as modern foreign languages, mathematics and the physical sciences (which, ironically, may be the subjects in which the country most needs more graduates). Primary schools are criticised for narrowing the curriculum in response to the pressure of targets set on national test results in a limited range of subjects. All of these are rational responses by schools to the performance indicators on which they are judged and the targets they are set. Badly chosen performance indicators warp professional judgements and undermine the professionals making them. Performance indicators for schools should be chosen in a way that minimises perverse incentives.[15]

Higher education

Universities are also subject to performance management, but not to government-sponsored league tables, which in that sector are created by newspapers and other sources, using their own criteria. The official performance management system for research is based on an assessment of research quality. The significance of the University Research Excellence Framework[16] is that funding decisions are made as a result of the performance assessment. While a small amount of school funding is tied to performance, for successful universities research performance determines a large proportion of their income. It is probably a special case of performance-based budgeting, since the beneficiaries of the funding, initially at least, are the members of staff of the universities themselves, although ultimately students are presumably better served at well-funded institutions.

INDIVIDUAL AND ORGANISATIONAL PERFORMANCE

Almost all public servants have an appraisal process through which their individual contribution to their organisation's performance is assessed. While the appraisal process has other objectives, such as to identify people's training and development needs, the emphasis is normally on individual performance, sometimes with an element of performance-related pay. In principle, the targets which individuals are assessed on should aggregate into the performance targets of the organisation as a whole. In centrally-managed services there is a direct relationship between targets set by ministers and the targets in individuals' work plans, targets and assessments. Sometimes the individual targets are not related to those of the organisation itself, especially if managers are free to decide their own priorities.

Performance-related pay has been applied in many parts of the public sector in an effort to increase productivity and to improve service quality. Of senior civil servants, 60% have a performance-related element in their pay; there is a scheme for teachers to link theirs and their pupils' performance to the teachers' pay; general practitioners' earnings are linked to their performance against fixed targets. The intention is that the targets used in determining individuals' pay are the same as the high-level targets for the organisations.

The Office of Manpower Economics commissioned a study[17] of performance-related pay in the public sector, looking at the Civil Service, healthcare workers and teachers specifically. In teaching, the review found that there are three sorts of incentive schemes in operation: subjective performance evaluations of teaching quality; pay schemes based on measures of pupil performance; school-level incentives based on performance measured at school level. The measured targets were the ones used as high-level targets by the government, especially 'value added' (the degree to which pupils progress) and the absolute achievement of targets such as the proportion of pupils achieving grades A–C at GCSE. Their review concluded that incentives to achieve particular outcomes do work, and they work mainly by improving the performance of pupils who previously performed badly, rather than improving the performance at the top level.

For general practitioners, the studies show that performance-related pay can improve performance in the selected indicators, but that doctors often over-achieve the targets even when this does not generate additional income. The use of performance-related pay for general practice added 25% to the core funding of practices when it was introduced in 2004.

Evidence from the Civil Service also suggests that some people do respond to incentives and that they will adjust their behaviour to meet the priorities expressed in the targets. One example is the Jobcentre Plus incentive scheme whereby people are paid bonuses based on the outcomes of the job placement process.

The use of performance to determine pay progression is less prevalent in the public sector than the private. The 2010 Reward Management Survey by the Institute of Personnel and Development[18] found that 50% of public-services workers' pay progression was based on individual performance, compared with 77% in private services and 73% in manufacturing. Of public sector workers, 66% still have in place some system of pay spine and increments, compared with 6% in manufacturing and 4% in private services, and length of service was one criterion for progression in 46% of the public jobs, compared with 14% in private services and in manufacturing.

Bonuses as a concept received bad publicity in the aftermath of the banking crisis of 2008, as bankers soon resumed their very large bonuses long before the banks got back into profit. The House of Commons Public Administration Select Committee made the point in their report in 2009:

> Regardless of the arguments for and against a greater proportion of senior salaries being directly linked to performance it is clear that such a move would not be acceptable in the current political and economic climate. The word 'bonus' has acquired a toxic quality and become associated with unjustifiable reward…[19]

PERFORMANCE MANAGEMENT AND POLICY EVALUATION

Once it has been decided that a set of outcomes is the objective of the organisation, the next question is how their achievement is to be measured. There are two approaches to this.

One is to search for some global indicator, such as the quality-of-life changes as a result of a service, such as a health intervention, or an environmental improvement. Employment policy may be measured by the level of unemployment in an area. This is essentially a top-down approach in which the change in the state of a person or a population is defined by the organisation and then measured.

The other is to start with the individual service encounter and start a discussion between the service provider and the service user about what outcomes they expect from the service. A good example of this has been the health authority in East London which developed outcome measures for the treatment of leg ulcers by asking nurses and patients what results they expected from treatment. Or the employment service can measure the numbers of people with whom it deals who find employment, rather than measuring the level of unemployment in its area.

Once the problems of defining the desired outcomes have been solved, there is then a third question: the organisation needs to evaluate how best to achieve those outcomes. Here the distinction between policy and management is not clear. Politicians may decide on the services to be provided, such as sentencing policy on criminal justice, that education should take place in particular sorts of institution or that health treatment should take a particular form. After those decisions have been made, managers implement them. However, the policies themselves may have as big an impact on the outcome as the way in which the service is managed. Even the most well-managed workhouses probably had negative effects on their residents.

This aspect of performance management is the process of policy evaluation. This might involve scientific studies of the impact of medical interventions, teaching methods, treatment of people convicted of crimes. It also involves dealing with the opinions of politicians about what works and what does not work. It may be politically attractive to favour harsh treatment in prisons even if criminologists can show that rehabilitation produces lower recidivism rates. Mixed ability teaching may be shown to produce better overall educational outcomes but some politicians believe in streaming. Low public transport fares may reduce road congestion and improve passenger movement but politicians may prefer balanced budgets for transport operators.

Evaluation has two aspects. One is to find out what works best in producing the desired outcomes: this may indeed be technocratic. Although professionals may continue to claim that only they know what works, because only they have the training and experience to make judgements, empirical scientific methods can produce results which allow people other than professionals to use their own judgement about policy choices. Such science is normal in the medical professions, where blind testing of drugs and treatments gives a good idea about the effectiveness of different approaches to diseases. In other services such an approach may be less appropriate if the outcomes are less measurable, although if outcomes are definable, it ought always to be possible to see whether they have been achieved. Indeed it could be argued that if outcomes cannot be identified, the service has no purpose and should not be provided.

The second aspect is the preferences which service users have for different services. For example, police forces claim that deploying their resources into 'rapid response' units with cars produces higher rates of crime detection and solving than having foot patrols. Surveys have shown, however, that visible police have the effect of reassuring people about their safety. The same is true for certain aspects of school education: parents have preferences for styles of discipline, uniforms and teaching method which are not scientifically-based judgements.

The Labour government's pragmatism to some extent promoted the idea of policy evaluation. The idea that ideology or populism should not distract services from 'what works' was widely promulgated. 'Evidence-based' practice was to be preferred to prejudice. The nature of the evidence on which practice was to be based was contested. The government's view was that evidence was represented by a national view of all evidence, rather than local experience, and that 'what works' should be defined from above and handed down. National Service Frameworks for treatment in the NHS are an example, as are the guidelines for probation services. Centralised interpretation of policy analysis became another way of controlling the organisations delivering services.

MANAGERIAL DISCRETION

Performance information is used for two main purposes: to judge the effectiveness of policy and the performance of organisations and their managers. Managers may also use measurement to judge and improve their own performance. The degree to which measures are able to offer a judgement of managerial performance is partly determined by the degree of discretion which managers have. Figure 6.5 represents a simple flow from inputs to outcomes. The ratio between inputs and outcomes or results is a measurement of a mixture of policy effectiveness and managerial performance. If the choice of outputs to achieve the outcomes is made by either politicians or professionals, then managers can be judged only on the efficiency with which they produce the outputs. If managers have little discretion in the choice and arrangement of inputs, any judgement on their performance is in practice a judgement of how well they manage a given set of people and equipment.

For example, let us consider what is being judged in a league table of school examination results. If a headteacher has no control over which teachers are hired, what equipment is purchased and how the school buildings are built and maintained, his or her discretion is limited to the organisation of the school and the motivation and skills of the staff. As personnel policy and budgets are delegated to schools, more discretion is given to headteachers and governors about the uses to which the budget is put and the results achieved are more subject to their efforts.

Satisfactory performance management requires a balance among all of these elements. Organisations that concentrate on a narrow range of targets, especially efficiency targets, are likely to look away from important elements of their work, such as the nature of their relationships with their service users.

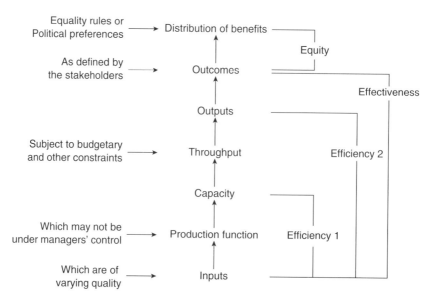

Figure 6.5   Elements of performance measurement

LEAGUE TABLES

Comparative performance information is published for most services. Schools and education authorities have their examination results made public each year. The local authority indicators are available to the public. The NHS has produced the Health Service Indicators since 1983. Universities are judged and ranked on the quality of their research and teaching.

The publication of these tables can have two effects. Managers may make efforts to achieve the targets contained in the league tables, to the detriment of other aspects of performance. In practice, there are trade-offs between elements of performance. For example, the Benefits Agency has targets for both the speed and accuracy with which benefits are paid. Accuracy can take more time. Universities teach and do research. Since resource allocation has been based in part on research output, some universities have recruited staff with a high volume of research output and not asked them to engage in much teaching: results in the Research Excellence Framework are improved with a negative effect on the quality of teaching for students.

The second effect is that managers may try to find out how they can improve their performance by looking at how people above them in the tables work. One way of organising this is through 'benchmarking', the systematic comparison with the best performer in a group. Benchmarking was first used by companies faced with competitors who could achieve much lower costs than themselves. It consists of comparing elements of the production process against a 'benchmark' performer. The benchmark may not necessarily be in the same industry. Benchmarking has grown in the public sector, both internally and using private sector benchmarks.

There is a national benchmarking project, based on the 'business excellence model' of the European Quality Foundation. Public sector organisations can check their performance on a range of criteria against each other and against those private sector organisations that have also signed up to the scheme.

THE COALITION

The Coalition government declared that it was not going to continue the process of target-setting, but would encourage service providers to be accountable 'downwards' to the users of services and taxpayers with a set of performance reports. It declared, in the White Paper on 'localism', that it was impossible for governments to be involved in the minutiae of service delivery and performance management.

CONCLUSIONS

The language of performance management, with targets, benchmarks and dashboards, was largely imported from the private sector, despite the fact that simple measures such as profitability and market share have no equivalents in the public sector. The evolution of the performance management system included the reduction in the number of targets and measures, and the transition from measures of input and output to measures of outcome or result. While the ambition was to have a seamless system all the way from high-level goals to individual targets for the people at the front line, this was rarely possible.

Further reading

Hans de Bruijn, *Managing Performance in the Public Sector* (London: Routledge, 2002) presents a useful framework for designing performance management and avoiding mistakes.

If you are engaged in devising performance measurement and management systems, Harry P. Hartry, *Performance Measurement: Getting Results*, 2nd edn (Washington DC: The Urban Institute Press, 2006) is a useful practical guide.

POINTS FOR DISCUSSION
- What are the obstacles to a comprehensive performance management system?
- What mode of governance does the UK performance management system represent: market, hierarchy or clan?

NOTES

1　John Bourne, *Public Sector Auditing – Is it Value for Money?* (Chichester: Wiley, 2007), p. 319.

2　Audit Commission, *Performance Measurement as a Tool for Modernising Government: Using the PSAs to drive continuous improvement* (London: Audit Commission, 1999).

3　For example, J.J. Laffont and D. Martimort, *The Theory of Incentives* (Princeton and Oxford: Princeton University Press, 2002).

4　M. Barzelay, *Breaking Through Bureaucracy: A new vision for managing in government* (Berkeley: University of California Press, 1992).

5　Ibid., p. 120.

6　Peter Jackson (1995) 'Reflections on performance measurement in public service organisations', in Jackson, P.M. (ed.), *Measures of Success in the Public Sector* (London: CIPFA, 1995), p. 4.

7　HM Treasury, Outcome Focused Management in the United Kingdom, General Expenditure Policy, London: HM Treasury, 2001.

8　National Audit Office (2010) *Taking the Measure of Government Performance*, HC 284, Session 2010–11.

9　For details of the measures and the data sources, see Local Government Performance Improvement Framework 2011–12, Public Accountability Measures, Guidance for local authorities, Local Government Data Unit 2011.

10　Departments of Communities and Local Government, Health, Education and Skills and Home Office, *Developing and implementing the new comprehensive area assessment and associated inspection arrangements*, April 2007.

11　There were 198 indicators, as set out in *The New Performance Framework for Local Authorities & Local Authority Partnerships: Single Set of National Indicators*, Department of Communities and Local Government, 2007. There were previously 1,200 indicators, so the new approach was claimed to be offering more freedom to local authorities.

12　Ruth Thorlby and Jo Maybin (eds) (2010), *A High Performing NHS? – A review of Progress 1997–2010*, London: The King's Fund, p. 9.

13　*Developing the NHS Performance Regime*, NHS, 2008.

14　Department for Education (2010) A Technical Guide to Contextual Value Added (including English and maths) Key Stage 2 to 4, 2010 Model.

15　Secondary Heads Association, *Towards Intelligent Accountability for Schools. A Policy Statement on School Accountability*, Policy Paper 5, March 2003, p. 3.

16　A process previously labelled the Research Assessment Exercise, it is a periodic thorough review of the quantity and quality of university research output.

17　Graham Prentice, Simon Burgess and Carol Propper, *Performance pay in the public sector: A review of the issues and evidence* (London: Office of Manpower Economics, 2007).

18　Chartered Institute of Personnel and Development, *Building Productive Public Sector Workplaces* (London: CIPD, 2010).

19　House of Commons Public Administration Select Committee, *Top Pay in the Public Sector*, HC 172–1 (2009), p. 27.

CHAPTER 7

E-government

SUMMARY

Information and communication technology is everywhere in the public sector. This chapter looks at its use in informing people about services, enabling transactions with government and in creating databases to make services more effective. It finds that there has been a good deal of success in the relatively simpler applications, such as running informative websites that are well used by the public. It finds that there has been a mix of success and failure in the creation of databases: the more reported are the failures, such as those for the NHS and the National Offender Management System, but there have also been successes in, for example, the Department for Work and Pensions. The chapter tries to explain, through official reports, what makes for success and failure.

LEARNING POINTS

- Designers and sellers of ICT systems often over-claim their usefulness and value.
- Government has spent very large sums of money on ICT systems, some of which failed to live up to expectations.

THE AMBITION

Winston Churchill once claimed that the National Health Service cared for people 'from the cradle to the grave'. The ubiquity of information and communication technology in public services means that the technology is involved in public service all the way from the birth certificate to the death certificate. Databases store information about every citizen, websites provide information about every service and enable transactions for a wide range of them, from tax collection to passport applications, booking garbage collection, making appointments with doctors, applying for a university place.

As well as enabling interactions between citizens and services (or at least, those citizens with access to the internet)[1] ICT is used by managers to plan and control services and by policy makers, potentially, to join services together and transform the way they are designed and delivered. The ambition of the UK government was set out in a plan in the year 2000 that all services should be 'available on-line' by 2005, and it was estimated that 75% of services were web-enabled by 2004. In that year the Spending Review set out ambitious goals for the increased efficiency that technology would provide, resulting in a reduction in public sector employment of 84,000 over the spending review period. In 2005, Tony Blair sponsored a review of strategy in the use of ICT in government, which set out the following ambitions:

> Overall this technology-enabled transformation will help ensure that:
>
> - Citizens and businesses have choice and personalisation in their interactions with government. Choice will come through new channels and more fundamentally through new opportunities for service competition.
> - Taxpayers benefit from efficiency gains.
> - Citizens, businesses and the voluntary and community sector benefit from the better regulation, reduced paperwork and lower costs from a leaner, modern, more effective public sector.
> - Public servants have better tools to undertake their jobs, and the opportunity to provide better service as a result.
> - Policy makers will be better able to achieve intended outcomes in practice.
> - Managers are able to free resources from back office to the front-line.
> - Citizens feel more engaged with the processes of democratic government.[2]

This was much broader than web access and efficiency: as the title of the paper 'Transformational Government' implied, technology was to enable the achievement of radical changes. All the ambitions are contained in this list, from choice and customisation, through efficiency gains, the search for effectiveness in achieving outcomes and even the spread of democracy.

THE ACHIEVEMENT

Websites

The COI commissioned a study of the use of central government websites:[3] the study showed that the costs of the site developments to that point came to £94,426,000 and that all sites had generated 568,321,965 visits. The five most visited government websites are listed in Table 7.1.

The National Audit Office had reported in 2007 that there had been good progress in the development of web access to government information and to some transactions. The results are summarised in Table 7.2.[4]

Table 7.1   Visits to central government websites 2009–10

	Total visits
NHS Choices	98,605,204
HM Revenue and Customs	81,134,411
National Archives	28,841,676
Transport direct information	19,905,725
Department for Work and Pensions	16,781,145

Source: COI (2010) pp. 18–20

Table 7.2   Some key achievements of government information and service provision online

Policy sector	Online achievement	Annual service users or visitors to websites (millions)
Local government	Websites run by local authorities provide a wide range of information on local services and issues	180.0
	Local authority websites accept e-payments transactions	4.0
	The Local Directgov service seeks to provide direct links between Directgov and online local services	n/a
Foreign affairs	The Foreign and Commonwealth Office website offers advice on travel and consular services	25
	The Foreign and Commonwealth Office sends emails alerting subscribers to changes of content including travel advice, press releases and job adverts	1.5
Labour markets	The Jobcentre Plus website, including job information accessed through public Jobpoints, is the biggest of its kind in the UK	67.0
	The 'Employer Direct' facility on the Jobcentre Plus website allows employers to upload their job vacancies online or by phone. The service now accounts for 27% of all notified job vacancies	n/a
Taxation	Import/export declarations have long been processed overwhelmingly online, with the service collecting £22 billion in import duties annually	26.0
	Income tax payers who need to file a self-assessment form with HM Revenue and Customs can do so online	3.0
	Employers' annual declarations (form P35) filed online during 2006–07	1.31
	Employers' annual summary of pay, tax and NIC details for individual employees (form PI4) filed online in 2006–07	45.7

(Continued)

Table 7.2 (Continued)

Policy sector	Online achievement	Annual service users or visitors to websites (millions)
Transport	An online journey-planning service is provided by the Transport Direct website	11.0
	Motorists can now renew and pay for their car tax or declare Statutory Off Road Notification online	3.7
	The Highways Agency handles emails to its enquiry service	0.017
Health	NHS Direct offers online health advice, now used by almost twice as many online visitors as phone users	13.5
	The NHS.uk site offers information to the public on NHS services	17.7
	The Department of Health website publishes extensive health policy and NHS performance information as well as departmental consultations and publications	10.2
Pensions	During 2006–07, 116,000 Real Time Pension Forecasts were processed online between April 2006 and March 2006	0.12

☐ Information provision	☐ Transactional service	☐ Mixed/other

Source: National Audit Office, *Government on the Internet: Progress in Delivering Information and Services Online*, HC 529 Session 2006–7, 13 July 2007

In this field, which is mostly about enabling people to access information and make some routine transactions with government, there seems to have been a degree of success. However, where more complicated ambitions have been pursued, especially in the field of large databases, success has been less frequent.

The Department for Work and Pensions, with its Chief Information Officer Joe Harley, later given a dual role in DWP as well as CIO for the whole of government, has the government's biggest ITC system. In 2008 it announced a programme of up to £3 billion of contracts for its IT systems. Paying out £148 billion to 20 million claimants through 27 benefits, it has 101,000 employees and 140,000 computer screens.

While there were the usual problems with some contractors, notably Fujitsu who were removed from a desktop management contract after a year in March 2011, most of the applications were installed and worked well. In January 2010 DWP announced that it had saved around £1.5 billion from its IT estimated spend through standardisation, use of Voice Over Internet and other savings.

These successes received less publicity than the failures. The problems of large projects in the ICT field have slowed down the development of better services and probably wasted around 70% of the government's ICT investments.[5]

THE CHALLENGES

Large scale ICT projects have a tendency to over-claim and under-perform. Shaun Goldfinch[6] has described the 'dangerous enthusiasms' of those involved in systems development and the dangers they pose to the success of ICT development. He claims that IT companies consistently exaggerate the benefits of IT developments and sweep up the technical employees in their enthusiasms, and the technical developments become detached from the operational experts in the departments.

The Office of Government Commerce diagnosed these reasons for the relatively poor performance of government ICT projects:[7]

1 Lack of clear link between the project and the organisation's key strategic priorities, including agreed measures of success.
2 Lack of clear senior management and Ministerial ownership and leadership.
3 Lack of effective engagement with stakeholders.
4 Lack of skills and proven approach to project management and risk management.
5 Lack of understanding of and contact with the supply industry at senior levels in the organisation.
6 Evaluation of proposals driven by initial price rather than long-term value for money (especially securing delivery of business benefits).
7 Too little attention to breaking development and implementation into manageable steps.
8 Inadequate resources and skills to deliver the total portfolio.

There has been no shortage of strategies on ICT, since the first 'e-government strategy' was published in 2000. There were eight major reviews in the following ten years,[8] setting out how government services could be provided online, how ICT can transform service delivery (the Varney Review), the establishment of a 'Power of Technology Taskforce' in 2008, a Treasury Operational Efficiency review in 2008 stating that the government could save £3.2 billion on ICT procurement, and another Treasury review in 2009, *Putting the Frontline First – Smarter Government*, culminating in the Cabinet Office's *Government ICT Strategy* in 2010.

The NHS National Programme for Information Technology

The NHS National Programme for Information Technology (NPfIT) was described as the world's biggest civilian IT project: the NHS was to be transformed by an inclusive, centralised IT system. The ambition of the system for improving patients' experience was set out:

Patient care will be transformed when all patients in England have an electronic care record which can be shared safely within the NHS and viewed, in summary form, by patients themselves.

The new technology will not only provide easier access to clinical information, but better support for diagnosis and treatment and improved communication between different groups of health professionals. These will all enhance patient care. If a GP decides with their patient that a referral is appropriate, the ability to 'Choose and Book' where and, more particularly, when they are treated will allow patients to plan around their work, family and carer commitments. This will also spare patients an anxious wait for an appointment and result in fewer appointments being missed.

Patients can also expect the right information about them to be available to the right clinician at the right time. Electronic records, results and scans are less likely to be misplaced and the new technology will enable test results to be communicated much more quickly – again, reducing the wait for patients. In addition, patients will no longer have to complete forms whenever they come into contact with a different part of the NHS and clinicians will be freed from repetitive administrative tasks, enabling them to spend more time with patients.

Electronic Transmission of Prescriptions (ETP) will bring benefits for patients, especially the large numbers of people who require repeat prescriptions. In future, patients will not always have to visit their GP surgery to collect a repeat prescription, but can have it sent electronically to a nominated pharmacy. ETP will also improve safety by ensuring that each patient's medication record is automatically updated.

New technology being introduced by the National Programme will also fulfil patients' expressed wish to become involved in, and more informed about, their care, through readily available information about health services, particular conditions and their own specific care regimes.

Patients will eventually be able to access their own electronic health record via a secure Internet link into the NHS. They will be able to check their record for accuracy and, in time, will be able to add their treatment preferences and information about their needs, such as wheelchair access requirements. Patients will have their own personal online health organiser, HealthSpace. This will act as a calendar, allowing them to record appointment details and set up reminders. It will also enable them to keep a record of their blood pressure, weight and height. It will store self-care programmes on, for example, stopping smoking or managing diabetes. HealthSpace will incorporate a search feature, allowing patients to look for up-to-date, reliable health-related information, and offer guidance and information on healthy lifestyles.[9]

These ambitions for patients were matched by claims for the benefits to 'the NHS family' (GPs, hospitals and PCTs). Announced in 2002, the project was a classic, in that the claims were that the technology would solve a multitude of human and social problems, and in the sense that cost overruns and delays were rife, leading finally, upon the change of government in 2010, to the redesign and scaling down of the project.

The programme was originally conceived as a series of projects at national and local level, costing overall over £12 billion. The breakdown of the spend is shown in Figure 7.1.

While parts of the system, such as the project to share X-rays electronically, a broadband network, most of 'Choose and Book' and an electronic prescription service, were delivered, the core of the programme, the development of a national patient record system, was not, by a long way, delivered by 2011, when it had been planned for 2010. Two of the main

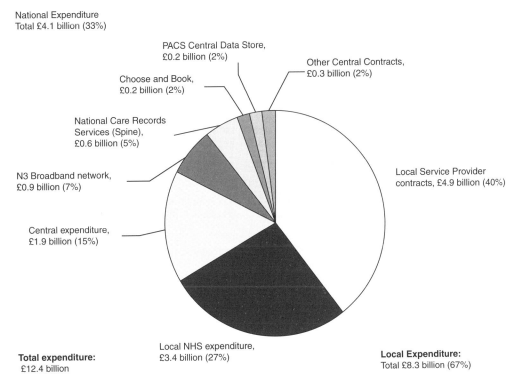

Figure 7.1   National programme for information technology planned spending

Source: Public Accounts Committee (2007) report 2006–07, *The National Programme for IT in the NHS*

contractors, Accenture and Fujitsu, withdrew or were removed from the project and delays were normal. An NAO Report in May 2011[10] summarised the value for money:

> Central to achieving the Programme's aim of improving services and the quality of patient care, was the successful delivery of an electronic patient record for each NHS patient. Although some care records systems are in place, progress against plans has fallen far below expectations and the Department has not delivered care records systems across the NHS, or with anywhere near the completeness of functionality that will enable it to achieve the original aspirations of the Programme. The Department has also significantly reduced the scope of the Programme without a proportionate reduction in costs, and is in negotiations to reduce it further still. So we are seeing a steady reduction in value delivered, not matched by a reduction in costs. On this basis we conclude that the £2.7 billion spent on care records systems so far does not represent value for money, and we do not find grounds for confidence that the remaining planned spend of £4.3 billion will be different. (p. 13)

National Offender Management Information System

Another ambitious IT project to create an inclusive and integrated database was the National Offender Management Information System, designed to join up all information on offenders held in Probation and Prison Service records. The contract was let in June 2005, with Canadian company Syscon Justice Systems Ltd and EDS, with an estimated lifetime cost of £234 million to the year 2020. By July 2007, two years after signing, the contract was already subject to two years' delay and the National Offender Management Service had spent £155 million, while the estimated lifetime costs had risen to £690 million, nearly three times the original estimate. A review was made and a new contract signed, not for a single integrated system but for five different systems, for delivery by March 2011, at a lifetime cost of £513 million.

Reporting on the failed contract,[11] the NAO found several causes of the failures:

- NOMS significantly underestimated the **technical complexity** of the project, particularly the need to customise TAG[12] for both prisons and probation services;
- NOMS did not get to grips with the **business changes** required to design and implement a single offender database across both services;
- NOMS' **contractual arrangements** with its key suppliers were weak and its supplier management poor;

- NOMS did not put the **appropriate resources and governance** in place to deliver such a complex project; and
- **Project management** was poor in key aspects, such as planning, financial monitoring and change control.[13]

THE COALITION'S RESPONSE

The combination of the need to reduce spending and the high profile of some of the IT failures provoked the Coalition into taking action on ICT. It continued the time-honoured process of conducting a review that would get costs under control and bring about more effective use of ICT. Its policy was set out in a Cabinet Office paper, 'Government ICT Strategy'. This paper re-issued some previous policies, such as the need to save money through using open-source software, an idea first proclaimed in the Cabinet Office's 2002 paper, 'Open Source Software use with UK Government'. But it also tried to reverse the process of letting large contracts with big suppliers, on the premise that the creation of the oligopoly of large suppliers working on very large contracts was the cause of the previous failures and cost-overruns. The new policy included:

> Where possible, government will move away from large ICT projects that are slow to implement or pose a greater risk of failure. Additionally, the application of agile ICT delivery methods, combined with the newly established Major Projects Authority, will improve government's capability to deliver projects successfully and realise benefits faster. (para 13)

The policy went on:

> The Government will also put an end to the oligopoly of large suppliers that monopolise its ICT provision. The Government will streamline the procurement process to break down the barriers that impede SMEs from bidding for contracts. The Government will also create a level playing field for SMEs and system integrators by creating a platform based on common standards. The platform will enable SMEs to invest in new government ICT solutions and allow government to buy directly from them. (para 14)

This policy had first been put forward in the 2003 paper, 'Government: Supporter and Customer?' from the Better Regulation Task Force, which recommended making it easier for small and medium-sized businesses to bid for contracts, including ICT contracts. The policy continued:

Building on the success of these measures, the Major Projects Authority has been established as the central scrutiny body to control ICT spending and advise departments at the earlier design stage how best to approach ICT solutions for business delivery needs. (para 19)

What this means is that the new policy will consist of the development of much smaller, local systems, but with interoperability and central control of the decentralised procurement, with no project costing more than £100 million.

In March 2011 the Government announced that it was closing 32 ICT contracts and 'reshaping' 68 others. It would appear that the age of the large contracts for integrated databases and applications with very ambitious objectives may have come to an end with a combination of parsimony and rethinking of the best approach to ICT.

CONCLUSIONS

There have been some very ambitious expectations and large budgets for ITC in government. The more ambitious plans, such as the universal identity card scheme or the database joining up all patient records in the NHS, seem to be the product of a well-developed imagination of an omniscient state, with records of everybody and everything, providing data for policy, for control and performance.

There has been a variety of success and failure in buying ICT systems. Part of the problem lies in the way that the buying has been done, the skills of the purchasers and the suppliers, the complexity of the transactions and the relationship between the technology and the nature of the service and its relationships internally and externally. Some of these issues will be considered further in Chapter 12.

Further reading

Richard Heeks, *Implementing and Managing eGovernment* (London: Sage, 2006). A text on the design and delivery of systems.

TOPICS FOR DISCUSSION

- What are the main reasons behind success and failure in ICT application in the public sector?
- Is the Coalition's solution, of multiple small contracts, likely to be successful?

NOTES

1 According to *Transformational Government* (Cabinet Office 2005), just over half of households had internet access at home in 2005.

2 Cabinet Office (2005), *Transformational Government – enabled by technology*, CM 6683, pp. 3–4.

3 Central Office of Information, *Reporting on progress, Central Government Websites 2009–10* (London: CO, 2010): report available at coi.gov.uk/websitemetrics 2009–10.

4 Source: National Audit Office, *Government On the Internet: Progress in Delivering Information and Services Online*, HC 529, Session 2006–2007, 13 July 2007.

5 A 2005 estimate by Joe Harley.

6 Shaun Goldfinch, 'Dangerous enthusiasms and information systems development in the public sector', in Shaun Goldfinch and Joe Wallis (eds), *International Handbook of Public Management Reform* (Cheltenham: Edward Elgar, 2009).

7 Royal Academy of Engineering and British Computer Society, *The Challenges of Complex IT Projects*, 2004, p. 8.

8 National Audit Office, *Information and Communications Technology in Government: Landscape Review*, HC 757, Session 2010–2011, February 2011.

9 NHS, *A Guide to the National Programme for Information Technology* (London: NHS, April 2005).

10 National Audit Office, *The National Programme for IT in the NHS: an update on the delivery of detailed care records systems*, HC 888, Session 2010–2012, May 2011.

11 National Audit Office, *The National Offender Management Information System*, HC 292, Session 2008–2009.

12 TAG was the software that the Prison Service had already bought from SYSCON, and that was being adapted for the new, integrated information system.

13 NAO (2010) *The National Offender Management Information System*, HC 292, p. 16.

CHAPTER 8
Customer–Citizen Orientation

SUMMARY

The interaction between people and government takes many forms: sometimes people are customers, at other times they may be in custody, paying taxes, voting. This chapter is about how government agencies can define and manage the variety of relationships. They can set standards that staff have to live up to, they can enable choice by the service user, empowering them, they can carefully design services to meet or exceed expectations. There will always be some residual contradictions in the relationship: when budgets are diminishing, service quality will probably suffer; customisation or personalisation will inevitably lead to unequal treatment of individuals.

LEARNING POINTS

- Citizenship and being a customer create two different sets of rights.
- Public sector organisations can design the way services are provided to better match the citizen's and customer's expectations.
- Because of the realities of rationing, customer–citizen orientation in the public sector is different from customer-orientation in business.

CUSTOMERS, VOTERS AND CITIZENS

It has become common for managers of public services to try to make them more 'customer-oriented'. This applies both to services which are for the public and to those which are for internal 'customers', such as personnel or accountancy services. A pure definition of customer would exclude many of the relationships between public organisations and the people who use their services. Customers normally have a choice about what to buy and from whom, they provide the revenue from which businesses generate profits and they have certain rights as customers. These conditions only apply to a small proportion of public services. There is a wide range of relationships between public services and the people who use them. At one extreme is the prison–prisoner relationship in which the prisoner is an unwilling user of the service with no option of exit. At the other extreme, users of public sports facilities have many of the attributes of customers: they pay for all or part of the cost, they can choose to go elsewhere or do something else. In between are relationships with varying degrees of ability to exit; if geography permits, children can change schools, patients can change general practitioner. In practice choice is limited: inner city areas, for example, have fewer GPs per head of population than the suburbs; travel prevents choice of primary school in rural areas; the district hospital system provides a natural catchment area for hospitals in small and medium-sized towns.

The right to exit is an important determinant of the way in which competitive businesses treat their customers. If they can go to another supplier when dissatisfied, they will. One measure of customer satisfaction is whether they come back or not. Without the option, there is neither the direct incentive to generate satisfaction nor the obvious measurement of whether it has been achieved. That is not the same as saying that competition and a customer relationship are sufficient to produce customer orientation: whole sectors can be equally poor at customer service, such as budget airlines that compete on price, not service quality. Nor does it imply that competition is necessary for customer orientation: there is no reason in principle why monopolies could not be responsive to their customers – in the case of many public services which are a monopoly, this is indeed the management task.

In addition to the question of whether or not there is a choice of provider, relationships vary according to the nature of the service. Some services are protective (fire, child protection) while others are concerned with organising access to entitlements (social security), yet others are concerned with helping people to have fuller lives (adult education). These services all require different ways of thinking about developing and maintaining a relationship which gives the recipients or users of the service as much control over the service as they want (and can be allowed to have). It is not necessarily the case that services can be more responsive if there is a consumer relationship than if the relationship is one of dependency. A consumer relationship might be very responsive if there is a monopoly (the only library in the village, the only golf course) if there are empowered and sensitive managers.

Responsiveness can occur at different levels. At its most trivial, a customer care approach is limited to providing a welcoming attitude, including a smile and a presentable reception area. While this may be pleasant, it makes only a small contribution to the service. A more responsive approach would be designed to 'deliver' the service in a way which reflects people's wishes. For example, whether they have to travel to get it or it is delivered at home, whether transactions are carried out by letter or by telephone. Even greater responsiveness would give the service user control over the level of service they can receive, such as the frequency of home help services. In the next section we examine those aspects of customer orientation in more detail.

APPROACHES TO CUSTOMER ORIENTATION

Standards

One way of managing the relationship between 'front-line' staff and the organisation's service users is to create a set of standards of behaviour and performance and then manage the people to make sure that they meet those standards. Usually this approach implies creating a manual that sets out what staff are expected to do in some detail. These expectations can then be translated into customer expectations and can then be communicated to the service users. There was a flurry of this approach across European public services in the 1990s, first in local authorities and then taken up by national governments. The statement of expectations was sometimes called a 'Charter', a word used both in France and the United Kingdom.

Standards can be developed either by the organisation in isolation, or in partnership with its service users. One model of service quality, the SERVQUAL process, aims to measure expectations and then create services to meet or exceed those expectations. Such approaches were rare in the early days of Charters in the UK, where standards were generally decided by the service providers. This led, after many years, to the realisation that even though the self-defined standards were steadily improving, satisfaction was lagging behind.

The use of standards as an approach has merit in certain contexts: where the service can be standardised, where there is a relatively fast turnover of staff and where there is little scope for staff discretion.

Vouchers, cash and customer control

There have been examples of the use of vouchers and/or cash to give service users customer control of their services such as the allowance for people with disabilities to buy their own vehicles, the disability living allowance, or vouchers for home care which are offered in some local authorities. Representatives of people with disabilities argue for the extension of such schemes, rather than having to choose services which have been designed and provided by somebody else. The law[1] allows local authorities to make direct payments to people assessed as needing community care, but as we saw in Chapter 4, very little use was made of this power in practice.

At various times, there have been arguments for vouchers for education and they were introduced for nursery education in 1996. Voucher schemes or cash allowances work if certain conditions apply. First, supply has to be available in a way that offers choice. Without that, the voucher is simply a token of funding. For example, if there is one nursery school in an area, the introduction of vouchers simply adds form filling and paperwork to the previous process of applying for a place. Second, for equity the voucher must be adequate to cover the cost of the service. If vouchers require additional payments, services are available according to how much money people have, rather than need. Third, people should be both willing and able to organise services for themselves, researching the options, making choices, entering agreements. Tradition and familiarity play a part here. Not everyone is used to the idea of acting as a consumer in relation to doctors or schools, or home helps or residential homes.

Empowerment of service users

While cash and vouchers represent a form of empowerment, there are other ways of enhancing people's control over the services they use. These include the establishment of tenant management committees on housing estates, consultative processes when services are planned, market research to find out what aspects of service are important to people. Sometimes the arrangements are formal and constitutional, such as the Community Health Councils, a set of organisations designed to represent patient interests in the NHS, abolished by Labour. A new version is planned by the Coalition, Health Watch.

Empowerment of front-line staff

If all services are provided according to a detailed manual, there is little discretion for the service delivery staff to respond to individual needs and preferences. If there is to be responsiveness, then management needs to allow more discretion, with boundaries set by the budget and the need for equity.

Customer-oriented service design

Services are intangible and therefore quality standards can only be measured by the customer's perception. While standards of manufactured products also have to meet customer requirements, once that requirement has been defined there are objective measures of whether they have been met. This is true of services only to a limited extent – through measuring response times, for example. In fact response times and waiting times are a common element of all charter-type standard setting, precisely because it is something that can be measured. Other aspects of the service experience, such as the degree of anxiety caused, the confidence the customer has in the abilities of the service provider, the politeness or empathy level during the transaction, are all important parts of customer satisfaction but cannot be measured continuously. Because of that, people designing and managing services have to find ways of ensuring that the exchanges take place in a consistent way without being able to check on every member of staff all the time.

The second main difference between services and products is that services cannot be stored, but have to be made available when the customers want them. Matching the timing of service availability with customer preferences sometimes requires work outside 'normal' hours and often requires seasonal variation in supply. More recently, people have come to realise that most industries have a service element to them, whether this consists of after-sales service or the service elements of the process of buying a product, and many of the ideas of service management have been applied in sectors which are not service industries at first sight.

These developments have been commented on and supported by academics and consultants on service management and service marketing. They need careful interpretation in public services because of the different relationships between the organisations and their service users and because of the frequent need for equitable treatment and the exercise of entitlements which derive from citizenship rather than the market.

Who is the customer?

The first aspect of service design which managers in the public sector have had to cope with is the definition of the 'customer'. While the people who receive the services are the most obvious customer, public services have other people to satisfy. For example, the Benefits Agency decided early that claimants of social security benefits should be called customers and treated as such. Managers argued that the customer relationship was an appropriate one as a model for the way in which claimants should be treated, even though some of the features of the supplier–customer relationship were absent. They said that the respect, politeness and concern which good customer service implies were appropriate and would be well understood by staff dealing with members of the public. They also had to acknowledge the interest in the service relationship of ministers, the Treasury and other parts of government.

Similarly, the Probation Service has a relationship with offenders which has elements of a customer–supplier one. At the same time, the service is reliant on magistrates to give non-custodial sentences. The service also has had to respond to the Home Secretary's ideas about what probation orders are. Service design therefore has to take account of the expectations and preferences of a range of 'stakeholders' or people who have an interest in and influence on the organisation.[2]

Service concept

Different stakeholders have their own ideas about the benefits of the service being provided. While people on probation may see the service as an intrusion, magistrates see it as a way of preventing reoffending and the Home Secretary sees it as a punishment. The service concept is defined by Normann[3] as the benefits of the service as defined by the customers. Clearly the public sector, with its multiple stakeholders, has to design services for many different definitions of benefits. For public services, there are multiple definitions of benefit, as defined by the people using or affected by the services, the taxpayers who pay for them, the politicians who decide on their shape and volume. Service by service, these definitions may vary greatly. During 2011, for example, there was a debate about the purpose of public libraries, as the Coalition government's spending reductions made many local authorities target libraries as an easy cut. Pro-library campaigners enlisted authors to claim the great educational and cultural benefits of having books available free. Librarians pointed out the importance of libraries as free internet access points for people with no other available computer. Teachers proclaimed the importance of libraries as homework resource places. Criminal justice services clearly have different service concepts for victims and criminals and the taxpayer. Even the benefits of education services will be defined differently by parents, pupils, employers and politicians.

Market segment

As well as having multiple stakeholders, public services have service users with different characteristics. One of the dilemmas which managers face is how to meet the different expectations of different types of service user while maintaining equitable treatment. Should doctors give as much time to people with minor ailments as they do to people with serious complaints? Fairness would suggest that everyone should have the same time spent on them, while creating an equal outcome would dictate that the serious cases get more time. In social security, should all claimants have the same access arrangements or should routine enquiries about pensions and child benefit be dealt with differently from social fund applications? Should gifted children receive more attention from teachers than children with difficulties?

Service delivery system

Once the service concept has been defined, and differences between groups of service users identified, the service delivery system can be designed. The delivery system has many elements: physical things, such as buildings, vehicles and telephone systems; staff; processes of access and rationing. Most services can be seen as having 'core' and 'peripheral' elements. The core is those parts of the service without which the service would not happen at all, while the peripherals may be designed to make the services attractive or accessible.

In the private sector, a lot of the competition among service organisations is based on the quality of the peripherals. Airlines, for example, have similar service cores: aeroplanes which take people from one airport to another. They differentiate themselves from each other partly by their schedules, so that people can go where they want at the time they want, and partly by the peripherals. The booking system can be very easy or tortuous. Treatment on the ground can vary: some airlines provide business class passengers with chauffeurs from their office to the airport; they build special lounges at the airports. Treatment in the aeroplane can also vary, with different grades of food and drink and entertainment. The no-frills airlines compete on price and schedules.

The public sector attitude to the peripherals is somewhat different, especially in periods of budget cuts. Managers and professionals defend the core services more than the peripherals against cuts. So, if there is a choice between reducing the number of staff and delaying re-decorating the waiting area, the core service is preserved.

Where there is competition for customers, these attitudes change. Schools which have to attract pupils to maintain their budget often concentrate on the attractive peripherals, as well as the core service of teaching and learning. Uniforms, school plays and music lessons may not be essential to the core service but they differentiate one school from another in the eyes of parents and potential pupils. Specialist schools all teach the national curriculum. What distinguishes them from each other and from the 'bog-standard' is the extra facilities available to help teach their specialisms.

The call centre is a cost-effective way of providing access to services. It represents a relationship with the customer that is in practice entirely impersonal, although it has some superficial aspects of real human contact. Call centres handle calls for a range of businesses, and workers access information on customers and services through databases that can be accessed during the conversation. Banks, utilities, cable companies and many others operate their customer interface through this method. The Blair government saw call centres as the 'modern'[4] way to provide services. It established NHS Direct in 1998, a way of accessing advice from the NHS over the phone as an alternative to visiting primary care providers.

The NAO reported on the use of call centres by government in 2002.[5] The report found a high degree of public satisfaction with the 133 call centres that were operated by both direct employees and outsourcing operators. Service quality and customer satisfaction are measured in a variety of ways, including measuring the time it takes to answer a call (84% are answered within 20 seconds), satisfaction polling (satisfaction ratings ranged from 71% to 00%), mystery shoppers and call monitoring.

The government has also set targets for the proportion of services that can be accessed through the internet. In 2000 the Prime Minister pledged that by 2005 all services that *could* be accessed through the internet *would* be. Promoting this access was one of many tasks taken on by the 'Office of the eEnvoy', a post created in 1999 (and deleted in 2004 when the function was transferred to the Prime Minister's Delivery Unit) to co-ordinate investment in information and communication technology in government. The portal through which services would be accessed (DirectGov) was launched in 2004 and by 2006 was getting 2 million visits a month and included links to 11 government departments. In 2006 responsibility for DirectGov was taken over by the Central Office of Information, as a main route for communication with citizens.

Customer co-production

All services involve a partnership between the service provider and the service user. In fact the expression 'service delivery' implies that the user of the service is a passive recipient who has the service delivered to them. School children have to participate in the education process, doing most of the work, or the service will fail. Medical services also require active participation by patients to effect a cure. The degree to which service users wish to participate varies, and sensitive service design and management will take this into account.

Image

The fourth element of service design is how the organisation is to present itself to the outside world. In private services, designers work on the whole set of ways in which an organisation communicates with its customers, from the appearance and attitudes of staff, through the colours used in the premises, to the letterheads used for letters.

Many public-sector organisations have had similar design makeovers. The creation of NHS Trusts, grant-maintained schools, competitive white-collar services and Executive Agencies has promoted the flourishing image-management industry, producing logos, 'corporate dress' (staff uniforms), glossy brochures and repainted signs.

Just as the other elements of design need to be interpreted in a public sector context, so does image management. The reasons are also similar: different messages may be appropriate for different stakeholders. Even glossy brochures may give the impression of profligacy to funders while instilling confidence in service users. The police have a particular problem in projecting a consistent image to members of the public, transgressing drivers and criminals.

Values

There is a debate about the role of values or organisational culture in service design and management. Normann, for example, argues that without shared values, service delivery cannot be of high quality and consistent. If there is to be discretion at the point of contact between the organisation and its customers, that discretion cannot be exercised by reference to a rulebook, rather to the customer service ethos of the organisation. When price competition called for cost reductions, rulebooks about the limits to customer service were introduced.

The opposite view is that if there is a high turnover of staff and especially if they are poorly paid and uncommitted to their organisation, staff cannot be expected to use their discretion and express the organisation's customer service values. Rather they can learn routines of behaviour which match most customer expectations. This is especially true in services which are relatively routine and where little discretion is required. Operatives in fast food outlets have not internalised an ethos of desiring general well-being when they tell us to 'have a nice day'. They have learned a routine, in which communication with customers is as regimented as portion size and uniform clothing. Such routine service produces customer satisfaction because it matches expectations.

In the public sector, there may be values and a collective ethos which are more than a desire for customer service: many public sector workers say that their motivation for working is to provide a service for people, to high standards and with equity. If, together with these values, they also have the necessary skills, then the service management process can rely on their appropriate use of discretion.

However, if the people in contact with the service users are not inspired by a desire to serve the public but regard the work as 'just a job', and a low-paid one, managers have a dilemma. Do they try to engender an appropriate set of values, perhaps through a training programme, or do they design a set of behavioural routines which simulate a good ethos? Approaches such as quality circles, in which people collaborate to find better ways of doing things, rely on the willing and perhaps enthusiastic participation of people in service improvement. If willingness is in doubt, such approaches are a failure.

Once these elements are put in place, they reinforce each other. The delivery system reinforces customers' expectations. The image reinforces staff attitudes to the organisation. Different segments have a modification of the delivery system. In well-managed services there is consistency among the elements.

Quality

Public service organisations have all had initiatives about service quality. There are two main approaches to quality, implied by two definitions of it. One is that quality is defined as 'conformance to specification', a definition clearly derived from manufacturing. Management's main effort, using this definition, is to make sure that the specification is met, either by employees or contractors. Quality control, through inspection and monitoring, will ensure conformance.

Another definition is 'fitness for purpose', which implies that it is the person using the service who makes the judgement about what would make it fit for the purpose and whether that has been achieved. This approach implies that service users are involved or control the quality assurance process, reacting with those providing the service to ensure that it does what it is supposed to do. This implies that the specification may be ignored or modified, to make sure that the service is what the user wants. Inspection of conformance to specification would not achieve this.

Quality assurance is an approach to quality which emphasises the importance of making sure that all the processes and activities involved in producing services are working properly, from planning to delivery and feedback. There are certification procedures, such as the international quality standard ISO 9001, which check whether all the right sorts of procedures are in place. Many firms and public authorities will only deal with organisations which have such a certificate.

Citizen-oriented service design

We have already seen that a private sector service design and management model cannot be directly applied to the public sector without interpretation. The underlying reason is that people who use public services are citizens as well as customers. Their access to services is frequently a right which derives from meeting eligibility criteria, or simply from being a citizen, rather than from the ability to pay.

There are several implications of this. First is that overstretched services may not wish to make themselves too attractive, because they cannot cope with existing demand. On the contrary they may want to engage in 'demarketing' their services, especially to those in least need. Second, in those services that are available as a right, the organisation cannot decide that they do not want to provide a service for a particular individual or group. Inclusiveness may obstruct good service design and delivery. Third, decisions about what to produce, in what quantity and for whom are not in the hands of the managers. All public services are ultimately under the control of politicians, whether directly or indirectly. A pure customer orientation is affected by politicians' attitudes.

In addition, accountability is more diffuse in the public sector. Managers of private services are accountable to shareholders for attracting enough customers at the right price to make a profit. Public sector service managers are accountable, ultimately, to their customers through the political process. They are also accountable to people who are not customers but taxpayers, and to their elected representatives.

CONTRADICTIONS IN CUSTOMER–CITIZEN ORIENTATION

Budgets and quality

These special characteristics of public services present managers with dilemmas. One is the balance between service quality and cost. In private services, generally, a higher-quality service can command a higher price and stay profitable. In the public services, high quality does not necessarily generate more revenue, but may be more expensive. If there are insufficient resources to meet overall demand, there is a temptation to provide a mediocre standard of service to as many people as possible, rather than a high standard to a few. An example is the homecare service, through which people with disabilities or infirmities are helped with certain tasks at home. With a given budget for this service, the options are to give as many people as possible a small amount of help (a relatively low quality of service) or concentrate the service on those in greatest need and give them a high quality. Politically, withdrawing small amounts of help from large numbers of people is unpopular.

Politicians, citizens and consumers: limits of arm's-length control

The relationships within public services involve at least three participants. Politicians vote the funds, decide what services should be provided and take decisions about the nature and style of service delivery, as representatives of the electors. At the same time there is a direct relationship between the service providers and the users, which can itself change the nature of the services. There can be tensions between decisions made by politicians and decisions made by managers.

The problem is even more complicated when contractors are involved in service delivery. Politicians do not have direct control over the operations of contractors which are managed through a series of contracts and specifications. Contractors have to refer to the specification and the purchaser before changing a service in response to a service user's preferences or requirements. It is more difficult to have a responsive service in these circumstances.

Equity, equal treatment and customisation

Another serious dilemma is that between equity of treatment and customisation.[6] David Miliband, then schools standards minister, called for more customised approaches to education, and the Prime Minister included 'personalised learning' in his speech to the Labour Party conference in 2003. Miliband said:[7] 'It means building the organisation of schooling around the needs, interests and aptitudes of individual pupils.' He did not go into detail about how this might be done in the classroom, but the 2008 Cabinet Office paper *Excellence and Fairness* said that it was about subject choices and out-of-school activities: 'Children and parents also need and want choice of curriculum and qualifications, more personalised learning and the offer of a far greater range of out-of-school activities'. (p. 19).

Private sector services can be customised, as long as the customer is willing to pay and is satisfied with the result. If the service design is to recognise and respond differently to different sorts of people, the implication is that managers and workers respond in different ways to each group, or even to each individual, which implies a greater degree of discretion than standard, routine treatment. Some people have described the process of designing services for individuals, rather than producing a standard service, as 'post-Fordism', an analogy with flexible production methods making manufactured products more individual. It is possible to overstate the existence of such individual treatment. An example sometimes quoted is the creation of 'packages of care' in community care. The range of alternatives to residential care is in practice not large: the combinations may be individual but the services are quite limited in scope. In other services there does not seem to be a trend towards customisation. Standardisation through national standards and procedures leads to less individual treatment, and the growth of contracting leads to less flexibility.

Excellence and fairness

The Cabinet Office paper of 2008[8] set out its view of the nature of public services and how they should be managed. Although the paper was partly designed to claim credit for the improvement of public services since the 1997 election, it also set out an approach to public services, personally endorsed by Gordon Brown, the Prime Minister at the time. There were three principles. The first was about the nature of the relationship between the service provider and the service user: 'Wherever appropriate, people should not be treated as the passive recipients of standardised services, but as active partners, able with tailored support to solve many problems themselves' (p. 12). This principle expresses the notion of 'customer co-production', an idea proposed by Richard Normann, among others, in the 1980s. It also challenges standardisation, a challenge which the government used in its policy towards specialist schools, a mixed economy in social care, competition for service provision.

The second principle was fairness and equity: 'World class services promote a fairer society – this means that they actively reach out to all, regardless of wealth, background, gender, ethnicity or assertiveness. A core purpose of world class services should be to reduce inequality, not to tolerate second-rate services or significant variations in quality between various locations' (p. 12). Clearly this principle cannot be applied to all services: the Jobcentre Plus, for example, does not 'reach out' to everybody, only to people with particular needs, and certainly does not deal with people regardless of their wealth – all means-tested services operate precisely to target people on low incomes. Perhaps the principle applies to health services.

The third principle in the paper was a restatement of the need to seek value for money, while 'allocating resources to people in greatest need and by adopting the most effective approaches' (p. 12).

Looking towards the next phase of service improvement, emphasis was laid on the need for diversity of provision: 'services will be provided by a wider range of organisations and offer greater choice, which remains a central driver of improved innovation and performance' (p. 13). Again, the market, or quasi-markets and competition, are seen as an essential element of the public service.

There is continuity from these ideas to the Coalition's proposals in its White Paper *Open Public Services*.

'Open Public Services'

This White Paper spelled out the Coalition's policy towards services, as we saw in Chapter 2. It is somewhat lacking in detail, but two principles are relevant to the customer–citizen orientation: there will be more competition in service provision, enhancing the market solution; there will be more direct accountability to citizens and service users.

CONCLUSIONS

There has been an increasing emphasis over the years on the 'consumer' as opposed to the 'citizen'. At local level, local authority powers have been constrained by central government, and local authorities have become a weaker and weaker way of people exercising their citizenship at local level. People have a wide variety of experiences of relationships to the state at local and national level, but there is not a clear set of constitutional principles setting out citizen rights and obligations: to a large degree each service and its managers have to design how they relate to their service users, how to empower or consult them and generally how to manage the relationship.

Further reading

Clarke, J., Newman, J., Smith, N. et al. (2007) *Creating Citizen-Consumers*, London: Sage. A book that brings together a large research project on the 'citizen-consumer'.

Simmons, R. et al. (eds) (2009) *The Consumer in Public Services: Choice, Values and Difference*, Bristol: Policy Press. Discussion of the different kinds of relationships individuals have with state institutions.

DISCUSSION POINTS

- Think about the design of a public service that you use, and suggest improvements that would better meet your expectations
- What are the main differences between public and private services?

NOTES

1 The Community Care (Direct Payments) Act, 1996.

2 For an analysis of the stakeholder approach to public services, see Bryson, J.M. (2011), *Strategic Planning for Public and Not For Profit Organizations*, 4th edn, San Francisco: Jossey Bass.

3 R. Normann, *Service Management,* 2nd edn (Chichester: Wiley, 1991).

4 I asked a senior manager of a major out-sourcing company if they ran call-centres for government. 'Ah', he said, 'you mean the modernisation agenda.'

5 *Using call centres to deliver public services*, report by the Comptroller and Auditor General, HC 134 Session 2002–2003, 11 December 2002.

6 Demos, the think-tank, published a pamphlet by Charles Leadbeater called 'Personalisation through participation' (London: Demos) in 2004, with a foreword by David Miliband.

7 In July 2006 at an OECD conference.

8 Cabinet Office, *Excellence and Fairness: Achieving World Class Public Services* (London: HMSO, 2008).

CHAPTER 9
Audit and Inspection

SUMMARY

The framework and arrangements for performance management were set out in Chapter 6. We saw there that the system has been based on a contractual hierarchical relationship. Incentives, disincentives and sanctions have been based on performance contracts. Compliance was supposed to produce both additional resources and autonomy from heavy control. In this chapter we look at the use of the audit and inspection functions, both established in a previous era of public administration, in the performance regime. The chapter shows that the style of audit and inspection has changed as the functions changed. Audit and inspection were originally conceived as ways of assuring conformity to a set of financial and professional standards, and have developed into a different function as part of the effort to improve performance.

LEARNING POINTS

- Both audit and inspection can be used by managers to diagnose problems and improve performance.
- There are some intractable problems that seem to be impervious to the impact of inspection.
- Managers still find ways to comply with inspections that do not necessarily improve performance of their organisations.

FROM CONFORMANCE TO PERFORMANCE

Both audit and inspection were originally set up to ensure that institutions conformed with a set of standards. Financial audit was mainly concerned with checking whether the right procedures have been followed, in allocating money to purposes, in spending, and then recording and accounting for how the money was used. Standards of procedures and of accounting were set down, known to both the auditors and those being audited and trusted to ensure probity in dealing with public money. Auditors were recruited mostly from the accountancy profession.

Inspections were also traditionally concerned with standards, established and accepted, normally by professionals from the sector being inspected: school inspectors were recruited from among teachers and heads, social services inspectors from among social workers, and so on. Ensuring conformance to standards was the purpose of both audit and inspection; identifying lapses in standards and reporting them were designed to make sure that money was handled safely and properly and that people were doing their jobs properly. The standards in both cases were established within the professions, rather than established and imposed from outside. This approach to inspection can be seen as part of the 'clan' approach to governance, since those inspecting and those being inspected share a professional training and through that a set of professional values.

The search for improved performance by governments has changed the purposes of both audit and inspection: their main aim has changed from ensuring conformance to a set, minimum standard to encouraging better performance both of individual institutions and the sectors as a whole. The Audit Commission was established in 1983 explicitly to examine and improve the performance of local authorities by the then Secretary of State for the Environment Michael Heseltine. Compared with the District Audit Service, which became one of many auditors along with the private firms, the Audit Commission was given the task of assessing performance, making comparisons, recommending changes in management practices. It was instructed from the beginning to use the McKinsey management model to look for local authorities' performance in relation to the '7 S's.'[1] Its remit also included the National Health Service. The use of a particular management 'model' is less significant than the fact that the Audit Commission's brief included investigating and commenting on management, using a particular approach, as opposed to checking the probity of the financial systems of its 'clients'. At the same time, the National Audit Office, since 1983 a Parliamentary institution not accountable to the executive, turned its attention to performance. When we look in detail at both audit and inspection in particular sectors, we will see that each institution has an idea about what is good management.

Management as a set of practices is subject to the influence of the organisation's environment, its 'socio-technical system', its staff's competencies and skills as well as to some element of fashion: business academics, management consultants, self-promoting business leaders all have an interest in putting forward their own approach to management to attract attention, students and sales of books. If an auditor or inspector is to make a judgement about an organisation's management it can only do so within a particular model or paradigm of management.

The inspectorates were also used as part of the performance management movement, and started to rank, assess and compare institutions' performance, rather than their conformance to minimum standards. They were helped in this by the performance measurement system.

A changing landscape of audit and inspection[2]

Like most other public institutions, the inspectorates and auditors have been subject to structural change. A series of mergers was implemented in 2007, producing four inspectorates in education, health and social services. A similar merger was planned for the inspectorates in the criminal justice system, but this merger was rejected in the House of Lords in 2005. The main inspectorates and audit bodies in England, Wales, Scotland and Northern Ireland are listed in Table 9.1.

Table 9.1 Audit and inspection bodies, England, Wales, Scotland, Northern Ireland

	England	Wales	Scotland	Northern Ireland
Audit	National Audit Office, Audit Commission (to 2012–13)	Wales Audit Office	Auditor General, Accounts Commission, Audit Scotland	Northern Ireland Audit Office
Health	Quality Care Commission (also adult social care)	Health Inspectorate Wales	Quality Improvement Scotland (a special health board)	Regulation and Quality Improvement Authority
Education	OFSTED	HM Chief Inspector of Education and Training in Wales	HM Scottish Inspectorate of Education (an exec. agency)	Education and Training Inspectorate
Children's services	OFSTED	Care and Social Services Inspectorate Wales (also adult social care)	Social Work Inspection Agency (but, joint inspections)	Regulation and Quality Improvement Authority
Housing	Tenant Services Authority	Wales Audit Office	The Scottish Housing Regulator	Department for Social Development Regulator of Registered Housing Associations
Criminal justice	HM Inspectors, Constabulary, Crown Prosecution Service, Court Administration, Prisons, Probation	(with England)	As E and W, separate inspectorates for Scotland	Criminal Justice Inspection Northern Ireland

AUDIT

The Audit Commission, abolished in 2011, had been established to broaden the remit of audit from probity and compliance to effectiveness in local government and the NHS. The National Audit Office had a similar remit for national government, with similar arrangements in Scotland under Audit Scotland. Its remits are listed in its annual report:

Financial audit

The C&AG audits the financial statements of all central government departments, agencies and other public bodies, and reports the results to Parliament.

Value for money audit

Our value for money studies focus on how government projects, programmes and activities have been carried out, and whether they have achieved value for money. We recommend how services can be improved.

Performance improvement

Our programme of discretionary work focuses on key aspects of public service performance and financial management.

Support to Parliament, the public, and other organisations

We support Parliament in holding government to account for taxpayers' money through our work for the Committee of Public Accounts and other select committees.

International

We also carry out some activities overseas, auditing major international bodies and contributing to the development of public sector financial management and accountability around the world.[3]

The fact that the NAO reports to Parliament gives it an independence from the Government that allows it to be free from interference about what and how it reports. We have seen already how the NAO's reports are an authoritative, independent source of assessment and evaluation of government actions, management methods, financing arrangements and the effectiveness of government organisations within its remit.

CHILDREN AND EDUCATION

The Office for Standards in Education (Ofsted) was set up by the Education and Inspections Act 2006, and took over the functions of four previous bodies[4]. It is responsible for inspecting children's services as well as education. Its inspections of children's homes cover the following matters:[5]

1   overall effectiveness including areas for development
2   outcomes for children and young people
3   quality of care
4   safeguarding children and young people
5   leadership and management
6   equality and diversity.

The way that schools are inspected was changed radically in 2005. The inspections (about 4,000 a year in England) are conducted quickly, over usually no more than two days, and at short notice. The inspection starts with examination of the school's self-evaluation form, and the school's performance data, including textualised value added (see Chapter 6).

Schools are subject to inspection, and an assessment is made using a four-point scale, 'outstanding', 'good', 'satisfactory' and 'inadequate'.

The inspections are designed to judge the processes of teaching, the outcomes, measured by examination results and 'value added' (the results, taking into account the ability of the pupils on arrival), and the quality of management in the school. They also provide an opportunity to express ideas about how the schools could improve. An example of an extract from a report will illustrate the contents of an inspection report:

> Elizabeth Garrett Anderson is an outstanding school in which each and every pupil really does matter. The exceptional care, guidance and support provided by the school are real strengths. Parents praise the school highly for its work in this area and in the words of one, 'EGA has transformed my child and no words can explain what it feels like.' A great deal of excellent work, particularly outside the classroom, has been done to ensure that vulnerable girls, those with specific, moderate, behavioural and emotional needs, and those girls with English as an additional language are cared for, protected and supported exceedingly well. Equally, the needs of those higher attaining girls are considered carefully so that they are challenged effectively. Some girls do not always arrive in school ready to learn. However, because the school has a consistent approach to behaviour management and high expectations, behaviour is exemplary. The result of this work is that the vast majority of girls make outstanding progress in their learning and that standards are rising steadily, both in national tests at the end of Year 9, and at GCSE in Year 11. Overall, standards are broadly average but considering their starting points, girls' achievement is excellent. The currently good teaching is being developed further through systematic and rigorous monitoring. Good teaching in class combines with excellent tracking and support for any girls whose progress might be in danger of slowing. This leads to their outstanding achievement. The school has already identified that the highly effective practice, supporting girls so very well outside the classroom, should be extended to work in class.[6]

This extract illustrates that the inspection is concerned with the ethos of the school, the quality of the teaching and the behaviour of the pupils. It takes account of the intake the school has, when making its judgements. It also looks at the systems (monitoring and tracking) and activities outside the classroom, as well as during class lessons. The inspection process seems to be more of a peer review process, inspectors and leadership teams collaborating towards improvements.

The National Foundation for Educational Research published a report[7] on the impact of inspection in 2007. Based on a survey of 1,597 schools and visits to 36, their research findings were generally positive about the effect that the inspections had on schools, from the schools' point of view. Among respondents, 88% were 'very satisfied' or 'quite satisfied' with the inspection. The inspection process includes a self-evaluation form, which is completed by each school and can be compared with the results of the external inspection. The two sets of results were mostly similar. Schools reported that they made improvements after the inspection, but not necessarily because of it.

Ofsted itself conducted a review of the impact of inspection in the same year. Perhaps not surprisingly, the review found that the impact of inspection was positive:

By their very existence inspection and regulation keep institutions on their toes. Inspection and regulation help make providers accountable to their users and to the public. Reports have a high profile, and can have serious implications when outcomes are poor. Providers may, for example, lose funding, lose customers or be shut down. Through changes to its inspection regimes in recent years, Ofsted has unashamedly 'raised the bar'; as children, young people, parents, and the public have come to expect higher standards of performance, so has Ofsted.[8]

PRISONS

Prison inspections have often been highly critical of the conditions, routines and management of prisons. HM Prisons Inspectorate has been headed by outspoken Chief Inspectors, such as Sir David Ramsbotham (1995–2001) and Anne Owers (2001–2010). Prisons have been subject to a very tight series of control mechanisms from NOMS, including a Strategic Plan, a Public Service Agreement, a Framework Document, Key Performance Indicators, Key Performance Targets and regular inspections. Ramsbotham, whose previous career had been in the military, was not convinced that the formal control processes were adequate to the task of ensuring good quality prisons. In an interview in January 2001 he expressed doubts about the purpose of inspection:

I have never seen an organisation with so many rules, operating standards, instructions, visions and mission statements. You name it. It is a horrendous amount of bureaucracy, it is not hands-on management. In the Army, the purpose of inspection was to ensure that the organisation being inspected was ready for its operational purpose. If not, you asked why not. This presupposed that someone was listening, which is not always the case in Whitehall.[9] © Telegraph Media Group Limited 2001

His successor was also critical of prison management, but reported, in her valedictory speech in 2010, that she had observed improvement in the Prison Service during her tenure. She said that there had been improvements in health and especially mental health facilities, in education and rehabilitation and in activity in prisons:

> Over the last nine years, there is no doubt that prisons became better places – better able to keep prisoners safe, provide a decent environment, offer some purposeful activity and provide some resettlement opportunities. To do this, they have drawn in money and professional expertise from outside. But they have also drawn in 27% more people. There are 20,000 more adult men incarcerated than there were when I started. That is one of the underlying reasons why progress has been slow and patchy, why recidivism remains obstinately high, and why hard worked-for changes often do not stick.[10]

As an example of prison inspections and their impact over time, we can look at Wandsworth Prison, which was inspected in 1999 and again in 2009. In 1999, Sir David Ramsbotham was highly critical in his inspection report:

> Regrettably I have to report that, in no prison that I have inspected, has the 'culture' that we found caused me greater concern than that in HMP Wandsworth. This is not just because of the grossly unsatisfactory nature of the regimes for many different types of prisoner that are described in the report, but because of the insidious nature of what the 'Wandsworth way' – as the local 'culture' was described to us – represents, in terms of the attitude of too many members of staff to prisoners and their duty of care for them. What we observed, and learned, confirmed that too many staff do not seem to think that the phrase 'look after prisoners with humanity', enshrined at the heart of the Prison Service Statement of Purpose, applies to them, and continue to pursue an agenda which, if it ever was authorised, is not only long out of date but far removed from current and acceptable practice.
>
> There can therefore only be one 'way' in prisons, and that must be the 'Prison Service way'. Those who think, or presume otherwise, preferring such as the 'Wandsworth way' should get out, or be got out, of the Prison Service now, and leave it to the decent minded majority, who hate what is happening, but feel, or have been rendered, powerless to do anything about it…[11]

The 2006 Inspection Report recorded that much had improved in Wandsworth, but that there were still problems:

> This inspection found an effective and united management team that was taking steps to move the prison forward. They had inherited a prison that was performing even less well than it had been at the time of the last inspection, in spite of having undergone a performance improvement programme. Since then, the prison had clearly improved: with greater confidence among staff and managers, more time out of cell and more activities for prisoners, and an improved focus on safer custody. There were, for example, effective first night and induction arrangements, and improvements to fundamentals of cleanliness, hygiene and food. All prisoners were out of their cells for a period of time each day; and, for the first time, Wandsworth offered vocational training opportunities – even if these were available to only 96 out of 1400 prisoners. However, this inspection also revealed the distance still to travel, and the residual problems that remained. The most important of these remained the attitudes and behaviour of some staff.[12]

This extract illustrates the matters with which a prison inspection is concerned: the physical state of the prison, the processes, the relationships between the prisoners and staff, the opportunities for meaningful activity.

By 2009, the inspectors could report further improvement:

> The body of this report records those positive changes. First night and induction procedures had improved, as had prisoners' relationships with staff. There was some positive work on race, though work with foreign national and disabled prisoners was underdeveloped. For a local prison, there was a commendable amount of activity, with some good quality vocational training, and prisoners were out of their cells for a reasonable amount of time. Resettlement work was also developing well, with some good local and community links, though the needs of short-term and remanded prisoners (a considerable percentage) were not systematically met.[13]

This particular inspection was marred nevertheless by the prison management's strategy towards the inspection:

> However, the prison's reputation has been seriously tarnished by the irresponsible, pointless and potentially dangerous actions instigated at managerial level, in conjunction with managers at Pentonville, whose report is also published today. Together, they planned to swap a small number of prisoners for the duration of their respective inspections – in Wandsworth's case to remove five prisoners perceived to be potentially 'difficult'. The consequences at Wandsworth were particularly serious. Three prisoners from the segregation unit and two from the vulnerable

prisoner wing were summarily told on the weekend before the inspection that they were to move to Pentonville. One was new to prison and already identified as in need of protection. Two others would miss medical appointments for serious conditions. Both were so distressed that they self-harmed. One, with a previous history of self-harm, tied a ligature round his neck, cut himself and was forcibly removed from his cell. He was taken to reception, bloody, handcuffed and dressed only in underwear. He attempted self-harm a further three times immediately after his move to Pentonville. The other took an overdose of prescription drugs and needed to go to hospital. On his return, he was nevertheless later taken by taxi to Pentonville. Those men, and two of the other transferees, were returned to Wandsworth immediately after the inspection was over.[14]

This is probably an extreme case, and one which was discovered by the inspectors, but it does illustrate an important point about strategy towards inspection. There are incentives to do well in an inspection: it enhances career prospects, it removes pressure from management above, it makes for an easier life.

In her speech Anne Owers spoke of the 'virtual prison service', the one that Ministers and senior civil servants know, and which exists in reports, statistics and accounts of performance targets passed, as she put it, 'through a series of charcoal filters that have removed any impurities'.

CARE QUALITY COMMISSION

The Care Quality Commission was set up under the Health and Social Care Act 2008. For the first time combining inspection of health and social care providers, its first task was to establish a registration system for care providers, starting with all NHS Trusts by April 1st 2010, then social care and independent health care providers by October 2010, then dentists, ambulance services and General Practitioners. When it was established, the CQC set out its purpose:

Our job is to:

- make sure that essential standards of safety and quality are met wherever health and social care is provided;
- protect the rights of people whose freedoms are restricted under mental health legislation;
- encourage those who purchase and provide care to continue to improve services; and
- promote the efficient and effective use of resources in the provision of health and social care.[15]

In its first annual report, the CQC stated that it had saved money compared with the previous arrangements, cutting the number of offices from 23 to 8, the budget from £240 million to £164 million and the staff from 2,900 to 2,100.

To get an idea of the scale of the inspection operation, in 2009–10 they carried out 11,477 inspections of premises providing adult social care, 741 establishments providing independent health care, 250 NHS Trusts, along with other inspections of children's services and young offenders' services providing drugs.[16]

Inevitably the new inspection service was the subject of some public criticism, every time an establishment subject to inspection was found to be failing to comply with standards. Scandals in premises providing care for people with learning difficulties produced publicity questioning the effectiveness of the inspection regime and the capacity of the inspectorate.

Parallel with the CQC is Monitor, a regulatory body for NHS Foundation Trusts, a class of Trust with more autonomy than regular Trusts. Monitor was set up initially to assess Trusts' suitability to become Foundation Trusts, and then to regulate them. It takes a risk-based and self-regulatory approach to its work, and is careful not to duplicate what the CQC does.

The inspection regime for health and social care was designed to treat the private and public sectors in the same way, with an identical registration and inspection regime. This would facilitate the expansion of the private sector in healthcare, in the same way as private social care has all but taken over the publicly-owned social care sector.

Learning to deal with inspection

Davis and Martin reported: 'In 2006, 64% of officers agreed with the statement: "my authority has got better at managing the inspection process in order to get a more positive inspection report".'[17] Inspection can be seen by those being inspected as a game that is played in order to achieve a positive report. This may be true even if both players of the game genuinely believe that the process can bring about improvements in the way that the establishments are run. While performance improvement may be the agreed objective, reputation and funding depend on the results of inspection, whether those inspected are in the private or public sectors. Nobody wants a bad report which, in the extreme, can lead to a career-limiting intervention and replacement of the local management. As the Audit Commission said: 'Centrally imposed targets and the associated performance monitoring and intervention are perceived to stifle innovation, addressing the failures of the worst performers while holding back the majority.'[18] In any case, there may be insufficient powers in the inspectorates to ensure that improvement takes place.

The Audit Commission called for 'greater incentives for improvement through a more varied approach which recognises the different starting points of different local authorities and which recognises too that local government is not just about the delivery of services.'[19] This was a polite plea that there are insufficient incentives available to the inspectors, in this case the Audit Commission, to bring about improvements. We have seen the frustration of the Prison Inspectorate on this same issue.

There are differences in approach according to whether the scrutiny is a professional inspection, an audit or a management inspection. While excuses may be found for poor professional practice, the only acceptable argument is a lack of resources, such as cash or trained staff. A standard response to adverse reports on individual prison performance is to use the report to make the case for more money or staff. The only credible response to criticism in an audit report is to put things right, or even better to claim that things have been put right between the audit visit and the report.

Strategies for coping with scrutiny on performance or the quality of management, such as the Best Value inspections, which used to be compulsory for local authorities, were more complicated. One approach is to join in wholeheartedly with the latest initiative and try to become a shining example, or beacon. This brings prestige and possibly extra resources and should be good for a manager's career. To achieve this, the organisation needs to get involved early, become a pilot for whatever the initiative is and take part in shaping the process. This requires that the existing arrangements are in line with the current thinking and that the existing managers are well connected with the scrutineers.

Less adventurous is a policy of conformance whereby the manuals are studied and the procedures followed in preference to existing ways of managing. In practice this should not be too difficult as the prescriptions offered are not usually too far removed from existing practices in well-managed organisations. Conformance involves work on presentation, possibly representing existing processes using the new language. For example local authorities have been doing various forms of performance review for decades and it should not be too hard to present this as the sort of performance review implied by the Best Value process. The response by the Chartered Institute of Public Finance and Accountancy[20] to the government's consultation on inspection reform included this warning: 'CIPFA is concerned that performance inspection regimes may distract focus away from improvement towards "inspection compliance". For example, many senior managers in local government…have developed a very detailed knowledge of the Audit Commission CPA [Comprehensive Performance Assessment] framework. They know exactly where additional points need to be earned in order to secure a more positive overall rating for the authority.'[21] Inspection compliance is a sensible reaction to inspection used as a way of assuring conformance to pre-set standards. If the purpose is improvement, then compliance will not be enough.

Less submissive is an approach that involves a dialogue with the scrutineers to persuade them that there are viable alternatives to their prescriptions. This requires confident management and an evaluation process that enables it to demonstrate that its ways of working are producing results. It also requires some political courage when the regime being imposed has strong government backing, but if the local authority members think that what they do has value, they need to protect it from the visitors.

Less drastic organisations can harness the external influences to help bring about change. Often managers know what should be done but they need help to overcome obstacles to change. An adverse report can be used to get extra resources. When the Benefit Fraud

Inspectorate make a visit they are very explicit about the resources required to combat fraud, and specify the shortfalls in staffing. Similarly the capacity of management is a legitimate reason for non-compliance and can be used to strengthen the management team. A report can also be used to gain legitimacy for changes some managers wanted to make in any case. An alliance can develop between like-minded people among the managers and the scrutineers.

CONCLUSIONS

Audit and inspection can fit within any of the main modes of governance: they can be used to reinforce hierarchy by ensuring standards set at the top, they can be used to ensure that markets are functioning (although regulation is more commonly used for that mode), they can be a part of 'clan' control by which professions reinforce their own values. In the UK public sector, the role of both has been to improve performance and quality of service.

Further reading

John Bourne, *Public Sector Auditing – Is It Value for Money?* (Chichester: Wiley, 2007).
Howard Davis and Steve Martin (eds), *Public Services Inspection in the United Kingdom* (London: Jessica Kingsley Publishers, 2008).

POINTS FOR DISCUSSION

- What are the factors that make schools respond positively to inspection but prisons to respond negatively?
- Why is 'inspection compliance' a problem?
- Can inspection adapt to the three main forms of governance, market, hierarchy and clan?

NOTES

1   I once interviewed the Chief Executive of the Audit Commission in the early days: he asked, lightly, 'what am I supposed to do if I find that the Chief Executive has no "style"?' The 7 S's were a heuristic device created as a consulting tool by the management consultants McKinsey and adapted by the Audit Commission to examine the management arrangements in local authorities. The first Chief Executive of the Audit Commission was previously a McKinsey consultant.

2   Government inspectorates have a history dating to the beginning of the 19th century, with the Factory Inspectorate set up in 1833, followed by Her Majesty's Inspectors of Schools (two of them) appointed in 1839.

3   National Audit Office, Annual Report, 2011.

4   The new arrangements brought together the existing remit of Her Majesty's Chief Inspector of Schools in England, the children's social care remit of the Commission for Social Care Inspection, the Children and Family Court Advisory and Support Service inspection remit of Her Majesty's Inspectorate of Court Administration, and the inspection remit of the Adult Learning Inspectorate.

5   Ofsted, *Framework for Inspection of Children's Homes,* 2011.

6   Ofsted Report, Elizabeth Garrett Anderson Language College, 2008.

7   National Foundation for Educational Research, *Evaluation of the Impact of Section 5 Inspections*, 2007.

8   Office for Standards in Education, *Review of the Impact of Inspection*, 2007, p. 2.

9   *Daily Telegraph*, 16.01.2001, p. 15.

10 Anne Owers, Speech to Prison Reform Trust, 2010.

11 HM Inspector of Prisons (1999), Report on Wandsworth Prison.

12 HM Inspector of Prisons (2006), Report on Wandsworth Prison.

13 HM Inspector of Prisons (2009), Report on Wandsworth Prison.

14 Ibid.

15 Care Quality Commission introductory leaflet, undated.

16 Care Quality Commission, Annual Report 2009–10, p. 21.

17 Howard Davis and Steve Martin, *Public Services Inspection in the UK* (London: Jessica Kingsley Publishers, 2008), p. 30.

18 Audit Commission (2006) 'The Future of Regulation in the Public Sector', Corporate Discussion Paper, p. 4.

19 Ibid., p. 30.

20 The main accounting body for the public sector in the United Kingdom.

21 CIPFA (2005), 'Response to ODPM Consultation on Inspection Reform', CIPFA homepage: www.cipfa.org.uk.

CHAPTER 10

Collaboration and 'Joined-Up Government'

SUMMARY

One of the consequences of a managerial approach based on performance targets for individual organisations is that the public services become fragmented and their staff develop narrow visions. Governments have tried to make public services more holistic, both at central government level and at neighbourhood level. While the co-ordinating mechanisms at central level have been subject to many reorganisations and rebrandings, at local level there has been a long series of experiments with area funding, partnerships, regeneration budgets, special zones. Some have worked better than others and there is a wealth of evaluations of these experiences.

LEARNING POINTS

- Centralised government will look to central units close to the Prime Minister and Cabinet to solve problems of co-ordination.
- Services at local level can be fragmented and not have shared objectives.
- There have been experiments to co-ordinate service delivery and policy at local level for many years.

FRAGMENTATION AND CO-ORDINATION

All governments face the problem of co-ordination of policy and of services. The institutions of the public sector have grown and developed over a long period and each has its own ways of working, of dealing with its client group and to some extent of managing. The norms of behaviour and even the ways of understanding and responding to problems differ widely across the public sector. As we saw in Chapter 4, the Probation Service went through an imposed change from being an organisation that befriended and supported offenders to one that was part of their punishment, and was put into much closer collaboration with the rest of the criminal justice system through the creation of a single organisation. Collaboration across organisational boundaries can be difficult because of the differences in behaviours and values between, for example, police and teachers, or social workers and doctors.

There are other aspects of the way the public sector is organised that separates out the services: the most important is the narrow focus on efficiency, and the use of performance targets and measurement as means of governance and control. Much of the managerial effort that we saw in Chapters 5 and 6 was directed at achieving efficiency: establishing what costs are, trying to reduce costs and to produce as much as possible for a given quantity of resources. The division of policy making from service delivery was done to enable managers in the service delivery operations to concentrate on a narrow range of tasks and do them well and efficiently. Financial management was delegated, along with a target regime, to enable managers at low levels in the hierarchies to manage their resources in a cost-effective way.

This combination of delegation and specialisation presents a problem of central control and central direction: the target system will, if it works, make managers concentrate on meeting their targets: exam passes, waiting times, arrest rates and so on, each with their organisational and individual incentives, direct managers' and workers' efforts. But what if there is a change in priorities that cannot be expressed through a change in targets? Or what if there are policy issues that are not susceptible to solution by setting a target for an agency?

The Labour governments responded to these questions in two ways: they set up a series of 'Units', usually attached to the Cabinet Office, to improve co-ordination; they established initiatives at local level to deal with policy issues that involved more than one agency.

Central co-ordinating institutions

The Blair governments were ambitious to implement a range of social policies that, ministers thought, required changes in the machinery of government. The party had been out of power for eighteen years and had few ministers with experience of running departments and policies. As is frequently the case, there was a suspicion that the civil servants were loyal to the previous governments and ruling party. They appointed special advisors, operating outside the normal Civil Service structures, to implement initiatives. There was a managerial tone to the way the incoming government operated, with an emphasis on 'driving through', 'delivery', 'strategy' and other language, but based on a curiously antique management approach: 'management by objectives', an approach made popular in business in the 1950s.

In addition to special advisors, the government also created special 'Units' that were designed to implement policies that required collaboration among central government departments and institutions outside central government, especially local authorities and the NHS. In most cases, the Units were attached structurally to the Cabinet Office, which was seen as the centre of government. In addition to the Units, later on, individuals were given jobs to 'drive' policies, and given titles that often included the word 'czar', such as the 'drugs czar'. It was an odd metaphor, especially as the appointments rarely brought with them any direct power, and the 'czar' initiatives soon fell back into obscurity. Their way of operating was to write strategy documents, which would set out an analysis of the problem and a list of institutions and the contribution that they should make to policy implementation.

Central Units included the Social Exclusion Unit, later downgraded to a Task Force, to try to integrate social inclusion policies; a Women's Unit, itself soon turned into the Women and Equalities Unit; then the Government Equalities Office, an Anti-Drugs Coordination Unit, a Sustainable Development Unit.

The Neill Committee[1] counted the number of units that had been set up at the centre of government: by February 1998 there were 113 review groups and 37 task forces. Between February and July 1998, 69 review groups and 18 task forces had reported, but 48 additional reviews and seven additional task forces had been announced (making net totals of 92 review groups and 26 task forces). For issues concerning public management the Performance and Innovation Unit was set up in 1998 with this remit:

> The PIU's aim is to improve the capacity of Government to address strategic, cross-cutting issues and promote innovation in the development of policy and in the delivery of the Government's objectives. The PIU is part of the drive for better, more joined-up government. It acts as a resource for the whole of government, tackling issues that cross public sector institutional boundaries on a project basis.[2]

The PIU reported on issues such as energy policy, waste, policy analysis, leadership in government. It was later re-named the Strategy Unit.

The model that all of these institutional initiatives shared was that of a small central unit, in or close to the Cabinet Office, that would 'drive' (a commonly used piece of management jargon) policies through the departments. They were all concerned with policy matters that required action by more than one department and policy instruments that were considered inadequate to the policy problem.

Efficiency and Reform Group

The Coalition continued the tradition of establishing what were in effect ad hoc units with the establishment of a new unit between the Cabinet Office and the Treasury, reporting to Francis Maude, Minister for the Cabinet Office, to co-ordinate initiatives on efficiency and reform. It was given both a narrow focus on efficiency savings and a broad focus on radical changes within the Big Society idea:

1 Making Government more efficient: reducing operational overheads to give tax-payers better value and allow resources to be focused on key priorities; and
2 Radically reforming the way public services are provided to ensure they meet rising public expectations: using transparency to improve accountability; shifting power to people and creating the Big Society.

Integrating health and social care

Apart from in Northern Ireland, health services and social care services have been delivered by different organisations, with separate budgets, very often to the same individuals. Adults requiring support and children's services often need elements from both the NHS and social services, and their integration has been an ambition of policy makers and managers for at least forty years.

For community care services, where an individual is entitled to and needs a combination of services from the NHS and local authority social services departments, there was an ambition that 'joint commissioning', involving both sets of organisations, would provide a seamless service. This ambition was never achieved, as a review by Bob Hudson[3] has shown. One of the reasons for the failure of joint commissioning was that social care commissioning is done mostly at the level of the individual service user, while health commissioning is done through large contracts with acute care providers. Whatever the reasons, by 2009, only 3.4% of the combined NHS and social care budgets was spent through joint commissioning.

Joined-up government at local level

Area-based initiatives have a long history in the UK, dating back to various experiments and pilots in urban renewal in the 1970s. The assumption at the centre has been that policy and service delivery would be more effective if only the individual institutions, such as schools, police, health authorities, social services, local authority departments would work together. The last such initiative from a very long list was Total Place,[4] an attempt to identify all the public services, and their costs, in a geographical area and rationalise them, eliminating duplication and focusing resources better on problems. An experimental project set up in

2009 in 13 areas of England with a combined population of 11 million people, Total Place was sponsored by the Department of Communities and Local Government. It was discontinued as a pilot by the incoming Coalition government in 2010, making it possibly the area initiative with the shortest life.

Action Zones

Health Action Zones were set up through a bidding process for permission to operate a zone, with local partnerships established for the process of bidding and the implementation of the action zone. Different localities chose different partnerships and different action plans. While there was not a fund to finance successful bids, the creation of the zone offered an opportunity to work within a more flexible set of rules. HAZs preceded the establishment of the Social Exclusion Unit, so there was not a central steering equivalent of the HAZs. Ken Judge was commissioned to evaluate the success of Health Action Zones and reported to the Health Committee of Parliament. In summary, he said:

> HAZs were born at a time when anything seemed possible for a New Labour Government desperate to make things work and quickly. But the tide of enthusiasm for change outran the capacity to deliver it. Too many hugely ambitious, aspirational targets were promulgated. The pressure put on local agents to produce 'early wins' was debilitating. A sense of disillusionment began to set in relatively early in their lifespan, and HAZs soon lost their high profile as the policy agenda filled with an ever-expanding list of new initiatives to transform public services and promote social justice. By the beginning of 2003, much earlier than expected, they were to all intents and purposes wound up.

The evaluation found that the sheer complexity of the initiative and the extent of policy change that HAZs experienced meant that drawing simple conclusions about their impact was difficult. It suggested that there were some benefits: HAZs made a valuable contribution to building partnerships and raising awareness about inequalities in health, and progress was made with individual programmes and projects. However, in general the conclusions were negative, finding that HAZs made little impact in terms of measurable improvement in health outcomes during their short lifespan. HAZs did not – probably could not – do what they set out to achieve:

> … this was supposed to be a seven-year initiative, launched by one secretary of state, dramatically changed by the next, abandoned by the third, subject to different parliamentary and political timetables, where guidance from the centre was not clear, [or was] …contradictory. People competed with each other in terms of their aspirations. One of the Health Action Zones, which covered an entire conurbation and was given

£4 million or £5 million a year, proposed to transform the life expectancy of the entire population such that it was in the top 10% for Western Europe in seven years. These things are simply not achievable.[5]

New Deal for Communities

New Deal for Communities was an Area Based Initiative aimed at general improvement of 39 selected deprived areas, each with a population of about 10,000 people and a budget of £50 million over ten years, with an outcome programme spend of £1.7 billion. Three of the aims were expressed as place-based outcomes (crime, community and housing) and three as people-based (education, health and worklessness). The programme required local collaboration among agencies. Over the ten years that the programme ran from 1998, the programme consisted of projects in the proportions shown in Figure 10.1.

According to the Department for Communities and Local Government evaluation, the programme achieved improvement in 32 of the 36 outcome indicators, as shown in Figure 10.2.[6]

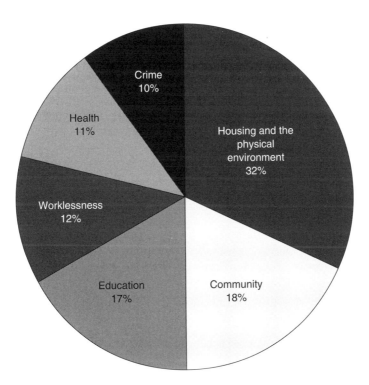

Figure 10.1   New Deal for Communities, expenditure

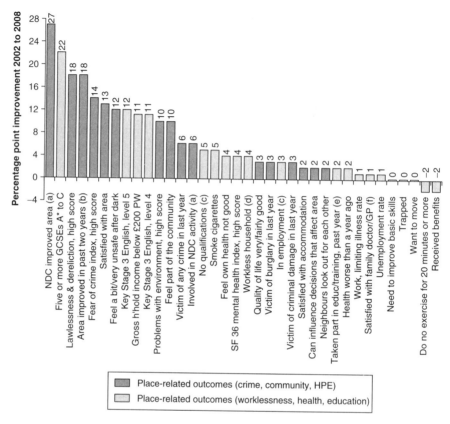

Figure 10.2   New Deal for Communities, outcome indicators: improvement 2002–2008

Source: A New Deal for Communities Experience: Final Assessment, p. 8

In the spirit of experiment, an element of all Area Based Initiatives over the forty years in which they were implemented, the final evaluation drew conclusions for future Area Based Initiatives. These were as follows[7]:

- It is important to set realistic targets for regeneration schemes: NDC Programme investment into these areas amounts to no more than 10 per cent of existing mainstream spend.
- The types of NDC areas which have seen relatively little in the way of change may not be those where there are the greatest opportunities to deliver longer-term transformation.
- NDC areas have seen more net change with regard to place-related, rather than people-related, outcomes over the 2002–2008 time period covered by this evaluation. Education has been one outcome where not only has it been difficult for NDC partnerships to

make an impact, but there are also, (albeit weak) negative associations between higher rates of spend and change in general.

- More emphasis needs to be given to determining what works at the neighbourhood level, if education is to be incorporated into similar ABIs in the future.
- Increasing proportions of owner-occupiers will help achieve outcome change and will dilute the scale of problems in regeneration areas; but existing residents in social housing schemes are unlikely to be able to purchase new owner-occupied dwellings.
- The time-frame for regeneration schemes should reflect their objectives.
- There is an argument that had NDC areas been larger, partnerships might have found it easier to engage with mainstream delivery agencies.
- There is a case for a year-zero for all regeneration schemes; NDC partnerships had to deal with a formidable array of 'setting-up' tasks.
- Continuity in relation to senior staff is associated with positive benefits.
- Staff involved with regeneration schemes need good informal, inter-personal skills.
- NDC partnership boards have run better when they have been chaired effectively, focused on strategic issues, and provided training for community representatives.
- Elections to boards may not be the best way of getting the 'right people in the right places', but they have been seen by many NDC partnerships as an important means of legitimising resident representation.
- Regeneration bodies need to be instrumental in gaining delivery agency support.
- Relatively small amounts of regeneration funding used flexibly can lever in larger sums of money from other agencies.
- Partner delivery agencies may be useful in informing the way regeneration bodies should spend their money, but be less inclined to bend their own resources into defined regeneration areas.
- From the outset regeneration schemes need to establish what the community dimension actually means and to set objectives accordingly: consultation, involvement, engagement, empowerment, or delivery?
- It is vital to manage expectations; local residents can have inflated views in relation to the speed with which projects can be delivered, and the degree to which benefits from regeneration projects will be distributed across all of those living in the area.
- Communities can play an especially strong role in defining needs and validating the 'additionality' of new proposals emerging from mainstream delivery agencies; they tend to be less interested in, and may lack the skills for, delivering projects.
- It is never too early to address issues of sustainability: regeneration programmes need to provide guidance in relation to legacy and succession at an early stage; the whole arena is fraught with financial and technical problems.
- New, neighbourhood-level, physical developments can provide guaranteed rental income after regeneration funding ceases, but the management costs of such projects can be underestimated; it may be difficult to maintain full occupancy rates, and rental income will not be sufficient to maintain the same scale of activity.

The long quotation from the evaluation of the NDC programme illustrates almost all the lessons that have been (or should have been) learned about neighbourhood-level policies aimed at improving conditions in a particular locality. If there are to be any future initiatives of this kind, it is to be hoped that they will learn from this valuable experience of the potential and limitations of area-based initiatives.

SURE START

Sure Start was a policy designed to end the process by which children of poor parents get a bad start to life which follows through into school and later life. It was a series of services for parents and children, which were not means-tested: everyone in a Sure Start area could benefit from the services. An evaluation was carried out in 2010 and concluded:

> The main impacts identified for children were that:
>
> Children growing up in SSLP[8] areas had lower BMI[9]s than children in non-SSLP areas. This was due to their being less likely to be overweight with no difference for obesity (using WHO, 2008, criteria).
>
> Children growing up in SSLP areas experienced better physical health than children in non-SSLP areas.
>
> The positive effects associated with SSLPs for maternal well being and family functioning, in comparison with those in non-SSLP areas, were that:
>
> Mothers residing in SSLP areas reported providing a more cognitively stimulating home learning environment for their children.
>
> Mothers residing in SSLP areas reported providing a less chaotic home environment for their children.
>
> Mothers residing in SSLP areas reported greater life satisfaction.
>
> Mothers residing in SSLP areas reported engaging in less harsh discipline.
>
> On the negative side, however, in comparison with those in non-SSLP areas:
>
> Mothers in SSLP areas reported more depressive symptoms.
>
> Parents in SSLP areas were less likely to visit their child's school for parent/teacher meetings or other arranged visits, although the overall incidence of such visits was low generally.[10] (p. vi)

The programme was launched with 21 outcomes, and the evaluation found that 8 of them were achieved.

Sure Start was the central policy instrument, along with the working family tax credits, of the policy of removing children from poverty. As such it was an important element of the highest priority policy of the Blair and Brown governments. The policy had many features of the preferred policy instruments, in that it was targeted, it was area-based and it was founded on the achievement of defined and measurable outcomes.

Local Strategic Partnerships

Another area-based initiative was called 'Local Strategic Partnerships', created to bring together participants from many organisations in the private and public sectors at local level. The official evaluation of Local Strategic partnerships in 2008 concluded:

> Many of the spheres in which survey respondents reported progress are process ones, ranging from developing a collective vision and co-ordinated strategy and understanding partners' priorities to widening the range of interests involved in local decision making. Other areas of progress include joint funding of projects, services better meeting needs in priority areas, levering in additional resources and quality and efficiency gains through joint working.

> Areas in which less progress has been made include pooling budgets, mainstream co-commissioning, efficiency gains through more strategic and collaborative commissioning, and mapping partners' spending programmes. The barriers to aligning mainstream programmes were, again, less to do with lack of local will and more to do with constraining central government priorities and targets as well as limited time and resources. When asked if there are examples of initiatives benefiting local people that would not have happened without the LSP, less than 10 per cent reported that there were no such initiatives. Features of some of the examples given are that, first, they are often deliberately setting out to be innovative and, second, they are taking advantage of partnership working either to focus on policy areas that cut across different agencies and for which no single body would otherwise have responsibility (such as climate change or cultural strategies), or to streamline activities in which several have to engage (such as community consultation) or enhance outcomes by bringing together different policy dimensions that all affect the same target group (for example, in working with children and young people). Overall, although only 10 per cent of LSPs had undertaken any cost benefit analysis, 84 per cent of respondents strongly agreed or agreed that the benefits of LSPs outweigh their costs in time, energy and resources.[11]

Single Regeneration Budget

The Single Regeneration Budget was a regeneration scheme, with funds attached, designed to combine all the separate regeneration budgets for the areas making a successful bid. It was the most comprehensive attempt to produce 'joined-up' regeneration at local level. The institutions involved included public, voluntary and private sectors in an effort to co-ordinate actions with a shared strategy and vision. An evaluation was conducted by the Department of Communities and Local Government in 2007. Its conclusions about the process are quoted here:[12]

The key features that have been important are:

- The partnership based model of delivery. Over its lifetime SRB brought most of the required key players to the table. How each then contributed to the process of regeneration varied, but there are numerous examples of good practice detailed in the report.
- SRB provided a workable and popular format for private sector engagement and there was a relatively high level of financial leverage and commitment as a result. This was a good design feature of the SRB approach.
- The experience of the voluntary sector varied more, but improved steadily over the successive rounds largely because of the attention given by the Government Offices (GOs) to help build the capacity of voluntary sector representatives to engage in the process of regeneration.
- SRB aimed to provide a co-ordination mechanism through which mainstream programmes (education, health, housing, crime and safety) could come together to help solve the problems of these areas, in a strategic, co-ordinated and cost effective way. This is often referred to as 'bending' mainstream activity, in terms of providing both customised policy delivery and more funding into the areas concerned. Overall the volume of mainstream funding into SRB areas remained disappointing. However, there was evidence of a strengthening, virtually across the board, throughout the successive rounds of SRB, in both the breadth and depth of mainstream player commitment to these areas.
- Engagement of the community was more variable, but again there are many examples of good practice, described in the report.
- The ability to submit regeneration bids for thematic schemes, which focused on the needs of particular groups of individuals, was of great value and allowed tailored approaches to be developed.
- Partners found the flexibility in the SRB funding format allowed regeneration schemes to be customised by geography, size, duration and objective. This was conducive to securing innovative and well-designed approaches and enabled matched funding.
- The lack of formally defined boundaries under SRB was a strong feature of its design and greatly assisted the regeneration process. It enabled a bid for funds to be submitted by a partnership in any location in England and for virtually any sort of regeneration activity. This meant that some areas with no tradition of making bids or receiving funds for regeneration could apply. It was a change from the essentially 'boundary' driven approach that had characterised much of previous

regeneration activity (ie Urban Programme, City Challenge etc). Leaders locally were responsible for demonstrating the relative need for the regeneration scheme for the locality they defined and in a way that they identified as being appropriate.

The SRB was the last in a long series of area-based initiatives for regeneration, dating back over three decades. As the above evaluation shows, lessons had been learned from the previous efforts and the SRB scheme was more flexible with regard to organisational arrangements and funding than previous efforts.

As well as evaluating the process the CLG report also measured outcomes from the SRB and found success in improving household incomes, satisfaction with accommodation, satisfaction with the areas from parents as a place to bring up children, feelings of mutual support and safety. The only negative outcome was that people reported less good health in the evaluations, not as a result of the SRB but because of trends in differences in health outcomes between areas.[13]

THE COALITION GOVERNMENT AND COLLABORATION

Sure Start was one of the first schemes to be cut as a result of the 2010 budget reductions. The area focus of the Comprehensive Area Assessment was abandoned. At the time of writing there have been no new announcements of area-based local collaborative initiatives.

With respect to health and social care, the Coalition's plans to abolish PCTs and the strategic health authorities remove the existing institutions that enabled collaboration between local authorities and healthcare. As Bob Hudson concluded:

> This is not simply a matter of numbers and administrative boundaries: it is also about the inter-personal relationships upon which so much joint working is based. All restructuring exercises damage networks, but the latest proposal to abolish the main NHS commissioning organisations of the past decade (PCTs) for a new and largely untried alternative (GP Consortia) will be especially damaging. Each restructuring not only destroys established networks, but it also re-focuses energy and attention upon internal reorganisation rather than external relationships. The cultural damage created by this endless change is rarely assessed. Rather the restructuring model is based upon a formal, hierarchical and mechanistic view of how organisations work, which downplays the importance of culture, norms, values and relationships.[14]

With regard to central co-ordinating mechanisms, so far the Coalition has established the Efficiency and Reform Unit, a central co-ordination unit for initiatives, but has avoided the 1997-plus plethora of central co-ordination units.

Further reading

Victor Bogdanor (ed.) *Joined-up Government* (Oxford: Oxford University Press, 2005).

T. Clarke, 'New Labour's Big Idea: Joined Up Government', *Social Policy and Society*, 1, 2, 2002, pp. 107–118.

POINTS FOR DISCUSSION

- Do performance targets for individual services inevitably cause fragmentation?
- What are the limits to co-ordinated policy of a small central unit close to the Cabinet Office?
- What are the main lessons about what works and what does not work to bring about co-ordination at local level?

NOTES

1 Neill Committee (2000) *Reinforcing Standards: Review of the First Report of the Committee on Standards in Public Life*, vol I, Cm 4557–I.

2 Press release on the establishment of the Performance and Innovation Unit, 1998.

3 Bob Hudson, 'Ten years of jointly commissioning health and social care in England', *International Journal of Integrated Care*, 7 March 2011.

4 HM Treasury and Department of Communities and Local Government, *Total Place: A whole area approach to public services*, March 2010.

5 http://www.parliament.the-stationery- office.co.uk/pa/cm200809/cmselect/cmhealth/286/28608.htm.

6 Department of Communities and Local Government (2010) *The New Deal for Communities: Evaluation: Final Report*, Vol. 7.

7 Ibid., pp. 8–9.

8 Sure Start Local Partnership.

9 Body Mass Index, an index of over and under weight.

10 *The Impact of Sure Start Local Programmes on five year olds and their families*, Department for Education, Research Report DFE – RR067, 2010.

11 Department for Communities and Local Government, *Long term evaluation of local area agreements and local strategic partnerships*, Report on the 2008 survey of all English local strategic partnerships 74–75 (London: Department for Communities and Local Government, July 2009).

12 Department for Communities and Local Government: *The Single Regeneration Budget: Final Evaluation*, London: CLG, 2007, p. 3.

13 Ibid., p. 4.

14 Bob Hudson, 'Ten years of jointly commissioning health and social care in England', *International Journal of Integrated Care*, 7, 11 2011.

CHAPTER 11
The Use of the Market in Public Services

SUMMARY

One of the devices for governance that has been used repeatedly is the market. It has been used to promote efficiency both in the sense of pushing costs down and to a lesser extent in the sense of producing a set of services that match people's preferences. Both Labour and Conservative governments pursued competition within the public services, for example among schools and among hospitals, and both forced public services to compete with private sector providers. Managers have had to respond to these competitive pressures in the way they manage, either to cut costs or improve quality. However, many of the markets have been a long distance away from pure markets with a high level of competition.

LEARNING POINTS

- Markets and arrangements that look like markets have been used for a long time and for a variety of reasons in public services.
- One way that markets have been used is to create choice for consumers.
- Competition and outsourcing have been used in many parts of the public sector, and the Coalition extends their coverage further into central government and the NHS.

MARKETS AND 'QUASI-MARKETS'

The use of the market in the public sector has been pursued both as an alternative to 'clan' control by professions and as an alternative to hierarchical control through a bureaucracy.

The superiority of markets was an important part of Conservative opinion and part of the ideological effort to counter the post-war development of planning and public services. 'Third Way' thinking was less ideologically enthusiastic about markets but promoted their use as a way of allocating resources: later Blair governments, leaving 'Third Way' notions behind, were at least as keen on markets as the Conservatives had been.

In practice the markets which were constructed by the Conservative governments rarely conformed with the features of the economists' 'perfect competition', with freedom of choice as to what to purchase and from whom, free entry for new competitors and perfect information for consumers. In fact they were mostly very limited in comparison to this ideal. One reason for this difference is that the motives for establishing markets, whatever the rhetoric, were not only to improve the allocation of resources or efficiency. One motive was to distance politicians from decisions which would be unpopular with the electorate: having a market to blame is convenient, whether for the closure of a popular facility, or a reduction in workers' incomes or the number of jobs. Later Labour governments, beginning towards the end of the second in 2004, became keen on the idea of free choice by service users, offering choice of hospital service provider and attempting to offer some choice of schools.

The Labour governments claimed to be less dogmatic about the advantages of markets and competition: they did not believe in them in principle but rather only if they worked. Very early the new government changed the internal market in the NHS, the competitive tendering regime in local government and the market testing arrangements in the civil service. While there was talk about partnerships and trust, the new arrangements subjected at least as many services to market pressures as the old ones and were designed as much to encourage private firms to provide services as to limit the destructive effects of competition.

The markets that were created before 2004 mainly excluded the element of free choice of service or supplier for the service user. The market within the NHS was an internal market, transactions being made between NHS employees without involving patients. Under local authority compulsory competitive tendering, the authority rather than the citizen had the choice of service provider. Market testing in central government is an internal matter designed to reduce cost and increase private sector participation in public services. In the community care markets, consumers do have a limited choice of services which is subject to their assessment as being in need.

The internal market in the NHS means that all activities have to be treated as if they were being bought and sold, even when they are in practice funded internally, thus creating very large transaction costs, and work unrelated to treating patients. Given their artificial nature (no chance of a supplier failing, no shareholders putting pressure on managers to perform) these internal markets have been defined as 'quasi-markets'.

As well as these internal markets, market mechanisms have also been introduced by getting the private sector involved in financing capital projects and in the market for labour. We will look at private finance for capital projects in Chapter 13, Public–Private Partnerships.

The Coalition government introduced the most extreme form of market competition yet seen to the NHS, in its Health and Social Care Bill of 2011, and in proposals to remove the cap on undergraduate places in the university funding regime, so that a free market would allow universities to expand and contract with market demand. The market as a form of governance and control was back in centre stage with the arrival of the Coalition.

WHY RULE BY MARKETS?

Ideology

To 'modernisers' the bureaucratic and professional organisations that were built as part of the welfare state, the NHS, local authorities, nationalised industries, powerful government departments, are part of the pre-modernised way of managing the state and delivering public services. The 'Third Way' rhetoric, a prominent feature of the first Labour government, could not simply propose the same market-type solutions but had to find an alternative, apparently softer and more collaborative version. Their coyness about proposing competition soon waned and by the third term, competition had become central to policy again. Towards the end of 2004, in the prelude to the 2005 general election, 'choice' became more central to government policy. Led by Alan Milburn, Minister of Health and a central figure in the election campaign, the new policy put choice for its own sake at the centre. Speeches were delivered berating the lack of choice and 'one size fits all' approach in public sector service provision. In one speech Alan Milburn even used the very old story of council tenants not being able to choose the colour of their own front door as a reason for allowing choice of hospital. Choice was not sold as a way of bringing costs down or quality up, rather as a good thing in itself, which would produce more consumer satisfaction. Professor Julian Le Grand[1] of the London School of Economics, and advisor to the Prime Minister at the time, was an enthusiastic proponent of the intrinsic value of choice to service users.

Before the idea that choice was a benefit, the main argument was that markets allocate resources more efficiently than bureaucratic rules. Efficiency is defined in two ways. First, goods and services will be produced at the lowest cost. Any high-cost producers will be replaced by lower-cost producers as new entrants seize the opportunity to make profits. Secondly, only those goods and services are produced which people demand. Producers' response to individuals' demands are more likely to produce what people want than some bureaucratic mechanism deciding what people might want or need. The first type of efficiency is known as 'productive efficiency' and the second as 'allocative efficiency'. To enable these two aspects of efficiency to prevail, there are certain prerequisites: consumers must know what is available in the market and at what price and be able to gain access to alternative suppliers; producers must be able freely to enter any particular market; existing producers should not have insurmountable advantages because of their existing operations; capital markets must operate in such a way as to allow investment in profitable opportunities.

Proponents of markets argue that even if these conditions do not prevail, partial market solutions are better than none. If there can be a competition among a small group of producers, this is likely to produce efficiency gains even if there is no free choice for the ultimate consumer. Alternatively, even if there can only be a small element of consumer choice this will make producers more responsive to consumers than if there is no choice. In other words, even if there is not an optimal solution, the less than optimal solutions will be better than having no markets at all.

A COMPETITIVE SPECTRUM

As we saw in the previous chapter, markets have been introduced in different forms in different parts of the public sector. It is useful to think of the markets as having degrees of competitiveness which in turn require different responses from managers. This is illustrated by Figure 11.1. At one end of the spectrum the service is outsourced, after competition among potential suppliers, but there is no internal bid. The second degree of impact on the competitive behaviour of the internal managers is simply an internal transaction in which each side plays at buying and selling services. At the other end there is a market in which purchasers have a free choice of provider, and service providers have to compete. The requirement from managers changes according to how far along the spectrum the markets lie.

Figure 11.1   Degrees of competition

While the 'Best Value' arrangements did not prescribe the details of how the market should be used, the government believed that competitive tendering was the best solution to performance improvement:

> While authorities have discretion over how individual services are provided, the highest standards of service provision are more likely to be achieved where there is genuine competition, choice for service users and a mixed economy rather than where any one supplier dominates the provision of services.[2]

Outsourcing with no internal bid

In certain, mainly internal, services a decision was made to outsource to a company without a bid from the internal team previously supplying the service. This applied particularly to central government, and some of the information technology contracts between the government and software and facilities management companies. Internal teams were transferred, at least partly, to the new employers and often had the same middle management. The impact was to remove some of the rigidities imposed by internal systems and to make staff make themselves attractive to their new employers, if they wanted to be transferred.

Internal trading

A minimal approach to the development of markets is to establish a supplier–customer relationship within an organisation. This idea became fashionable in parts of the private sector during the 1980s as a way of helping people who are not in direct contact with customers to define what it is they do and for whom. In manufacturing and service industries, the development of internal relationships in this way became part of the quality improvement effort as value chains were defined, each part of the production process being identified as adding value to the product or service and each link in the chain being described as a market relationship. Only the relationship between a 'supplier' and a 'customer' was felt adequately to result in good service or value for money. The idea was applied in the public sector through contracts on the volume and quality of service to be offered. In local government these were called 'service level agreements'.

The first impact of internal trading is that managers have to define their position in the value chain, and decide who is the customer and who is the supplier in each relationship. Sometimes this is very complicated. For example, an accountant working in a local authority may have a large number of customers: line managers for whom s/he provides management information, the chief finance officer who receives finance data, members who receive advice. S/he might also be a customer of the personnel department, the legal department and the car park. Or the chain may be long. A software maintenance person may be a supplier to a school but the school has a contract with a purchasing division of the local authority which commissions work from internal and external suppliers. If in turn the software maintenance section has subcontractors, the supply chain may be longer still. In other cases the process is more simple. Grounds maintenance is clearly a service to a school, personnel advice on disciplinary matters clearly a service to line managers. In these cases the definition of who is working for whom is useful: the school gets its cricket pitch rolled before the match, not after. The process can make the relationships more appropriate for good service delivery: rather than the personnel department dictating what managers can do, they are there to support management. One example is recruitment advertising, which can be a source of long delays for managers trying to replace staff. A customer–supplier relationship can help to ensure that managers are supported.

Once the supply chain has been established, the next task is to define what is being bought and sold. Taken to the extreme, the definition of the service provided by professionals can be an elaborate and lengthy business. However, the process can be useful, especially if it makes it more obvious what professionals do. A negative aspect of professionalism is that individuals can create a mystery. A definition of the service provided both makes the activity explicit and allows others to judge the value of the service. Such definitions also expose the power relationships in the organisations. Traditionally, people in charge of money have been powerful, whether directors of finance or principal finance officers. They have controlled the flow of financial information and in many cases the flow of funds used by people providing services. They have also created the impression of crisis, only to solve the problem by mysteriously finding an extra pocket of money at the last minute. Defining their job as a service to other people in the organisation addresses this power and provides a starting point for discussions about who is in control.

The third requirement for an internal market is the need to estimate costs. It sometimes appears odd to outsiders, but it has often been the case that managers have no clear idea about how much services cost: they may know how much cash a department or unit consumes but have little idea of how much a particular service costs. Internal trading forces people to make these calculations. In some cases, the allocation of costs is necessarily arbitrary but even estimates are valuable. The calculation of costs itself puts managers under scrutiny. Even if there is no competition, the fact that costs are known makes people question the value of what is provided for those costs and whether that value could be obtained more cheaply. In some cases, questions are asked about whether the service is required at all.

Once the suppliers and customers have been identified, the services defined and the costs calculated, internal markets can then be accounted for in a series of trading accounts. In traditional public sector accounts, departments or units are allocated funds, usually at the beginning of the year, and the accounts are prepared to show how those funds are spent. Trading accounts are different: they have an income side as well as an expenses side. Credits are made to the account as work is performed according to the contract. In practice, most purely internal trading accounts are fictitious in that income is entered in regular monthly sums whatever work is done. Where the income side of the account represents real transactions, trading accounts become an important means for managers to see whether their trading activity is successful. It is surprising how much difference this change makes: managers no longer see themselves accountable only for money spent but also for work done and therefore income received. This change in attitude occurs even when there is no competition, although competition brings with it other changes as well.

Internal trading with price testing and benchmarking

A variation on this approach is to make an internal contract and then check the costs of providing that service against what might be offered by an alternative supplier. While there may not be a formal competition, the fact that alternative prices are estimated sets a 'benchmark' figure for the service. For example, it is possible to estimate how much a bank would charge for running a payroll system, which could be compared with the internal charges. It is also possible to define the quality standards that an outside supplier would conform to.

Price testing with outside suppliers generates more change. The costing exercise has to be more precise: if prices are to be compared, the units in which trading occurs have to be defined. For example, if the recruitment part of the personnel function is to be compared with the cost of hiring a recruitment agency, the relevant comparison is between the cost of hiring one member of staff internally and the charge which the agency would make for this. Then, the costs of the department which is hiring need to be included in the total cost of the exercise and the difference in that cost between using the inside personnel department and an agency.

The next step is to compare the internal costs with the external prices. This always starts an argument about the allocation of costs and managers' discretion to affect their own costs. For example, one central government training department had its costs compared with the cost of outsourcing the training function. One of its major costs was the rent it notionally paid on a very expensive central London office, which had a lease signed during the property boom. Unable to vacate the premises or negotiate the rent level, it was placed at a competitive disadvantage. Similarly, people always argue about the level of recharging for central departments. As more and more services are subjected to internal market regimes, these costs become more visible and what is provided for the money becomes more clear. There is a sequential process of questioning costs: those first exposed to comparison question the cost and value of the services which they receive from others, who in turn begin to ask the same questions of their internal suppliers.

Comparing quality with outside suppliers can also have an impact. In some cases, the internal customers for a service are convinced that the quality of outside suppliers would be higher, and it is worth testing that proposition. Conversely it is often the case that existing services are of too high a quality and have too many refinements that internal customers rarely need and do not want to pay for.

Limited freedom to choose suppliers

A further step is when the customer end of the customer–supplier relationship is allowed, within defined limits, to choose an alternative supplier. An organisation may have a printing unit, for example, but people who need printing may be allowed to shop around with a proportion of their printing budget. In community care, people making assessments and allocating care may have a proportion of their budget to spend on the open market. Once those exposed to price comparisons are exposed to actual competition, the pressure is even greater. Faced with the threat of losing their job, managers have to look seriously at their costs compared with the prices of the competition.

Both sides of the internal trade also look at the relevance of the services being provided and their quality. Some internal services are of a quality which is not required by the customer: for example, some payroll systems have a level of potential sophistication in reporting which is never used. Line managers question whether they need some services at all. When legal costs are attributed through a service level agreement to a unit which never receives legal advice, they wonder why. If they face competition and those legal costs are a contributory element to their uncompetitive price, they protest. Such activity has its advantages: people are forced to think whether they are doing a useful job. It also has its disadvantages, in that it splits the organisation into divisively competitive elements.

The transfer of budgets to the customer side of the transaction changes the power relationships. Take the accounting function – if there is an allocation of funds to the accountants, with no accountability to line managers, they are in a strong position. Such a position is difficult to imagine in the private sector, in which an accountant arrives at a firm, announces that she has been appointed as accountant, defines what she is going to do and how much the customer is to be charged. Once the customer–supplier relationship is established and the customer has a budget for accountancy, the relationship changes. It can even change to the extent that the provider side starts to sell itself to the customers. This certainly happened in the education service. Education department employees produced glossy brochures and made sales visits to schools when the budgets for support services were devolved. Some schools were surprised when previously haughty managers transformed themselves into humble salespeople.

There are also changes in the way in which services are provided, in line with customer requirements. For example, support staff are more likely to be physically sited where the customers want them, rather than in a head office building.

Competition for whole services

A more radical step is to put a whole service out to tender. Once the customer–supplier relationship has been defined, the customer side then seeks bids from people to become the supplier. They may do this because they have been told to (in the case of local government by legislation and regulations, in central government by ministerial edict) or because they see it as a way of reducing cost. The franchise approach is a variant on this. In London, bus routes were offered to bus operators by tender, as were individual train routes in the privatisation of British Rail.

When a whole service is put out to tender, there is a sudden-death competition in which the in-house team is given a single chance to keep their jobs. If they have already been through the processes we have just seen, the next step is to see whether they can reduce their cost to the likely price of the competitive bid. Since most services are labour-intensive this often means reducing staff costs. While the European Union regulations that protect workers' conditions when their work is transferred to a new employer limit the extent to which companies can reduce staff terms and conditions after winning a bid, there is still competitive pressure on prices. While the competitors' likely prices are not known, at least the first time, they do have access to published accounts from the organisations whose work they are bidding for and are likely to reduce costs.

The search for cost reduction may involve finding different ways of providing the service. For example, Capita provide council tax collection services on a series of centralised computers, rather than each council having its own. In-house teams have to try to find their own ways of matching such changes in service design if they can.

Sometimes, the in-house team decides that the constraints on its operations and its costs are such that it is unlikely to compete successfully. The only way to win is to make a management buy-out and put in a bid for the work as a new entity. An early example of this was a company called MRS which was established by managers at Westminster City Council to win the bid for refuse collection. An alternative is to find a 'host company', already established in the field, to employ the in-house team. This happened in local government, especially, as a way of avoiding going through the competitive tendering process. Tendering was compulsory only if the council wanted to do the work using its own workforce. Once the work had been privatised, the rules no longer applied. Similarly there were examples of local education authorities contracting out the management of their departments in advance of being ordered to do so by the Department for Education and Employment.

Complete choice of suppliers for individual purchasers

At the extreme, all budgets are moved to the customer side of the relationship and there is neither a commitment to the internal supplier, nor a periodic tendering process. Budget holders simply choose where to spend their money on each occasion on which they need services. The devolution of budgets from education authorities to schools has this effect. Once the purchasers have complete freedom, they may choose to exercise it by entering long-term contracts but how to purchase is their decision.

The generation of opportunities for individuals to choose their supplier of public services was an important theme of the last Labour government. A review of the impact of choice and competition was published by the Office of Fair Trading in 2010.[3] In its analysis of the availability of choice in health, secondary and further education, services for the long-term unemployed and individual budgets for social care, it pointed out the importance of the details of how the market is organised, on both the demand and the supply sides. The elements of each are summarised in Figure 11.2.

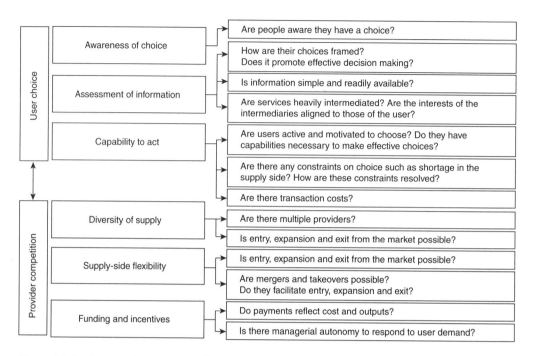

Figure 11.2   Factors determining effectiveness of choice and competition in public services

Source: Office of Fair Trading, 2010, p. 12

MANAGING IN THE COMPETITIVE ENVIRONMENT

Managers in services that are subject to competition first have to understand the rules of the game they are being made to play. First, they need to know where the buying decision is being made: how much choice do the consumers have and how much is the market managed by the purchasing or commissioning side of the organisation? The answer varies: in the case of schools competing for pupils and therefore funding, the marketing effort is directed at children and their parents and guardians. In the case of care homes for elderly people, state-funded residents have a choice of home, but it is restricted first by the requirement that an individual is assessed as needing and being entitled to residential care and then limited by the amount of cash the social services department is willing and able to pay. The case of refuse collection contains no contract with the end-users; the decision with whom to contract is made by the local authority. In the case of healthcare, 'choose and book' gives some choice of hospital to patients, where there is available supply within accessible distance, but most contracts are of a 'block' nature, negotiated and planned before an individual choice is made, so not much marketing effort towards individuals needs to be made.

Second, the managers have to understand the criteria on which the buying choices will be made, especially the relative weight given to cost, quality and reputation. With limited budgets, and with rules about how competition is organised, there is a strong tendency towards cost competition. It is admirable to create a high-quality public sector care home with well qualified and numerous staff, but given a fixed weekly price, quality as a competitive strategy will result in failure and closure. In this case and all those in which competitive success is based on price, managerial effort must be directed towards cost containment.

In the NHS market, under the regime of 'payment by results', prices for procedures are fixed in advance, and management has to concentrate on keeping cost below price. It is not necessarily the case that the cost of each individual instance of each procedure must be kept within the unit price, but overall cost must be equal to or below revenue. If the mix of procedures is skewed towards those which are unpredictable and likely to overrun the tariff, losses are likely. There was much debate during the passage of the Health and Social Care Bill about the possibility of private healthcare companies 'cherry-picking' or choosing only to compete for those procedures that produce easy profits. The debate missed the point that it is not the case that some procedures have high margins and others have low margins: prices can be set to reflect likely costs. It is rather the case that some procedures have predictable costs for a given outcome, and others have less predictable costs, because of unknown levels of complication. If a case mix is biased towards a high proportion of predictable costs, then profits are more likely.

Public sector managers in the same sector as private sector managers, such as refuse collection departments and companies, or healthcare providers, or IT or legal services suppliers, face different markets: in general the manager of the in-house team gets one chance to bid for their 'own' work, while the companies against which they are bidding have a large array of chances to bid, for a large number of opportunities, and therefore need a lower success rate to stay in business. It is also the case that they can spread their overheads over a bigger turnover: when, for example, Capita bids for a contract to run council tax collection, it can spread its system cost over many local authority contracts.

CONCLUSIONS

The use of the market has been a prime governance and control mechanism used by a succession of governments since 1980 to create efficient and effective public services. Markets have been seen as a solution to the rigidity of hierarchical bureaucracy, as a way of reducing the power of professional 'clans', of preventing 'supplier capture' of public services, of driving down costs, improving quality, increasing consumer choice and creating allocative efficiency.

As we have seen, the markets that were created were in the main a long way away from a real and competitive market, being mostly managed markets. With the election of the Coalition government, there is a new group of pro-market advocates in government. They have a wealth of history of the use of markets to learn from.

Further reading

Julian Le Grand (2007) *The Other Invisible Hand: Delivering Public Services through Choice and Competition*. Princeton University Press.

POINTS FOR DISCUSSION

- Is the use of markets in public services a matter of ideology?
- In which public sector markets do individuals have a choice of service or provider?
- Are there any circumstances in which the market solution is not appropriate in the provision of public services?

NOTES

1   Julian Le Grand was seconded to the Prime Minister's office from 2003 to 2005 and was brought into the Coalition government to advise on 'Open Government' in 2011. His ideas about choice can be found in his book: Julian Le Grand (2007) *The Other Invisible Hand: Delivering Public Services through Choice and Competition*, Princeton, NJ: Princeton University Press.
2   Office of the Deputy Prime Minister (2003), *Local Government Act 1999: Part 1, Best Value and Performance Improvement*, ODPM Circular 03/2003, p. 6.
3   Office of Fair Trading, *Choice and Competition in Public Services*, March 2010. The report was produced by Frontier Economics.

PART 2B   Outsourced and privatised services

CHAPTER 12
Managing Through Contracts

SUMMARY

Much of what we have seen of how the public sector in the United Kingdom is run hinges on a contractual relationship: the cascade of agreements down from the Treasury, through the Ministries and the service providers, are all some form of contract, although not necessarily regulated by contract law; the outsourced services, including the special case of PPP/PFI arrangements which we will look at in the next chapter, all involve real contracts between separate legal entities.

The ways that the contracts are written, agreed, implemented and monitored are important influences on the nature, quality and cost of public services. Poor contracting can lead to waste, inefficiency and in extreme cases service failure. Intelligent contracting can produce responsive services, innovation and improvement and can maintain a downward pressure on costs.

LEARNING POINTS

- Contracts can take many forms and the choice of contract can make a big difference to the outcome of the contracting process. The two extreme forms are 'obligational' and 'adversarial' contracting, the former involving close collaboration and trust, the latter distance and mistrust.
- UK government policy towards contracting is constrained by European directives.

THE CONTRACTING ENVIRONMENT

The public sector markets consist of a wide variety of market structures and institutional arrangements. At one extreme there is the purchase of complex weapon systems, such as nuclear submarines or fighter planes. The nature of this market is that there are few suppliers, since the investment required is large in relation to the total market size. There is also what is known as 'information asymmetry', which means that one side of the bargain knows more than the other; normally the company knows more than the Ministry of Defence, both about technical issues in the specification and about the costs of meeting the specification. Sometimes the companies know more about the specification than the military and the Ministry of Defence. The transactions are likely to be complex, each element requiring technical knowledge and judgement about whether what is produced meets the terms of the contract. We also know that in the purchase of items such as nuclear submarines, not everything is known about the whole product when the contract is signed: for example the precise weapon systems to be used may be decided after the contract is under way.

At the other extreme, purchasing is much more straightforward: in buying stationery for a school, for example, there is competition among suppliers, and the school bursar knows enough about the requirements to be able to make an informed choice and to judge whether the stationery works or not. If the price or quality is unsatisfactory, the transaction can be switched to another supplier.

Between the two extremes is a variety of contracting environments, each of which will have its appropriate contracting method to deliver a satisfactory outcome. Contracting authorities do not have a free hand to choose how they enter contracts, however; they are bound by legislation and regulation, which cascade from Europe to national level. These cover which contracts are to be subjected to competitive tendering, how the tendering process is organised and how the contracts are written.

CONTRACTING AND COMMISSIONING

The procurement process is supposed to enable the purchaser to get value for money by organising a competition, writing contracts and enforcing them and monitoring and evaluating the results. The technical part of this process consists of formal procedures, bound by rules that are designed to prevent collusion among suppliers and to enable the purchasers to take control of the process.

Before the procurement process comes the policy process which ends up deciding what to buy: in simple services such as street sweeping, waste collection, highway maintenance, this is technical but relatively straightforward in policy terms; all these areas can be defined as a set of service standards covering inputs (the kinds of staff and equipment), processes (frequency of work, where waste is to be collected from) and outcomes (how clean the streets are, how smooth a resurfaced road).

The less physical the service is, the harder it is to specify and measure, as we will see. But in policy terms it is also less obvious what should be purchased to achieve the desired policy result. This has been problematic in the areas of health commissioning, deciding what services are required to generate health outcomes, social care, designing (rationed) services to meet the needs of children, vulnerable adults and older people; defence, where the defence capability of procured equipment has to match the military's policy requirements; and drug and alcohol treatment, where outcomes may be degrees of harm reduction.

This higher-level part of the procurement process, translating policy objectives into definitions of what services need to be procured, is known in government language as 'commissioning', and has even been called 'strategic commissioning'. It clearly takes place on the 'purchaser' side of the 'purchaser–provider' divide and is part of the procurement process.

Influences on the type of contract

There is a variety of influences on the type of contractual relationship which people adopt within the public sector and between it and the private and voluntary sectors, including legal requirements, the structure of the market, managers' approach to quality and efficiency, and politics and the administrative rules under which contracting is done.

Law and regulations

A major determinant of the nature of transactions and contracts is of course the rules established by the government. Britain does not have administrative law, as such. There are laws, such as the Competition Act 1999, which apply to public authorities as much as to companies, and European Union laws and regulations and directives on business transactions and on the procurement of goods and services by the public sector in member states, which generally promote competition and therefore mitigate against the development of long-term and less competitive relationships. While European regulations apply to all sectors, the way in which the contracting process has been organised in Britain has not been consistent across the sectors, with regard to the bidding process, the length of contract or relationship, the mechanisms used for monitoring or the actions to be taken in case of default.

In the public services, there are those who believe that contracting is a matter for the law and lawyers. This view is especially held by lawyers, who get involved in writing the contracts and therefore think that they should also be involved in determining the relationships between the parties. They apply the same principles to contracting with civil engineering companies, cleaning companies and the local branch of a charity. While the purchasing side of local authorities needs to be protected, the law is not the only answer. As a standard textbook on the law of contracts says:

Writers of contract textbooks tend to talk as if in real life agreements are effectively controlled by the law as stated in their books. A moment's reflection will show that this is not so. There is a wide range of transactions where the sums at stake are so small that litigation between the contracted parties is exceptionally unlikely ... in substantial areas of business, contractual disputes were resolved by reference to norms which were significantly different from the theoretical legal position. The most important single reason for this seems to be that, in many business situations, the contract is not a discrete transaction but part of a continuing relationship between the parties and that insistence on certain legal rights would be disruptive of that relationship ... In other areas of business, strict insistence on legal rights is common.[1]

It would seem, then, that the law and legal obligations are not the whole explanation for contract forms or a sufficient guide to how to contract, except in cases where there are specific legal requirements which they cannot avoid.

THE NHS AND COMMUNITY CARE

The House of Commons Health Committee defined commissioning in the NHS thus:

The 1991 market reforms were based on the **purchaser–provider split**. It was thought that, whereas in the past providers, usually hospital doctors, had largely determined what services would be provided, now commissioning bodies would act on behalf of patients to purchase the services which were really needed. 'Purchasers' (health authorities and some family doctors) were given budgets to buy health care from 'providers' (acute hospitals, organisations providing care for people with mental health problems, people with learning difficulties, older people and ambulance service). To become a 'provider' in the internal market, health organisations became NHS 'trusts', separate organisations with their own management.[2]

The same House of Commons Committee were not impressed by the commissioning performance in the NHS, especially by the Primary Care Trusts:

As the Government recognises, weaknesses remain 20 years after the introduction of the purchaser/provider split. Commissioners continue to be passive, when to do their work efficiently they must insist on quality and challenge the inefficiencies of providers, particularly unevidenced variations in clinical practice. Weaknesses are due in large part to PCTs' lack of skills, notably poor analysis of data, lack of clinical knowledge and the poor quality of much PCT management. The situation has been made worse by the constant re-organisations and high turnover of staff. Commissioners do not have adequate levers to enable them to motivate providers of hospital and other services.[3]

The policy of purchasing residential and domiciliary care from the private sector created, or at least caused to grow, an industry. There are small proprietor-run businesses, often owned by an ex-nurse, providing residential care, along with similar, locally-based businesses contracting to provide domiciliary care. There are also large businesses, created by acquisition and by organic expansion. These businesses have been quite attractive to investors, as the revenue streams of local authority cash for care for people assessed as being eligible were a guaranteed flow of funds. The businesses became attractive to venture capital.

As the cuts in spending started to affect the local authorities' care budgets, the revenue streams became smaller and less certain, naturally causing some difficulties for businesses, as occupancy levels started to fall and costs started to exceed revenues. While many businesses struggled quietly to cut costs to meet the reduced revenue streams, there was at least one very public case of a care home company going broke, Southern Cross. Box 12.1 contains the story.[4]

Box 12.1   Southern Cross

'So how, given that the "eldercare" market is expanding briskly and enjoys a degree of revenue stability that would be the envy of many other sectors, did Southern Cross get into such a hole in the first place? And why is it apparently facing bankruptcy when it still has hefty income and only around £50m of debt? The trouble dates back to its ownership by private equity giant Blackstone, which bought the firm for £162m in 2004 and rapidly tripled its size by acquiring two rivals, financing the deal by a sale and leaseback of its entire property portfolio. To many investors this looked like a safer bet than the usual leveraged buy-out, but in reality it didn't make much difference – rent, like interest, still has to be paid every month.

Interesting to note also that both Blackstone and the then-management team did pretty well on the deal, extracting big bucks while the getting was good. Southern Cross floated on the FTSE250 in 2006, and its market cap peaked at over £1bn a year later. Then chairman William Colvin and three other directors sold their entire stakes in 2007, netting themselves an estimated windfall of £35m. As pension fund watchdog PIRC told the FT recently, this is hardly best practice. "Shareholders like to see directors maintain a meaningful stake in the business in order to achieve an alignment of interests. To sell an entire holding, however financially advantageous, doesn't send the best signal."

The size of the rent bill bequeathed to the current management, plus automatic increases annually for the 30-year terms of the leases, meant that it took only a modest drop in referrals from local authorities as a result of spending cuts to put the entire business in jeopardy. Hardly a ringing endorsement of private sector involvement in the healthcare sector, a business where the consequences of failure far exceed the purely financial ...'

The Southern Cross story illustrates the special nature of the Community Care market: some businesses are very dependent on public funding for their profits, which can be high when funds are sufficient. The market is subject to normal commercial pressures as people try to make money through financial engineering rather than service provision.

THE EUROPEAN UNION DIRECTIVES

Purchasing by governments and other public bodies in EU member states is subject to Directives of the European Commission. The Public Sector Directive (2004/18) applies to services, supply and works contracts for all of the public sector apart from utilities, which are covered by the Utilities Directive (2004/17). Contracts that are covered by the Directives must be subject to EU-wide competition and advertised in the *Official Journal of the European Union (OJEU)*. The competition must normally be organised according to either the 'open procedure' or the 'restricted procedure'. There are two sets of exceptions: where there is only one feasible supplier, the 'negotiated procedure' can be used; where the contract is very complex and there may be information asymmetry the 'competition dialogue procedure' may be used. Under the Utilities Directive the public body may choose any one of the four procedures, while under the Public Sector Directive the 'open' or 'restricted' procedures should be followed, unless circumstances are exceptional. Where there is only one legal entity and a contract is essentially internal, the competitive procurement rules do not apply.

There are rulings about the size of contracts that trigger the application of the rules, the contract sizes being revised every two years. The 2010 limits are shown in Table 12.1.

In addition to the two Directives on the procedures, there is also the Remedies Directive (2007/66) which sets out what companies can do if they think they have been treated incorrectly.

Local government

Local authorities have been subject to competition rules since the 1980 Local Government (Planning and Land) Act. This Act introduced rules for all UK local authorities about what

Table 12.1 EU contracts subject to competitive bidding

Contracting entity	Supplies €	Services €	Works €
Public sector bodies subject to World Trade Organisation rules (government departments)	125,000	125,000	4,845,000
Other public sector bodies (mostly local authorities)	193,000	193,000	4,845,000
Utilities	387,000	387,000	4,845,000

work must be put out to tender and how the tendering was to be organised. The process was later modified by the 'Best Value' regime, which was less directive about lower limits for compulsory competition since these were now specified by the EU, but set out principles that had to be followed to ensure that authorities considered contracting out for all services in its Best Value procedures. In England only, from 2003–2007 there was the 'National Procurement Strategy for Local Government', which aimed at improving the procurement process, mainly by setting up shared services ('Regional Centres of Excellence') to carry out the procurements for small local authorities. Slightly different approaches have been adopted in the devolved administrations.

The scale of local government contracting was estimated in 2007 as shown in Table 12.2.[5] Local authority spending in England for 2007–8 was £92 billion revenue expenditure and £20 billion capital expenditure, a total of £112 billion. The £42 billions spent on external contracts therefore accounted for about 37% of total spending.

'"New" Institutional Economics'

Once economists started to realise that the real world exhibited few of the features of the theoretical world of perfect knowledge and perfectly rational choices in a perfectly competitive market, the problem arose: how to explain market behaviour when these conditions do not apply. This problem is important in the context of government contracting, since only rarely do conditions of perfect competition arise in the field of government procurement: in relatively trivial purchases, such as stationery or vehicles, there may be a highly competitive market with many alternative suppliers competing, in which it is possible for governments to gather sufficient information and have the capacity to make well-informed optimal decisions.

In the procurements that typically absorb large amounts of public funds, such conditions do not apply. Markets for the supply of such things as military hardware and big computer systems are characterised by a small number of suppliers and complicated products and services about which the buyer will have less knowledge than the supplier. Local governments are often faced with small numbers of suppliers of services, especially in expensive services such as secure accommodation for difficult cared-for children or

Table 12.2 Contracting by local government in England 2007

£42 billion is spent by local government on external contracts, of which

£12 billion on commodities, goods and services

£13 billion on constructing and maintaining buildings and roads

£6 billion on adult social care

£3 billion on waste services

rehabilitation for drug abusers. It is likely that governments will not find it possible to collect, absorb and analyse sufficient information to make an optimal choice, even when there is a compulsory tendering system in operation.

The arrangement between a government or government department and a contractor is subject to the same pressures as any other contractual arrangement: each side wants the best outcome for themselves and will use whatever advantages they can to achieve them. Both sides will try to minimise the risk attaching to themselves from entering the contract. The contract will reflect the balance of knowledge and power between the parties and the nature of the relationship between the two.

There has been a body of economics concerned with the contractual relationships between parties in the real world (as opposed to the theoretical world of perfect information and large numbers of willing buyers and sellers, beloved of economic theory). This branch of economics is sometimes called 'The New Institutional Economics', although by now it is no longer new. The underlying questions of this branch of economics are:

- Why do firms sometimes choose to buy their inputs in the market place and at other times decide to make the inputs themselves?
- When is it best to organise production through the market and when is it best to organise it through a hierarchy of employees? And more broadly,
- Why do organisations exist, and what determines the boundary between one organisation and the next one?

Oliver Williamson[6] looked systematically at the problems posed by the fact that markets are not perfect: when is it better to purchase goods and services in the market and when is it better to produce them yourself, using your own employees?

This is essentially the question for government: when should they write a contract with an independent body for the supply of services, and when should they provide them using their employees? Under conditions of 'bounded rationality' not all information is known, or it is impossible to take account of all information in the decision process. The conditions in the market that Williamson considered were:

- *Complexity*: the transaction is so complex that it is not possible to consider all the options.
- *Uncertainty*: not all possible futures can be predicted, so it is not possible to write a contract that takes them all into account.
- *Language*: it is not possible to specify everything in language that both parties to contract can agree on.
- *Small numbers*: where there are very few suppliers, those in the market can engage in opportunistic behaviours to the disadvantage of the purchasers.
- *Information 'impactedness'*: where one side to the transaction has more information, especially about costs, than the other.

- *First-mover advantages*: by which winners of a contract gain information that puts future competitors at a disadvantage and reduces the impact of competition in all future transactions.
- *Atmosphere*: the moral stance that parties to the transaction take, which may not be perfectly economically self-seeking.

Williamson usefully draws these elements into a framework, which he calls the 'Organisational failures framework', which is illustrated in Figure 12.1.[7] We can use this framework to interrogate the way contracting has developed between government and companies.

In most markets, people involved in transactions are not normally able to make completely optimal decisions: they do not have perfect knowledge; they do not have the capacity to process all the available information for every transaction. Even if they had the information and capacity, there remains the problem in any transaction of trying to ensure that the person from whom one party is purchasing delivers what is expected and is motivated and enabled to do so in all the possible circumstances that might arise.

For managers, therefore, there are no simple answers to the question of how to establish and manage contractual relationships. On the one hand, there are market structure considerations and efficiency and effectiveness considerations which would provide some guidance as to the most effective way to do things. In some cases, these might lead to a preference for long-term contracting, in others for short-term. The nature of the market may lead to a desire to establish long-term close relationships with suppliers, or may lead to frequent competitions to keep prices down. Overlaid on these influences on practice are the legal considerations. The law itself and the regulations may force people to behave in a particular way, even though they know that the results will be less good than if they

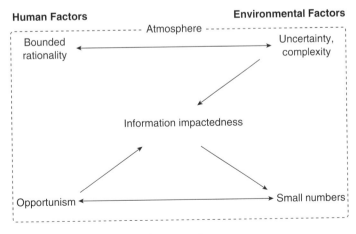

Figure 12.1   The Organisational failures framework

behaved in other ways. There are also more local legal influences. Legal advice may itself lead people to behave in ways which they do not think make managerial or contractual sense. Lawyers accustomed to caution may be more interested in generating apparently detailed and enforceable contracts which professionals know cannot be enforced in practice. Politics can also determine managerial decisions. While managers may know that it would make more sense to keep a service in-house, they are not able to exercise that choice. The opposite can also be true: managers may wish to contract out but are instructed to retain directly managed provision.

However, there is still some discretion. In the rest of this chapter we look at the elements of the contracting process and ask what would be the best approach to each of these elements in different circumstances.

OBLIGATIONAL AND ADVERSARIAL CONTRACTING

'Relational' contracts are sometimes referred to as 'obligational' contracts, in which the two parties have obligations to each other to make a success of their joint efforts beyond the terms of their immediate contractual relationship. 'Obligational' contracts are contrasted with 'adversarial' ones in which each side is out for their own advantage from the immediate contract and is unconcerned about the success of the joint enterprise.

Sako[8] has developed a framework for understanding contracting behaviour, using these two archetypal relationships. At one extreme is the Obligational Contractual Relationship (OCR), where the two parties trust each other, work together for mutual benefit, share risk and do things for each other which go beyond the details in the contract. The Adversarial Contractual Relationship (ACR) is at the other extreme, where there is low trust, the expectation that each side wishes to gain at the expense of the other, and contracts are used to protect each side from the other. Sako breaks down the contracting process into eleven elements: transactional dependence; ordering procedure; length of trading; documentation; the approach to 'contractualism' or contingencies; contractual trust; competence trust; goodwill trust; technology transfer and training; communication channels and intensity; and risk-sharing.

Transactional dependence

If a purchaser wants to be able to switch from one supplier to another, they will have contracts with a large number of people. They can then use the threat of switching to make suppliers do what they want. On the other side, suppliers may wish to maintain contracts with a large number of purchasers to minimise their dependence. In these circumstances, the relationships are likely to be distant. Under OCR, the purchaser may wish to develop closer relationships with a small number of suppliers and offset the dependency created by fewer closer relationships.

There is a variety of experience with regard to dependency. The large computer privatisations which have occurred in the H.M.R.C. and Driver and Vehicle Licensing have made the government very dependent on one supplier in each case. Local authorities which have established contracts for items such as refuse collection have sometimes become completely dependent on a single firm, which has won the contract for the whole of that local authority area.

We would expect high dependency to result in a close relationship between the two parties. In practice, the legal constraints and lack of experience on the part of purchasers led to the development of detailed contracts and specifications with complicated procedures for coping with default. As time went on, however, both sides realised that the interdependency which comes from having a single supplier and a single purchaser allows a relationship which is closer than those implied by spot contracts or frequent switching of supplier.

Ordering procedure

The stereotype of the adversarial approach to ordering is encapsulated in the compulsory competitive tendering legislation for local authorities: competitors have to bid for the work, the purchaser chooses the supplier as a result of the bid, rather than any other aspect of the bidder's work or reputation, and the price is fixed before the contract is let. The opposite, OCR way of ordering may not involve bidding, and if it does, the bid price is not the only criterion for placing an order and prices are finally settled after the decision about who will be awarded the contract. The way orders are placed has an effect on the relationship between the parties. If a long-term relationship is expected, both sides need to decide whether such an arrangement would be beneficial. This requires more than doing some pre-tender checks and then opening sealed bids. When Toyota was setting up its plant in Derby, the process it used to sign up component suppliers started with assessing the management capabilities of potential suppliers, then the manufacturing skills of the workforce. The end of the process was concerned with negotiating price.

Bidding is almost universal in the public sector, for reasons of propriety. Public accountability requires that contracts are awarded fairly, without corrupt favouritism. This is interpreted to mean that the only way to accept bids is through a procedure which keeps the two sides at arm's length. European regulations require that large public sector contracts are advertised in the *Gazette* and bids invited from companies in all EU states. These regulations imply an adversarial style of contract award, rather than the development of a close relationship.

There are occasions on which negotiations about price and quality continue after a bid has been accepted. The most notable of these was the post-tender negotiation for the

Inland Revenue computer contract, much to the displeasure of the unsuccessful bidders who were not given a chance to re-tender. Local authorities sometimes negotiate with the successful bidders for building and civil engineering contracts.

In the United States of America, some public authorities have a system of 'calls for proposals'. In this process, instead of the authority writing a specification and inviting bids to carry it out, they may state a problem, give an indicative budget and ask companies and the voluntary sector how they might solve the problem. This approach has been used in substance-abuse programmes and community care. It allows the suppliers of services to show what they can do, rather than waiting for the public authority to do all the work on service design and specification. It is similar to the system of commissioning buildings in North America, where it is normal practice to specify the required performance of a building and then ask architects to design and organise its construction.

The ordering procedure sets the tone for the nature of the relationship between the two parties. If contracts are based on a quotation against a specification which is the same for all bidders, the responsibility for developing the contract and specification rests with the purchasers, rather than being a joint effort between buyers and suppliers. After the contract is let, the process of contract management is therefore concerned with ensuring conformance to the specification.

Once a contract is let, purchasers may try to develop a closer relationship than that which existed prior to the award. However, contracts are normally for a fixed term at the end of which a new bidding process is started. The close relationships are stopped and the distancing implied by fair treatment begins again.

Length of trading

In an ACR contractual relationship, the parties expect to trade with each other only for the length of the contract. In OCR, there is an expectation that, if things go well, there will be further contracts and there will be a mutual long-term commitment between the parties. There is the possibility of 'roll-over' contracts in the public sector where contractors are allowed to continue for a further period. However, lawyers say that it is unwise to include clauses in initial contracts which imply that successful completion of a given contract would most likely result in another.

The length of trading can determine the type of company or charity with which the public sector trades. Large suppliers with a variety of contracts in the public and private sectors are more likely to be able to cope with a series of time-limited contracts with any purchaser than are small local suppliers. This applies especially in community care, where small local voluntary organisations become completely dependent on their local authority for their funds. They are, in other words, dependent on the one transaction, the failure of which would result in the end of the organisation. In practice, they often lurch from one short-term contract to the next.

Documents for exchange

In ACR, there is an attempt to write all the terms and conditions, including substantive conditions. Every possible item is written down. In OCR, the contracts concentrate on procedural rules which set out how problems would be resolved if they arise, and individual issues are dealt with when they occur. Contracts may even be oral rather than written.

In the public sector, contracts and their associated specifications have generally been long and detailed. In some cases, manuals of procedure which were in place when the service was directly managed were used as the basis for the contract and specification. For example, the original contracts between the Department of Employment and the TECs were the old department area office programme manuals. Hospital contracts and specifications consisted of a detailed description of existing procedures. However, people have realised that not everything can be written down and that in any case, the fact that the contract contains a long and detailed specification is no guarantee of service delivery. Contracts have become less detailed as people have learned that there are other ways of ensuring quality, such as involvement in the suppliers' quality assurance procedures or talking to the users of the services.

'Contractualism'

Sako refers to the treatment of contingencies as 'contractualism'. A contingent claims contract is one in which contingencies have to be defined, a procedure has to be established to agree whether a contingency has occurred, and the consequences of the occurrence are specified.

Most contracts have contingent elements: exceptional weather can affect highway maintenance contracts; sudden outbreaks of disease trigger health service interventions. The question is whether each possible contingency can be sufficiently defined in advance and whether the recognition of its occurrence can be spelled out in advance. The OCR option is to establish procedures by which both sides can agree on contingencies and what should be done as a result, relying on trust and an expectation that an agreement can be reached. The ACR option assumes that an agreement will not be reached or will be difficult, and that every contingency must be defined in advance. We will see in Chapter 13 that in the case of the maintenance contracts for London Underground, neither party could predict the state of the track and had to agree on a way to define the contingencies when they arose.

There is a mixture of approaches to this question in the public sector. Attempts to specify contingencies have not always worked. For example, in the care of older people, there are 'tariffs' for the cost of care according to people's degree of dependency, from a range of physical and mental disabilities. Local authorities usually have a 'banding' system in which progressive disabilities trigger progressively intensive care, but there have to be procedures by which the purchasers of care and the provider agree the extent of an individual's difficulties.

Trust: contractual, competence and goodwill

Sako distinguishes three areas of trust: contractual, competence and goodwill. An ACR approach to contractual trust means that suppliers do not do anything without a prior, written order. In an OCR relationship, supply or changes to specification can be started as a result of an oral communication. Competence trust is concerned with the degree to which the purchaser trusts the supplier to deliver the quality of product. If there is low trust, the purchaser will inspect heavily and presume that the supplier will try to skimp. In a high-trust relationship, the purchaser may be involved in the supplier's quality assurance procedures, but will not carry out much, if any, inspection. Goodwill trust refers to the degree to which each side is willing to become dependent on the other.

Trust is a very important element in public sector contractual relationships. The degree of trust depends partly on the sort of relationship established during the ordering procedure. If the order is placed on the basis of the bid price only, it is likely that the chosen supplier will be operating on low, or even negative, profit margins. In order to make a profit, suppliers have to shave the quality as close to the specification as possible, if not below it. The purchaser's main function then becomes one of trying to make sure that the specifications are met, requiring inspection and checking. If the winning contractors believe in any case that the purchaser did not wish to contract with them but was forced into it by the legislation, there is no initial basis for establishing trust, and adversarial relationships are probably inevitable.

Trust can develop during the contract period or as a succession of contracts is completed. It is natural for buyers to be wary of new suppliers until they have evidence that they can be trusted. Sometimes the voluntary sector may be trusted more than the private sector whose profit motive causes immediate suspicion by some public sector managers.

Technology transfer and training

In an OCR relationship, the purchaser is willing to help the supplier develop the best technology and skills. This may involve helping the supplier to organise training or allowing them to join in joint training, which may not be fully costed. In an ACR relationship, help is given only when it is fully costed and paid for. One area in which this is important is in the NHS. If purchasers do not fund the development of new technologies, research and development has to be funded in other ways. In practice, since prices are supposed to be equal to cost in NHS contracts, there is no surplus available for research, which is funded through a separate mechanism.

In community care, this is not the case. Providers have to make sufficient surplus from their contracts to fund research and development. This problem was recognised in the joint statement by the Association of Directors of Social Services and National Council for Voluntary Organisations, but there is no compulsion on purchasers to price contracts in such a way as to allow innovation:

> ADSS and Voluntary Organisations jointly recognise ... that VOs may include in the costs of service provision reasonable allowance for indirect costs properly associated with the maintenance and development of a cost effective quality service, as well as the direct costs of service provision.[9]

It is unlikely that there would be much transfer of technology and training in the mainly adversarial relationships which have developed – public accountability for funds, which pushes the relationship in an adversarial direction, makes it unlikely that free funding of development would occur as a routine part of a long-term contractual relationship.

Communication channels and intensity

In ACR, the communication channels between the two contracting parties are specified in the contract. Nominated officers on each side are allowed to speak about technical and financial matters, according to their individual competence. In an OCR relationship there are multiple channels of communication as each side tries to understand the other. As with other aspects of the relationship between public organisations and contractors, frequent contact is treated with suspicion, especially informal contact. Lunches are frowned upon as corruption. While there may be some basis for suspicion, it is unfortunate that the need for propriety stops beneficial exchanges between the two sides.

The National Audit Office found that joint working and good communication improved the contracting process in the NHS:

> The National Audit Office surveys of regions and trust monitoring outposts ... showed that both felt that health authorities and hospitals were still mainly concerned with achieving their own distinct objectives rather than coming to a jointly beneficial agreement. Both groups surveyed considered that forming joint long-term strategies and providing comprehensive and timely information as well as maintaining regular communications between chief executives, were most important in achieving good relationships.[10]

Risk-sharing

In OCR relationships, risk is shared, based on principles of fairness. In ACR, risk may not be shared but the acceptance of risk is defined in advance. There are three aspects of risk in public service contracts: risk of price changes, of changes in the volume of demand and the risk that arises from suppliers making innovations.

With relatively low inflation, the risk of price changes turning out to be much different from that predicted at the time of signing the contract is small. However, there are prices which may fall suddenly, because of technical changes. For example, the introduction of keyhole surgery, or much cheaper computer processing, may produce a 'windfall' increase in profits for a supplier. A risk-sharing approach would lead to such windfalls being shared between the supplier and the purchaser.

The second type of risk refers to the possibility that the volume of work predicted will not be forthcoming. The supplier sets up an operation to provide the predicted volume and incurs costs which are not recouped. Again, a risk-sharing approach would involve sharing a proportion of those costs. One way of doing that is for the purchaser to guarantee a certain volume of service will be purchased, even though it may not be required.

The third element comes from innovation; a supplier may invent and offer a new way of providing a service, which turns out to be unsuccessful. Without such innovation, the contracting process will stop the development of new services, as all specifications are based on already accepted practice.

Private Finance Initiative projects and Public–Private Partnerships, as we shall see in Chapter 13, are based on the premise that the contract can allocate the risk between the private and public sectors and the contract can be formulated to reward risk taking. In the case of unpredictable costs, this can provide incentives for the contractor to contain costs. In the case of unpredictable volumes, such as on a toll road or bridge where the revenue to the contractor depends on traffic volumes, the risk avoidance cannot be achieved by changing contractor behaviour.

SUCCESS AND FAILURE IN CONTRACTING

We saw in Chapter 7 that there has been multiple and repeated contract failure in the field of information and communication technology contracts. We can now use our framework to ask why some contracts are more successful than others. In the case of the NHS contract, there seem to have been two fundamental issues: the information asymmetry between the Department of Health and the contractors; and the market structure created by the contracting process by which the DoH was dependent on a small number of suppliers who therefore had an advantage in the relationship.

The other issue in the ICT field was the mistake of treating ICT contracts as if they were 'complete' contracts where everything can be specified at the beginning and contingencies can all be defined. This definition of the relationship led to a contractual form, essentially adversarial contracting, that was not fit for the purpose of contracting in this sector.

There is at least one good example of the appropriate use of obligational contracting by government. The Department for Work and Pensions had to organise the transformation of the Jobcentre service by merging Social Security and Jobcentre functions in 858 newly created or refurbished offices with new branding and design. The programme ran from

October 2002 to March 2006 and cost about £750 million. The department was pleased with the process and the results, and they attributed the success to a 'supply chain' approach to contracting. In a report[11] on the project, the DWP explained the elements of its collaborative contracting process:

- Open book price frameworks with active risk management
- Equalised overheads and profit with 14 contractors
- Payment of 'actual costs' to contractors
- Incentives through cost saving and performance targets
- No penalty clauses or retentions
- Allocation of workload, based upon performance against a balanced scorecard.

These are familiar elements of the 'obligational contracting' approach. The report emphasised the amount of effort required to create such a collaborative framework:

> Collaboration can and does work, but a great deal of hard work is required before the benefits are realised. Rushing the start of a project, and not having sufficient time to prepare the supply chain, results in errors, delays and additional cost. In selecting companies, a willingness and capability to operate in a collaborative manner is crucial. Companies will cooperate when they are given clear guidance and incentive.[12]

CONCLUSIONS

The markets created by governments looking for a governance mechanism both for outsourced services and for internal transactions were mostly characterised by small numbers of providers, by information asymmetry and, in many cases, by a skills deficit on the part of the purchasers. These markets mostly worked in favour of the suppliers, although there were sometimes skills deficits on their part as well.

There has been a tendency to assume that competitive tendering and complete contracts were the right solution to the issue of contracting, an assumption that has frequently been proven incorrect. Adapting the contracting form to the structure of the market and to the nature of the transactions would result in a greater variety of ways of letting and running contracts and to a higher success rate.

Further reading

M.P. Furmston, *Cheshire, Fifoot and Furmston's Law of Contract* (Oxford: Oxford University Press, 2006). A standard text on contract law.

M. Sako, *Prices, Quality and Trust* (Cambridge: Cambridge University Press, 1992). A comprehensive account of the different forms of contracting.

POINTS FOR DISCUSSION

- Do public sector organisations use the form of contracting that will generate best results?
- What are the main reasons for failure of public sector contracts with private sector providers?
- What are the obstacles to a more collaborative form of contracting?

NOTES

1   M.P. Furmston, *Cheshire, Fifoot and Furmston's Law of Contract* (Oxford: Oxford University Press, 2006), p. 24.

2   House of Commons Health Committee, *Commissioning*, 4th Report of Session 2009–2010, p. 9.

3   Ibid., p. 3.

4   From *Management Today* 10.6.11

5   Department for Local Government and Communities, *The National Procurement Strategy for Local Government*, Final Report, 2008.

6   Oliver Williamson, *Markets and Hierarchies* (New York: The Free Press, 1975).

7   Ibid., p. 40.

8   M. Sako, *Prices, Quality and Trust* (Cambridge: Cambridge University Press, 1992).

9   Association of Directors of Social Services and National Council for Voluntary Organisations (1995), *Community Care and Voluntary Organisations: Joint Policy Statement*, London: ADSS/NCVO, para 14e, p. 7.

10 National Audit Office, 'Contracting for Acute Health Care in England', Report by the Comptroller and Auditor General, London: HMSO, 1995, p. 19.

11 Department for Work and Pensions/Office of Government Commerce, *DWP Jobcentre Plus roll-out: Integrated Supply Chain* (London: DWP, 2006), p. 5.

12 Ibid., p. 7.

CHAPTER 13
Public–Private Partnerships

SUMMARY

A particular form of contractual relationship between a public agency and the private sector is the Public–Private Partnership, a way of sharing responsibility for funding, providing and maintaining buildings and other assets used to provide public services. Forms of PPP have been used for infrastructure, including the Skye Bridge and the private M6 motorway, for prison building and the provision of custodial services, hospital building and the 'Building Schools for the Future' programme of secondary school rebuilding. There has been mixed success: evaluations of school and prison PPPs shows that performance of the institutions funded by traditional methods was no better or worse that PPP ones, while there is some evidence that costs were higher under PPP. In some very large cases, such as the refurbishment of London Underground, there were spectacular losses. The future of PPPs is uncertain, both because of the Coalition government's reluctance and because of the illiquidity of the financial markets.

LEARNING POINTS

- PPPs were adopted for many reasons, as a financing method that did not directly add to public debt, as a way of managing facilities, as a way of exploiting private sector expertise and as a way of sharing risks.
- Risk sharing has proved to be illusory, especially in the case of the London Underground PPP, where the government guaranteed the banks' loans to the PPP consortium and was obliged to honour the guarantee.
- PPPs require skilled management and negotiation to make sure that the public sector achieves value for money.

WHY PPPs?

Between 1992 and the financial crisis of 2008, there were over 900 PFI/PPP agreements, with a total contract value of £66 billion.[1] At the beginning of 2011 there were a further £6,970 millions-worth of PFI projects in negotiation. HM Treasury's forecast of annual payments under PFI from 2011 onwards was just under £10 billion per annum.[2]

The 'Private Finance Initiative' was introduced by the John Major government, but was pursued enthusiastically by the Labour governments from 1997. The 'initiative' in the title referred to the push being given to the establishment of this sort of financing. The more normal nomenclature in the industry is 'Public–Private Partnership' or PPP, which is used in this chapter.

PPPs were seen as an attractive alternative to direct funding of infrastructure investment. Firstly, the borrowing was done by the PPP company, normally a 'Special purpose vehicle', or company established especially for each project, rather than by the government. While this meant that the interest rate payable on the borrowing was higher than it would have been for the government, the borrowing does not appear in the government's accounts.

Secondly, the PPP contracts normally include the maintenance of the asset over the contract period, transferring that responsibility to the contractor.

Risk is also formally transferred from the government to the contractor. In the special case of prisons, where the PPP agreement includes the provision of custodial services as well as the infrastructure and its maintenance, the contractor also takes responsibility for the service.

According to Jane Broadbent and Richard Laughlin,[3] the justification for using PFI/PPP for infrastructure investment shifted from a macro-fiscal one to a micro-value-for-money one after the fiscal impact of the long-term commitments under PFI were deemed similar to the costs of more conventional procurement. The decision, in each case, to implement a project through PFI/PPP was based on a comparison of the cost of doing it the PFI/PPP way and a 'public sector comparator'. All the costs of the PFI route would be compared with the costs of doing it the conventional way, plus an estimated element of cost for the risk implied by keeping the procurement within the public sector. The comparison is illustrated in Figure 13.1.

Figure 13.1 shows that some risk was expected to be retained by the public sector even under PFI. The estimation of the difference in risk between the two procurement methods became a crucial determinant of the outcome of the decisions. Alyson Pollock and her colleagues[4] investigated the cost comparisons of PFI and conventional procurement in the NHS and found a large degree of variation in the value attributed to the risk in the Public Sector Comparators. The differences are illustrated in Table 13.1.[5]

Against these advantages, there are also some disadvantages of PPPs compared with conventional funding. First, the cost is in principle higher than conventional funding, since it includes a higher cost of borrowing and requires a return to shareholders.

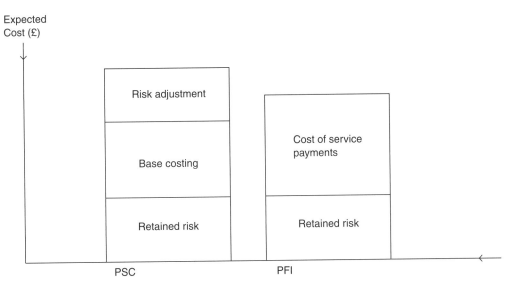

Figure 13.1   Cost elements in public sector comparators and PFI transactions

Source: Broadbent and Laughlin, p. 90 (see note 3)

Secondly, the contract period is normally very long, and removes flexibility in response to changing needs. Thirdly, as we will see in the case of the London Underground PPP, in practice government steps in to fund failure and does not transfer all the risk.

Table 13.1   How risk transfer closes the gap between the net present costs of a publicly funded scheme and those of a PFI scheme

Trust	Cost advantage to publicly financed scheme before risk transfer (£ m)	Value of risk transfer to the PFI scheme
Swindon and Marlborough	16.6	17.3
King's Healthcare	22.9	23.8
St George's Healthcare	11.9	12.5
South Durham	6.1	9.1
Hereford Hospitals	14.4	21.9
South Tees	28.8	67.8
West Midlands	8.4	13.5
University College London Hospitals	36.5	48.5
West Berkshire	36.3	41.8
Northumbria Healthcare – Hexham	3.2	4.8

Source: Pollock et al., p. 432 (see note 4)

TYPES OF AGREEMENT

PPPs have a great variety of structural forms, from very simple, with few players, to very complicated. The structure is in part determined by the complexity of the service to be delivered, especially if it involves a serviced building or, in the case of prison PPPs, the custodial and correctional services as well as the provision of a serviced building.

The relatively simple structure of the agreement for the M6 Toll Road (Figure 13.2)[6] has a Principal, 'The Authority'; a concession company, formed for this specific contract; and then a series of subcontracts for construction, operation and maintenance of the road. The banks fund the contract by lending to the concession company.

A more complicated structure is illustrated by the Stirling Water PPP, illustrated in Figure 13.3.

The common feature of all PPPs is that some of the financing is provided by equity stake from the contractors and some by debt borrowed from the banks. In almost all cases the prime contractor is a special vehicle company established for the particular deal.

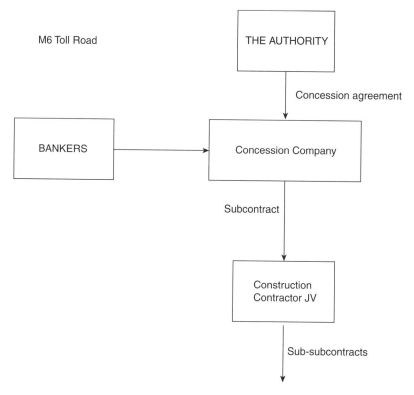

Figure 13.2   Structure of the M6 Toll Road PPP

Source: Partnership UK, Project database

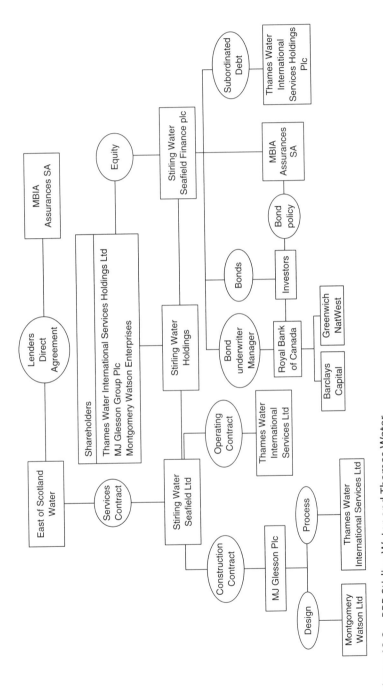

Figure 13.3 PPP Stirling Water and Thames Water

Source: Partnership UK, Project database

PRISONS

The National Offender Management Service provides an example of PFIs that include not only the construction and/or maintenance of the physical infrastructure, but also the core service, of incarceration and management of the prisoners in the PFI prisons. There has been a series of competitions for control of the prisons between the (then) Prison Service and a small number of private sector providers, with both sides having some success. At the time of writing there are nine PFI prisons.

Prisons are variously governed: publicly owned and run with or without Service Level Agreements, privately owned and run, and PFI prisons. The nine PFI prisons are subject to contracts containing 30–40 performance measures, about 40 performance targets and 61 prison service standards. The contracts, both within PFI and within the Service Level Agreements (SLAs) with the public providers, tend towards the 'adversarial' end of the contracting spectrum. There is an attempt at as complete a contract as possible, with specifications for prison regimes as well as some obvious outcomes, such as escapes. One aspect of the 'adversarial' nature of the contracts, as defined in Chapter 12, is that they are subject to periodic formal competitive bidding. Another is that there are penalty arrangements in the contracts that can result in payments being withheld for poor performance.

The National Audit Office reported[7] on the operational performance of PFI prisons in 2003. While the report points out that prison performance is affected by many variables other than the governance arrangements, such as the category of prison and prisoners and the age of the buildings, it was able to reach some conclusions about the impact of PFI management arrangements on the operational performance.

One conclusion concerns the rigidity built into the prison regime by a long-term contract:

> Prisons constructed and managed under PFI contracts, like those built and funded conventionally, may not be sufficiently flexible in design and operation to respond to changing penal priorities. Negotiating changes through a PFI contract or SLA adds a further level of complexity to this process. For example, there is now a greater emphasis on education and rehabilitation rather than employment in prison workshops, which was a priority when the earlier PFI contracts were let. (p. 6)

In general, the auditors could attribute neither good nor bad results to the PFI arrangements, showing that there were good and bad prisons under each of the governance mechanisms. The fact of competition has, however, had an impact on standards as both public and private prisons respond to the targets in the management contracts. Otherwise the main impact was on recruitment and the use of technology:

> The use of the PFI has brought innovation, mainly in the recruitment and deployment of staff and use of new technology; however, there appears little difference in terms of the daily routines of prisons. (p. 9)

The report's overall conclusion was non-committal:

> The use of the PFI is neither a guarantee of success nor the cause of inevitable failure. Like other forms of providing public services, there are successes and failures and they cannot be ascribed to a single factor. This report shows therefore what we should expect. A relatively new procurement method such as the PFI is associated with encouraging and disappointing results and that performance will improve over time. But a general verdict that the PFI is either good or bad in the case of prisons, or more generally, cannot be justified. (p. 9)

If the Auditor General's conclusions are accurate, this may suggest a general conclusion about the use of PFI as a way of managing services, as distinct from a way of financing them. The prison case seems to suggest that a system of service-level agreements with internal providers, and a periodic market test, in this case a real competition, is as effective in producing good (or not so good) management as the use of PFI. The PFI arrangement is not demonstrably better than the internal contract, backed by some external comparisons.

METRONET 2003–2007

'Metronet', as the PPP for the refurbishment and maintenance of London Underground track, signals and stations was called, was one of two large failures of the PFI/PPP programme, along with the National Physical Laboratory. The structure of the arrangement is shown in Figure 13.4. Essentially, the partners in the programme were a special company established for the purpose, divided into two parts for different tube lines and owned by five contracting firms. These companies borrowed money from a group of banks to carry out works in exchange for payment by London Underground Limited which in turn was paid a grant by the Department of Transport. The loans from the banks were 95% guaranteed by the government. Metronet was a £15.7 billion PPP signed in 2003 and personally championed by the then Chancellor of the Exchequer, Gordon Brown.

The government, as the ultimate Principal of the contract, was confused about what the contract consisted of. As Vining and Boardman[8] interpreted it:

> The government acted as though it had purchased an output-based fixed price contract. The private sector acted as though it had agreed to a series of heterogeneous, cost-plus contracts. Not surprisingly, this created ongoing conflict and was inevitably the source of much of the ex post transaction costs during the relatively short period that the contract was operational. This fundamental disagreement seems unbelievable in an enterprise of this magnitude.

Of the finance, 88.3% was provided as loans by the banks, the other as capital invested by the contractors in the special vehicle. The payments to Metronet were expected to be £8.7 billion over the first 7½ years (in current prices). There was another contract with another specially created company called Tube Lines.

The structure of the deal was complex,[9] in that the shareholders of the two Metronet special vehicles, Bombardier, WS Atkins, EDF Energy, Thames Water and Balfour Beatty, were also contractors to Metronet. The other feature of this structure is that the work was financed with debt from banks – the 'senior debt providers', which was 95% guaranteed, ultimately by government through the Department of Transport. The work was paid for by London Underground Limited.

By 2007, the Metronet companies declared bankruptcy and the government was forced to honour its guarantee of the debts and pay over £1.7 billion. The immediate cause of the bankruptcy was that the company spent more on the programme of station and line works than was available in the budget. The National Audit Office[10] attributed the failure to bad corporate governance:

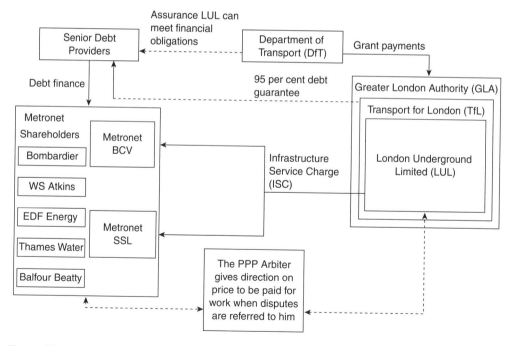

Figure 13.4   Metronet PPP relationships

Source: National Audit Office (June 2009), p. 5

The main cause of Metronet's failure was its poor corporate governance and leadership. Many decisions had to be agreed unanimously by five shareholders, which all acted as Metronet's suppliers and had different motivations depending on their roles. The executive management changed frequently and was unable to manage the work of its shareholder-dominated supply chain effectively. These suppliers had power over some of the scope of work, expected to be paid for extra work undertaken and had better access to cost information than the management. The poor quality of information available to management, particularly on the unit costs of the station and track programmes, meant that Metronet was unable to monitor costs and could not obtain adequate evidence to support claims to have performed work economically and efficiently. (p. 6)

BUILDING SCHOOLS FOR THE FUTURE 2004–2010

A special project was established in 2004 to either rebuild or replace all the secondary schools in England within a 15–20 year period. 'Building Schools for the Future' (BSF) was announced by the Prime Minister in 2004, a scheme whereby private finance initiative funding, plus receipts from selling land and buildings no longer required, would be used to finance the programme. The private sector would be involved in financing and building the schools, including the IT elements, through 'Local Educational Partnerships', of which 33 were established before the scheme was scrapped by the incoming Coalition government in 2010. The first of 185 schools redeveloped was opened on May 1st 2006, and schools in the last phase were opening through 2012. Overall the programme involved about £50 billions of expenditure. All major capital spending on secondary schools was organised through the BSF scheme, which was managed by a specially established Non Departmental Public Body, 'Partnerships for Schools'.

The House of Commons Education and Skills Committee[11] proclaimed the importance of this project and its potential problems:

It is worth emphasising the scale and scope of BSF; there is no project like it anywhere in the world. Not since the huge Victorian and post-war building waves has there been investment in our school capital stock on this scale, and of course the potential for new ways of learning has moved on considerably since then. Investment in the three decades before BSF was announced had been minimal, meaning that there were very few architects, procurement experts or head teachers in the system with experience to build on. (para 18)

Partly as a result of the scale of the programme and the need for many skilled people to make it work, the Committee heard evidence that there was a lack of capacity on the client side in managing the BSF programme:

> The CBI made a ... point about the capabilities of local authorities: 'The capacity and ability of local authorities to deal with the levels of commercial sophistication needed to create the type of partnership on which the success of BSF depends is of major concern. Anecdotal evidence suggests that there is a marked disparity in procurement capacity and experience between different local authorities. There are some very good local authorities but the overall picture is of shortages of skilled and experienced procurement staff. This has added to the complexity of BSF and increased delays.' (para 31)
>
> ...
>
> Secondly, there is the risk of a school becoming unviable through a fall in pupil numbers. While this is clearly the kind of problematic original procurement decision that PfS [Partnerships for Schools] was referring to, it can be extremely expensive if it happens to a PFI school. We are aware of three instances where PFI funded schools have closed or are closing leaving the relevant authorities with continuing financial commitments: a school in Brighton, which closed after three years, leaving the authority having to pay at least £4.5 million to release itself from the PFI contract, a school in Clacton which is to close after five years because of falling rolls, and a school in Belfast which is to close this summer after five years, for which the authority is committed to paying £370,000 a year for the next 20 years. (para 68)

An early Audit Commission report on PFI schools[12] showed that on all the criteria they used, PFI schools were on average less good than schools built through traditional financing and procurement, as illustrated in Figure 13.5.

The Public Accounts Committee, reporting in 2009,[13] found many shortcomings in the BSF scheme, including:

- The Department's poor planning and persistent over-optimism has led to widespread disappointment with the programme's progress and reduced confidence in its approach and ability to include all schools by 2023. Such over-optimism is systemic across the Civil Service's planning of major projects and programmes.
- The Department and Partnerships for Schools has wasted public money by relying on consultants to make up for shortfalls in its own skills and resources. The value for money of using Local Education Partnerships (LEPs) has still to be proved.
- The Department plans that most BSF schools will be procured without competitive tendering.
- Partnerships for Schools has yet to provide local authorities with enough information to build cost comparators and compare the price of each project.

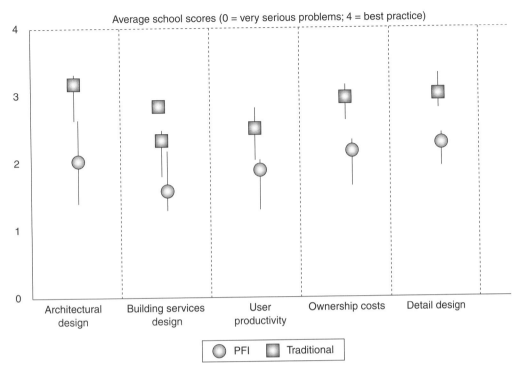

Figure 13.5   PFI and traditional financing performance

Source: Audit Commission (2003) 'PFI in Schools'

- The Treasury has recently announced that the Government will provide debt financing of BSF private finance initiative projects where sufficient private debt financing is unavailable and the project has started procurement. (p. 6)

A National Audit Office report[14] had, in the same year, concluded that PFI projects were no more delayed than conventionally managed projects, so the delays were presumably prior to the start of construction. Optimism seems to be a common hazard in major projects, but given the scale of BSF and the unprecedented call on the resources of schools, local authorities and the design and construction sectors, delays were perhaps inevitable.

The conclusions on finance were cause for concern: the lack of information on cost comparators, and the absence of competition for many projects, throw doubt on the value for money of the whole process.

Given the general doubts that we saw earlier in the chapter on the difference in costs between conventional and PFI procurement, the fact that there were neither competition nor cost comparisons means that no judgement can accurately be made.

A survey by Demirag et al. showed that the PPP-financed schools led to head teachers being frustrated about the lack of flexibility the contract offered once the school was running:

Many headteachers said that the fixed payments payable to the contractor have reduced flexibility in terms of management of their budget. For example: 'Unitary charge leaves no flexibility in budget for other costs. Facilities management providers need to be aware of how schools work. Internal fixtures and fittings need to be suitable for children's use, not the usual office type. There needs to be an efficient system in place to resolve snagging issues between the construction teams and facilities management'. [15]

HOSPITALS

Unlike the schools building programme, PPP only accounted for about 30% of the hospital building and refurbishment programme. The major PPP schemes for hospital construction consisted of a contract for the provision of the building plus building-related services including maintenance, cleaning, portering and catering. Medical services were never part of the PPP deal, unlike the case in prisons, where custodial services were included. The agreements were signed for periods of from 24 to 63 years.

The NAO reported in June 2010:[16]

> This report looks at the value for money achieved by hospital PFI contracts once they are operational. We found that most PFI hospital contracts are well managed. And the low level of deductions and high levels of satisfaction indicate they are currently achieving the value for money expected at the point the contracts were signed. However, as the cost and performance of hotel services are similar to those in non-PFI hospitals there is no evidence that including these services in a PFI contract is better or worse value for money than managing them separately. (p. 8)

Some hospital trusts have wished to buy themselves out of their PPP contracts, to save money. The first successful example was the Tees, Esk and Wear Valleys Mental Health Foundation Trust which decided in 2011 to buy itself out of the contract to supply West Park Hospital in Darlington. Its PPP contract required it to pay £2 million per year, but it decided that paying £18 million to exit the deal and take the hospital into ownership would save £14 million over the period of the remaining contract.[17]

URBAN REGENERATION/PROPERTY DEVELOPMENT

The other uses of PPP include urban regeneration, where local authorities enter a partnership with property development companies to redevelop urban areas. On example was the London Borough of Croydon.

> ## Box 13.1   Urban regeneration in Croydon[18]
>
> 'Croydon Borough Council has identified an opportunity to establish a strategic joint venture property partnership to lead, guide and influence development and investment and secure long-lasting and sustainable regeneration in the borough whilst addressing the accommodation requirements of the council for the short-, medium- and long-term. The council holds a substantial portfolio of development sites and owner-occupied estates in the town centre and throughout the wider borough. The portfolio includes a number of large strategic development opportunities in the town centre. It is proposed that a joint venture partnership, to be known as an Urban Regeneration Vehicle (URV), will be established between the council and a private sector partner to whom the council will initially commit a number of town centre development opportunities. In addition, the council will consider committing to a pre-let on new office accommodation to be developed by the URV in order to provide a strong covenant and income stream to assist in the redevelopment of other mixed-use sites taken forward by the URV'.

The scheme was a 50%:50% partnership PPP between the London Borough of Croydon and John Laing, and involved £450 million of investment over a 28-year contract.[19]

HIGHWAYS

The Highways Agency made use of PPPs for the construction of highways in Design, Build, Finance and Operate deals, since 1992. Early experience was judged to be positive. To understand the nature of the deals involved, look at the example of the first PFI highway scheme in Wales, in Box 13.2.

> ## Box 13.2   Example of PFI highway project
>
> 'The A55 Llandegai to Holyhead dual carriageway is the first PFI Design, Build, Finance and Operate (DBFO) road scheme in Wales. The scheme comprises the construction and maintenance of 31.5 km of trunk road and the maintenance of the two road bridges (Menai and Britannia) over the Menai Strait. The construction element was approximately £100m with a build period of 2 years and 3 months. The new dual carriageway across Anglesey was one of the main strategic objectives of the former Welsh Office and subsequently of the Welsh Assembly Government. It marks the final link in the improvement of the A55 from Chester to Holyhead. The road was opened to traffic in March 2001 and was officially opened by Rhodri
>
> *(Continued)*

> *(Continued)*
>
> Morgan AM, First Minister on 10 April 2001. Payments to UK Highways are by "shadow tolls" based on actual measured annual traffic volumes. It is estimated that payment will be about £16m per annum. The contract allows for a mechanism to cap the maximum amount of payment should traffic volumes greatly exceed the Assembly's forecast.'[20]

A typical privately-financed scheme, it involved the government paying for the highway by making 'shadow' toll payments for the actual volume of vehicles using the road. The use of PFI for highway construction continued at least until after the credit crisis. One scheme that was implemented over the 2008 credit crisis period was the widening of the M25. A report[21] by the National Audit Office found some contentious issues with this scheme. One was that the early signing of the contract to widen the road precluded other options, such as hard shoulder running in peak hours. Another was the increase in financing costs as credit dried up after the financial crisis. A third was the heavy reliance on advisers, who soaked up 7.5% of the contract value of the scheme, and made no contribution to the capacity development of the Highways Agency.[22]

IS THERE A FUTURE FOR PPP?

The financial crisis of 2008 led to a shortage of credit in all markets, including the market for PPPs. The National Audit Office published an assessment of the impact of the crisis on PFI[23]. The NAO found that no loan finance was available for the £13 billion of schemes in the pipeline, and the Treasury set up the 'Infrastructure Finance Unit', to behave, in effect, like a bank lending money for PFIs on commercial terms. The Unit only made one loan, for a waste disposal project in Manchester, but this seems to have given the market confidence and lending was resumed, to some extent, for 35 infrastructure projects. However, the margin on PFI loans increased from 1% or less pre-crisis to 2.5% or more after the crisis. This made PFI considerably less attractive than it had been as a financing option for infrastructure projects. As the NAO concluded:

> Higher financing costs eroded the value for money advantage that departments attribute to PFI. Departments initially seek assurance on the value for money of PFI procurement by comparing alternative ways of providing the same results. Although we have often expressed concern about these calculations, the typical estimate of the PFI cost advantage lay in the range of 5 to 10 per cent (and some cases we have audited showed smaller savings). We estimate that financing rate changes increased the annual contract charge by around 6 to 7 per cent. This finding suggests an increased risk to value for money resulting from the credit crisis.[24]

In opposition, the Conservative Party opposed PPPs as an unacceptable burden on future tax payers. On taking office in the Coalition, one of the first decisions was to cancel the Building Schools for the Future programme. The Coalition did, however, continue with other PPP projects.

PPP/PFI arose in a particular set of circumstances: for the Treasury it provided a way of borrowing off balance sheet, a piece of financial engineering that was popular in the private sector at that time; for the banks it was an opportunity to make profits on relatively safe loans which, whatever the rhetoric of risk transfer, were backed by the government. The Metronet case showed clearly that risk remained with government; and with high-geared PPP deals the banks put up a very high proportion of the funding at no risk at all.

From the point of view of the banks, PPP presented a way of lending to government at much higher rates than the normal process of buying bonds, partly because of the apparent risk involved. The secondary market in PPP contracts, where other financial institutions could simply buy the revenue stream with the PPP contract meant that the original risk, such as it was, could be passed on to the buyer of the contract. The buyers have mostly been funds, rather than operators or infrastructure providers, so the PPP process has not developed the companies that provide the infrastructure projects as major players in the PPP field.

CONCLUSIONS

The use of PPPs has sometimes achieved the objectives, in terms of delivery of infrastructure and services, although not in a way that proved even slightly better than conventional financing and contracting. There is a paradox in the inflexibility of the PPP approach: the way the contracts have been drawn up and implemented has been as if they were 'complete' contracts, with all contingencies defined. In the case of Metronet, this was clearly an erroneous approach as the physical state of the network was not known in advance of the contract. In the case of hospitals, contingencies, such as the future need to change the facilities, were eliminated from the contracts, making implementation more successful than Metronet, but producing inflexible facilities. We may well see the same in the case of the PFI schools, as educational technology and pedagogy change the way in which people learn in schools and the contracts for the facilities run for thirty years. Some of the schools demolished to make way for the new BSF schools were less than thirty years old and already marked out for replacement.

As a financing mechanism, PPPs probably did succeed in accounting terms, by the narrow definition of keeping the expenditures out of the definition of borrowing. It was almost certainly more expensive that more conventional financing mechanisms, and certainly did not remove the liabilities of continuing contractual commitments from the government's spending in future years. Given the state of the credit markets, and of the mid-term fiscal future, it is quite likely that the use of PPPs will be seen as a phenomenon of the period 1992–2010.

Further reading

Darren Grimsey and Mervyn K. Lewis, *Public Private Partnerships* (Cheltenham: Edward Elgar, 2004). A survey of PPPs worldwide, with good coverage of the United Kingdom experience.

Aidan R. Vining and Anthony E. Boardman, 'Public Private Partnerships: Eight Rules for Governments', *Public Works Management Policy* (2008), Vol. 13. Using a range of examples, the authors make policy prescriptions to make PPPs work better.

POINTS FOR DISCUSSION

- What are the main elements essential to a successful PPP?
- Why have some PPPs gone very badly?
- Under what circumstances should PPP be used for public investment?

NOTES

1 Peter Sheridan, 'PFI/PPP Disputes', *European Public Private Partnerships Law Review*, 2, (2009).
2 HM Treasury, PFI Data Summary, HM Treasury website (March 2011).
3 Jane Broadbent and Richard Laughlin, 'Striving for Excellence in Public Service Delivery: Experiences from an Analysis of the Private Finance Initiative', *Public Policy and Administration* 19; 82 (2004).
4 Allyson Pollock, Jean Shaou and Neil Vickers, 'Private finance and "value for money" in NHS hospitals: a policy in search of a rationale?', *British Medical Journal* 324, May (2002), pp. 1205–1209.
5 Ibid.
6 Partnerships UK, Project database: http://www.partnershipsuk.org.uk/PUK-Projects-Database.aspx.
7 Comptroller and Auditor General, *The Operational Performance of PFI Prisons*, HC 700, Session 2002–3 (18 June 2003), London: HMSO.
8 Aidan R. Vining and Anthony E. Boardman, 'Public Private Partnerships: Eight Rules for Governments', *Public Works Management Policy* 13; (2008) p. 149.
9 National Audit Office, 'Department of Transport. The failure of Metronet', HC 512, Session 2008–9 (June 2009), p. 5.
10 Ibid., p. 6.
11 House of Commons Education and Skills Committee, 'Sustainable Schools: Are we building schools for the future?', 7th report, session 2006–07, Volume 1, HC 140–1 (July 2007).
12 Audit Commission Report, *PFI in Schools*, 2003.
13 House of Commons Public Accounts Committee, 'Building Schools for the Future: renewing the secondary school estate', 27th report of 2008–9, HC 274 (2009).
14 NAO Report, *Performance of PFI Construction*, 2009.
15 Istemi Demirag and Iqbal Khadaroo (2010) 'Costs, outputs and outcomes in school PFI contracts and the significance of project size', *Public Money & Management*, 30: 1 (2010), 13–18.
16 National Audit Office Report, *The performance and management of PFI hospital contracts*, HC 68, Session 2010–11 (June 2010).
17 Reported on 'Health Direct' website, February 17, 2011.
18 Partnerships uk database: http://www.partnershipsuk.org.uk.
19 Partnerships uk database: http://www.partnershipsuk.org.uk.
20 Ibid.
21 National Audit Office Report, *Highways Agency procurement of the M25 private finance contract*, HC 566, Session 2010–11 (2011).
22 PFI database.
23 National Audit Office Report, *HM Treasury: Financing PFI projects in the credit crisis and the Treasury's response*, HC 287, Session 2010–11 (July 2010).
24 Ibid., p. 10.

CHAPTER 14
Regulation

SUMMARY

Regulation is used to control or influence services produced by private providers but where there is a public interest that would not necessarily be met by the market. The objectives of regulation include price control, security of supply, quality and sustainability. This chapter looks at the industries and their regulators in power, water and the railway. These are all examples of industries that at one time were part of the public sector and subsequently were privatised and subject to regulation. The purposes of regulation change as policy towards these industries changes, and as different policy instruments are created for the regulators.

LEARNING POINTS

- Regulation is not a single policy but a collection of policy objectives and policy instruments.
- The purposes of regulation can change as circumstances and priorities change.
- Not all privatisations produced the results that were expected at the time of privatisation, nor has regulation been entirely successful at producing the expected benefits.

REGULATION

Almost all activities and behaviours in the UK are subject to regulation of one sort or another. In this chapter we are concerned with the regulation of services, carried out to protect the public interest, in circumstances where governments consider markets inadequate in some way. There are some regulations that cover all productive activities, such as those policed by the Health and Safety Executive, which was set up in 1974. Other regulators have more distant origins, such as the Factory Inspectorate, established to police health and safety standards in factories from 1833. Employment practices, various aspects of trade such as what measures and weights are used and their accuracy, how much competition there is in the industry, vehicle safety, traffic rules, activities that might damage the environment, are subject to universally applicable regulations.

Some industries have their own regulators, including the building industry, the financial sector, food production and catering, mining, transport, broadcasting, who design and enforce specific regulations for the protection of the public. The Labour Government established a Better Regulation Executive, whose task was to review and suggest changes to the regulatory regime, with a view to simplifying the regimes and reducing the costs of regulation to businesses.

The professions also have their regulators, which have slowly evolved from internal, self-regulating bodies to independent regulators, as in the case, for example, of the lawyers, whose Bar Council for barristers and Law Society for solicitors have evolved into the Legal Services Board. The medical professions have traditionally regulated themselves, but have responded to suggestions that their regulatory bodies should include more non-professionals as members. Some occupations, such as journalists, continue to regulate themselves.

There is a distinct category of regulator created as part of the process of privatisation of the 'network industries', in telecoms, power, water and sewerage, buses and railways. Here, the regulators either make rules that are supposed to act as substitutes for competitive market forces, or try to manage the industries in such a way as to create competition.

One sector, community care, has also gone through a long and slow process of privatisation and now has a regulatory regime which covers both the private and public sectors, through the Care Quality Commission, which we saw in Chapter 9. This will be the precursor of the combined process of regulation for public and private providers if and when private provision of health services is expanded by the Coalition government.

Regulation is not a single policy instrument with a single set of goals: it consists of many and changing goals, and the instruments used also vary and change over time. The goals include price, quality, environmental impact, equity, sustainability, continuity of supply, safety and investment levels. The policy instruments used to pursue these goals include price controls, intervention in market structure, inspection of physical quality, subsidy and exhortation.

POWER

Since electricity privatisation in 1990 (England and Wales), 1991 (Scotland) and 1992–3 (Northern Ireland) the government has attempted to create a competitive market in Great Britain in the generation and distribution of electricity and the distribution of gas. Electricity has a supply chain that stretches from *generation*, the production of electricity in power stations, through *transmission*, carrying high voltage electricity from the power stations, *distribution*, delivering from the high-voltage system to the low-voltage regional redistribution system, to *supply*, buying electricity wholesale and selling it to end-users.

At privatisation the old Central Electricity Generating Board, a nationalised industry, was split into three generators, National Power, Powergen and Nuclear Electric. Transmission was handed to the Independent Transmission System Operators (TSOs), and the 12 Area Boards were sold as privatised Regional Electricity Companies to become the suppliers.

TSOs in gas and electricity are not allowed to get involved in buying and selling power in the wholesale or retail markets. However, there was no restriction on companies in the generation business from buying the retail suppliers, and generators now own all the retailers, effectively bypassing the wholesale market for electricity. By 2000, all the Regional Electricity Companies were owned by generators.

The regulator of the power industries in Great Britain,[1] the Office of Gas and Electricity Markets (Ofgem), works through issuing licences and by being a competition authority, working in parallel with the Office of Fair Trading. Rather than being set for domestic consumers,[2] retail prices are controlled by competition among suppliers.

The retailers compete for customers on price and service levels, and domestic customers are free to switch suppliers. At the network level, prices are fixed by the regulator, using a formula of Retail Price Index minus X, usually for a period of five years. Companies can make profits by reducing their costs below the formula, while still delivering specified outputs. Having several distributors allows the regulator to compare costs and set challenging 'X' levels based on the performance of the more efficient distributors. Network operating costs fell under this regime, by 30% in real terms, between privatisation and 2001.

The energy market operates through British Energy Trading and Transmission Arrangements, which allows for 'spot' trading of energy in half-hour segments. Competition in the energy market is the main mechanism for determining price and improving efficiency. The National Audit Office reported that the regime produced a 20% reduction in wholesale prices in the year after the introduction of the scheme[3] and that the system had produced a 40% reduction in wholesale prices between 1998 and 2003.

There is a debate about the extent to which the price reductions can be attributed to the market and regulation arrangements that were established. Steve Thomas[4] has two reservations about the competition arrangements and their impact on the prices. The first is institutional: he argues that there are confidential long-term contracts, rather than a real spot market; that the only real market is at the retail level, where consumers can switch their suppliers; and that there is not enough switching to affect the price. His second argument is that there were other factors at work to bring about the price reductions: the artificial rise in prices (by 7% more than the industry needed) prior to privatisation to make the privatisation more attractive to investors; the removal of the nuclear subsidy reduced prices by 10%; the ending of the high-priced coal contracts in 1998; the creation of over-capacity as new-generation plants were added after 1997; the cut in distribution costs; the price regulation calculations based on incorrect asset valuation at privatisation; and the world price of fossil fuels falling over the period of wholesale price reduction.

As Dieter Helm said, the internal competitive arrangements within the energy industry are not the main determinant of the price outcomes: 'Energy is now about the big oligopolists and their relationships with the upstream oil and gas companies in the emerging liquefied natural gas and international gas markets.'[5] The regulatory arrangements have no influence over those markets.

WATER AND SEWERAGE

In the case of water and sewerage, there are 'externalities' whereby access to supplies of water and sewerage services are good for the community at large as well as the individuals who benefit directly from them. Neither service was started as a state activity but in the nineteenth century, concerns about public health and monopoly led to the development of municipal organisation of these services. While in the middle of the nineteenth century only 10% of households were connected to piped water, by the middle of the twentieth century 90% of households were connected, mainly because of the efforts of the municipal water undertakings. The Public Health Act of 1875 gave responsibility to the local authorities for ensuring an adequate supply of water. The services were financed by a 'water rate', a property tax based on the 'rateable value' of domestic properties and charges for industrial users. For domestic water users, this method of charging represented a subsidy for poor consumers whose charges were determined by the value of their house rather than the volume of water they consumed. The water companies would never have made profits from a universal supply to all, including the very poor.

The water industry was nationalised in 1974, the municipal water enterprises being taken over, in England and Wales, by ten Regional Water Authorities, their boundaries determined by the natural water catchments. The government controlled the Water Authorities' capital programmes, and capital spending halved between 1974 and 1982 as part of the general cuts in public spending.

When the water supply and sewerage services were privatised in 1989, they were in poor shape. Pollution incidents were rising; there was proportionately more raw sewage being discharged into the sea than in any other European country; 3,000 km of rivers were so polluted that no fish survived in them; and the EU were legislating for drinking and bathing water quality.

Four models of ownership and three regulatory regimes were employed, based on the overall idea of dividing the industry among regional companies that were given 25-year monopolies. In England and Wales they were to be regulated by three bodies: price was to be controlled by the Office for Water Services ('Ofwat'), water quality by the Drinking Water Inspectorate and pollution by the Environment Agency. Box 14.1 shows the variety of objectives and policy instruments used by Ofwat. The monopoly structure of supply and distribution led Ofwat to a system of controls over the monopolies, while creating and maintaining competition where possible.

Box 14.1   Ofwat's strategy[6]

Ensuring a fair deal for customers

- Making sure that all customers receive the services they expect at a price that treats them and others fairly, is transparent and gives them choice and some control over the charges they pay.
- In the absence of customer choice, challenging monopolies to improve on all aspects of service and price they offer. And where there is choice, making sure that markets deliver benefits to customers and the environment.
- Making sure that customers now and in the future contribute their fair share – and no more – towards sustainable water.
- Making sure that our work takes account of customers' priorities, including those who need additional help and those on low incomes.

Keeping companies accountable

- Making sure the companies deliver the services they promise at the price they agreed, and meet their legal obligations.
- Making sure that monopoly suppliers listen to their customers, deliver their priorities and are honest about their performance. And, where there are open markets, ensuring that the companies operating in them do not break the market rules.
- Making sure that the companies meet their wider social, economic and environmental obligations.
- Where companies fail, taking fair and appropriate action against them to put things right to protect consumers, and deter them from further failures.

Making monopolies improve

- Challenging the monopoly companies to improve in all aspects of their performance, delivering their customers' priorities as well as their other legal obligations.

(Continued)

(Continued)

- Making sure that the way that monopolies operate does not interfere with efficient and effective markets – and that they are encouraged to learn, adapt and behave in ways that mimic competitive markets wherever possible.
- Making sure that monopoly companies help ensure water security and meet their wider social, economic and environmental obligations effectively and efficiently.
- Making sure that our system of regulation provides the right incentives to ensure that monopolies innovate to improve all aspects of their services.

Harnessing market forces

- Using regulated markets to reveal new information or new approaches to help deliver long-term water security.
- Introducing regulated markets where there are clear long-term benefits to customers and the environment.
- Monitoring markets to make sure they operate effectively and efficiently – and taking action where they do not.
- Designing markets, and the regulatory tools to harness them, in ways that promote positive social, economic and environmental benefits.

Contributing to sustainable development

- Making sure that customers continue to receive safe, reliable, efficient and affordable water and sewerage services that promote positive social and environmental impacts now and over the long term.
- Making sure that the companies meet their customers' needs and deliver long-term water security effectively and efficiently.
- Making sure the companies contribute towards wider social, economic and environmental objectives.
- Making sure that we make sustainable choices and our approach to regulation encourages others to do the same.

Delivering better regulation

- Effective regulation, delivered efficiently at a minimum cost to customers and a minimum burden to the companies.
- A system of regulation that encourages the companies to meet the needs of customers and the environment – and takes action against those that do not.
- Continually reviewing the tools, approaches and information we use to ensure that monopolies improve the services they offer and that markets deliver benefit to customers and the environment.
- Regulation that promotes positive social, economic and environmental impacts.

Water and sewerage supply and services in England are provided by a collection of private companies: ten water and waste companies and 13 water-only.[7] Like other private companies they have a history of business decisions, including mergers, acquisitions and diversifications, some of which have been more successful than others. An example was Southern Water, a company that after privatisation diversified unsuccessfully into a variety of businesses before it was taken over by Scottish Power. Scottish Power got into financial trouble in its operations in the United States of America and needed cash, so put the business up for sale. After the Competition Commission blocked the sale to Vivendi,[8] it was bought by a company established for the purpose, Southern Water Investments, whose ownership is shared by Southern Water Capital (80.1%) and Veiola. Thames Water, one of the biggest suppliers of water in the UK, was bought by a German firm, RWE, in 2001 and together they have become one of the world's large companies in the water industry.

In Scotland, since April 2002, water is supplied by Scottish Water, a nationalised industry created out of the old East, North and West of Scotland Water companies. Its investment programme is run through Scottish Water Solutions, a company set up for the purpose of implementing most of Scottish Water's capital programme and owned 51% by Scottish Water, 25% by United Utilities, the rest by a consortium of companies called the Stirling Water Consortium. The Scottish Executive established an independent Water Industry Commission to act as regulator.

In Wales, privatisation produced a company called Welsh Water, which went in for a spree of acquisitions, including the electricity company Swalec. It soon ran into financial problems and was bought by Western Power Distribution who soon in turn put it up for sale again. This time a not-for-profit organisation was formed to buy the water part of the business, Glas Cymru, running the water business through wholly-owned Dŵr Cymru/Welsh Water. Dŵr Cymru has a small staff, and operations are outsourced to United Utilities (which used to be called North West Water), while capital investments are outsourced to a variety of partners. The process through which the company provides water is by raising loan finance and organising a series of contracts at all points along the value chain. This process is similar in some respects to the way that London Underground relates to its PFI contractors for works on the infrastructure while maintaining public ownership of the operation: the water operation is similarly split between the not-for-profit organisation and its operational and engineering contractors.

In Northern Ireland, water is supplied by the Northern Ireland Water Service, a government department, funded through taxation. This is the last remaining 'traditional' publicly-owned water and sewerage service run as part of government.

Ofwat regulates water prices in England and Wales, while the Environment Agency monitors environmental quality. Scottish regulation is carried out by a Water Commissioner who reports to the Scottish Executive, and environmental standards are regulated by the Scottish Environmental Protection Agency. European regulations and standards on water quality are a major determinant of investment in sewage treatment. Regulation in Northern Ireland is done by the Water Management Unit, within the Environment and Heritage Service.

Drinking water is regulated by the Drinking Water Inspectorate within the Northern Ireland Environment Agency, the Drinking Water Quality Regulator in Scotland and the Drinking Water Inspectorate in England and Wales.

Colin Mayer has suggested that water privatisation and regulation occurred in three phases.[9] The initial privatisation was designed to get the Water Authorities out of government hands and secure infrastructure investment 'at almost any price'. The price was quite high: while the flotation raised £5.2 billion, there was a debt write-off of £4.9 billion and a cash injection of £1.5 billion.[10] In this first phase there was easy money to be made. Prices were set to allow rates of return well above the cost of capital to the companies.

The privatised monopolies in England and Wales had their prices set at periodic reviews for five years. Prices in England and Wales were set in 1990, 1994, 1999 and 2004 (with a revision in 2005) and in 2009. While they invested around £3 billion per year, these companies achieved very good returns on their capital. The average domestic water bill rose from £166 in 1989 to £242 in 1998–9, an increase of 46%. At the end of the first period of price setting the average return was 23%, the highest return being 31% for the company supplying Manchester's water. Profit margins by 1998 included 59.7% for Southern, 51.6% for South West and 46.7% for United Utilities. Total pre-tax profits for the ten companies grew by 142% between 1989 and 1998. These returns were very high by comparison with other countries' private water industries[11] but the investment produced improvements in water quality and environmental quality of the rivers.

In 1997 the newly elected Labour government called a 'water summit', partly in response to public concern about rising prices and big profits for the water companies. One result of the change of policy towards the industry was that the water companies were charged a 'windfall tax' that cost the industry £1.65 billion. In 1999, Ofwat declared that water bills should be cut by 12.3%, after an average increase since 1990 of 30% for domestic water users without a meter (and 19% for those with a meter). Share prices in the water companies fell by 50%, reducing the market value of the companies to less than the value of their assets.

One consequence of this change in profitability was a series of 'leveraged buyouts', financed by borrowing, as shareholders sold their equity in the water companies, seeing that the days of easy high returns were over. The capital structure changed from 20% debt in 1989 to 50% debt in 1999. The other consequence was that there was now pressure on the companies to control their costs. The only source of profits, once prices were fixed, was to increase operating efficiency. This was Colin Mayer's second phase: a period during which managerial efforts were directed towards the efficiency of the operations, and cutting running costs. The third phase is one of pressure on capital efficiency, making better use of the assets. The progression is from a regulatory regime in which both the firms and the regulator were committed to high levels of investment and high rates of return to one of control, where the regulator forces the companies to become more efficient. The change in the capital structure reflects the desire of investors to have an exit strategy, once the days of easy money were over.

However, the 2004 review announced an 18% rise for the next five years, soon to be superseded by an announcement of an 11.8% rise for 2005/6. At the same time the Scottish

Executive announced that domestic water prices in Scotland would rise by 0.5% less than inflation. It is not possible to conclude that a regulated privatised monopoly (England and Wales) produces big price increases while a regulated nationalised industry (Scotland) produces no real-terms increases in price, because the physical conditions of water and sewerage systems may be different. It is hard, however, to believe that average domestic water bills in England and Wales are more than twice the level that they are in Scotland only because of the physical infrastructure and the nature of the water capture and distribution systems. The actions of the regulator in England and Wales, allowing big price rises again, seem to be in response to the change in capital structure and a desire to continue to promote investment in infrastructure for the industry.

The lesson from the case of the water and sewerage industry is that the companies respond quickly to changes in the regulatory regime: when prices are left to rise and there is a monopoly, consumers have to pay both for the investment in infrastructure and the shareholders' dividends. When prices are held back, investors flee and share prices fall. As a mechanism for generating investment, privatisation depends on regulation allowing the companies to collect revenue from the consumers. Without competition, consumers have no choice but to pay up. For the companies, strategy depends on what the regulator does: incentives to invest, or to cut costs, or to exit the industry are all determined by what the regulator decides.

THE RAILWAY

British Rail, the nationalised industry that ran Britain's railway from nationalisation in 1947, was privatised through the Railways Act of 1993. The structure set up to run the privatised railway contained a variety of mechanisms to try to make the trains run. First, ownership and control of the track and signals were separated from all other parts of the railway business. A new company, called Railtrack, was floated to own the network, organise maintenance and improvements and lease the network to the people who ran the trains. The physical work of maintaining the network was contracted initially to 13 Infracos, soon whittled down through mergers and acquisitions to 4 companies. In turn they subcontracted to about 1,000 individual companies. The government initially paid about £1.3 billion annual subsidy to this disparate set of companies to keep the infrastructure running.

The present structure dates from 2002, with a state-owned company, Network Rail, running the infrastructure, a franchising system of periodic competitions whereby Train Operating Companies (TOCs) lease space on the tracks, and rent trains from Rolling Stock Companies (Roscos). Two Roscos, Eversholt and Porterbrook, were created as management buy-outs by former British Rail employees. The third, Angel, was a consortium. Within a few years all the Roscos had been sold to banks (HSBC, Abbey and Royal Bank of Scotland), incidentally making multi-millionaires of the management buy-out staff. Both economic and safety regulation are carried out by the Office of the Rail Regulator (ORR).

By 2001 70% of passenger revenue went to four groups, mostly companies in the bus industry. With franchise prices fixed for the period of the contract, leasing costs fixed and fares regulated, the main way that companies could improve their profits was to attract more passengers and cut the costs of running the trains. This mostly meant cutting the numbers of staff, with unforeseen consequences for reliability.

The total public subsidy to this collection of organisations rose to £6.8 billion in 2006–7, compared with a subsidy of £1.3 billion in the last year before privatisation. If privatisation had been seen as a way of reducing the government's expenditure on the rail system, it clearly did not have this effect.

It was a big task to co-ordinate all of these companies, over 100 main players, and well over a thousand if all the maintenance subcontractors are included, to run trains to a timetable, maintain and improve the track and run the stations and ticketing system. The mechanism chosen was licencing and incentive-based contracts. The Office of the Rail Regulator issued licences to everybody in the system, apart from the Roscos. The TOCs had a contract with Railtrack to use the tracks. If track problems caused delays, their fee to Railtrack was reduced. If trains caused delays by blocking the tracks, they paid a fine, by the minute of delay. This was all organised through the Train Running System (TRUST), with 2,900 'reporting points' and 1,300 'delay attribution points' designed not to make the trains run on time, rather to apportion blame when they were late. Some companies collected more money in compensation payments from Railtrack than their total operating profit.

Maintenance was organised by a cascade of contracts from Railtrack to the Infracos and from them to the subcontractors. These contracts were unusual in that the contractor rather than the client mostly specified what needed to be done, since Railtrack had little engineering expertise or up-to-date knowledge of the condition of the network. Since the contractor had more information and expertise than the client it should not have been surprising that the contractor was able to operate in its own interests.

While passenger numbers continued to grow after privatisation[12] the complexity of the contracting system and its incentives led to a decline in reliability[13] and safety. Railtrack's contracts with the TOCs, having to compensate for lost time, meant that they had an incentive not to close tracks for repair and upgrading. The Infracos, with their combined job of specifying the work necessary as well as carrying it out, had no financial incentive to create a safe and reliable network.

Three crashes causing multiple fatalities, at Southall, Ladbroke Grove and Hatfield (in 2000) brought the problem to the attention of those people who had not already noticed the deteriorating state of the railway. After Hatfield, Railtrack imposed speed restrictions and closure on many tracks to 'export the risk' of another accident and the whole system slowed down and became more unreliable. The government replaced Railtrack, handing over the ownership of the tracks and stations to a new not-for-profit company, and effectively re-nationalised the network by transferring the assets to Network Rail, after cutting Railtrack's funds and effectively bankrupting it. While the government defined Network Rail as a private, not-for-profit company, its revenues consisted of government subsidy and its borrowings are all backed by the Government, so in effect the company and its assets are publicly owned. The new company took over the assets in October 2002.

The White Paper published in July 2004[14] found five main structural problems:

- a complex and confusing public sector structure, with too many overlapping responsibilities and no clear command of strategy;
- a regulatory system and contractual structure which do not give the Government direct control of the level of public funding for the railways;
- an over-complex private sector structure, with Government often far removed from the impact of the decisions that it takes;
- a relationship between track and train companies based on false and sometimes perverse market incentives, that in many cases do not reflect customers' needs; and
- a lack of operational leadership in the private sector, with no-one clearly accountable for the delivery of improved performance and reliability. (p. 13)

In addition the White Paper brought maintenance work back in-house to Network Rail. 'This will allow it control over the work carried out, reducing management duplication and overheads…' (p. 20). The Strategic Rail Authority was wound up and its powers taken back to the Department of Transport.

The White Paper pointed to the failure of the relationship between the TOCs and Network Rail and proposed a new franchise contract, which would be awarded on the basis not only of cost but past records of reliability and 'provisions on train and crew availability, which are by far the largest factors in delays attributed to train companies, and are clearly within their control' (p. 47).

The story of the railway provides several lessons for public management. First, the replacement of hierarchical command structures by contractual relationships requires care. The relationship between Railtrack and the Infracos was always uneven, since Railtrack lost most of its expertise and knowledge. There was no capacity for Railtrack to be an intelligent client, however much such capacity was needed to make the contracts work. The contracts between the TOCs and Railtrack focused everyone's attention on blame, rather than making the system work.

Second, the main objective of the privatisation was to reduce the public subsidy to the railway, transferring the commercial risks to the companies with the assets and reducing public responsibility. Not only did this not occur, but the subsidy grew rather than shrank. The Roscos took very little risk, letting contracts to match the franchise periods, and yet the original owners were rewarded with very large profits when they sold the businesses, eventually to the banks. These profits were not a reward for risk-taking.

Third, despite the continuing and growing public liability, the government lost control of the railway. Taking strategy back in-house and virtually re-nationalising the infrastructure were eventually seen as the only way to get the railway back under government control.

There are differences between the arrangements put in place for the privatisation of the railway and the PPP for London Underground. The most obvious is that while private companies operate and maintain the Underground system, the ultimate control is with

Transport for London and the Department for Transport, a situation that was not the case with the railway, at least while the track and signals were in private hands.

The nature of the contracts is also different, in that the Underground railway contracts have an emphasis on outcomes, although in both cases there was a low level of information about the state of the infrastructure and the amount needed to be spent on it.

In 2011 Roy McNulty reported[15] on the value for money of the railway industry. He found that costs were 40% higher than comparable European railways and that the system itself was flawed in the way it created incentives for the TOCs and for Network Rail. Subsidy had grown since privatisation and had peaked at 49% of total costs in 2006–7. His report estimated that costs 'should be' 30% lower than existing costs, and that this should be achieved through a series of changes in practices by Network Rail and the Roscos rather than another structural reorganisation. Among the many reasons for the high costs, McNulty believed that the government itself took too much responsibility for the railway:

> The current level of rail subsidy inevitably brings with it a significant degree of Government scrutiny and challenge. However, the fragmentation of the industry, together with the absorption by the DfT of a range of functions from the Strategic Rail Authority (SRA), has resulted in a level of Government involvement in railway affairs which many observers consider is now greater than it was under the nationalised British Rail (BR).

> Within the current framework, much of the responsibility for the industry's performance, including costs, is seen to rest with Government, and the industry has not taken the responsibility that it needs to exercise for driving costs down.[16]

He proposed an enhanced role for the Office of Rail Regulation, including the enforcement of the Department for Transport's fares policies, and a strong role in managing the relationship between the TOCs and Network Rail.

CONCLUSIONS

Regulation is not a foolproof way of guaranteeing the public good in the network industries. Companies will concentrate on profits because that is what they are set up to do, while the regulator's job is to influence their behaviours and revenues to safeguard the public interest. In the case of water the companies were able to make very high returns on their capital employed, and companies made high profits from the railway. Power companies' prices were, for a while, held to prices that seemed to be in the consumers' interests, until the wholesale markets for energy turned against consumers. Regulation has been of mixed success.

Further reading

Robert Baldwin and Martin Cave, *Understanding Regulation: Theory, Strategy and Practice* (Oxford: OUP, 1999).

Jacint Jordana and David Levi-Faur, *The Politics of Regulation* (Cheltenham: Edward Elgar, 2004).

TOPICS FOR DISCUSSION

- Why did the privatised railway not succeed as expected?
- How would you rate the success of Ofwat and the ORR?

NOTES

1   In Northern Ireland the Office for the Regulation of Electricity and Gas, in the Northern Ireland Authority for Energy Regulation. At the time of writing there was only one electricity supplier, Northern Ireland Electricity, which was privatised in 1992 (power stations) and 1993 (the rest of the business) and discussions had started about opening up the market.

2   The regulator set retail prices until 2001, after which competition was to be the main determinant of price.

3   It was called the National Energy Trading Arrangements when it was introduced without Scotland in 2001: see National Audit Office, *The New Energy Trading Arrangements in England and Wales*, HC 624, Session 2002–2003, 9 May 2003.

4   Steve Thomas, 'The British Model: Failing Slowly', *Energy Policy*, 34, March 2006.

5   Dieter Helm, Editorial, *The Utilities Journal*, Vol. 8, March 2005, p. 1.

6   Water Services Regulatory Authority (Ofwat), Delivering sustainable water – Ofwat's strategy (2010).

7   The structure of the industry changes as mergers and acquisitions and divestments take place. For up-to-date information check: http://www.thewaterplace.co.uk.

8   'Veiola', briefly known as 'Vivendi' and 'Vivendi Environment', was previously Compagnie Générale des Eaux, the company that has 50% of the French privatised water market.

9   Colin Mayer, 'Commitment and Control in Regulation: The Future of Regulation in Water', in Colin Robinson (ed.), *Governments, Competition and Utility Regulation* (Cheltenham: Edward Elgar, 2005).

10 Karen J. Bakker, *An Uncooperative Commodity: Privatizing Water in England and Wales*, Oxford: (Oxford University Press, 2003).

11 Mohammed H.I. Dove, Joseph Kushner and Klemen Zumer, 'Privatization of Water in the UK and France – What Can We Learn?', *Utilities Policy*, **12** (2004) pp. 41–50.

12 The White Paper says that the number of passenger journeys grew by 26% between 1996/97 and 2004.

13 In 1992–93 British Rail achieved nearly 90% of trains on time; the system achieved 80% in 2002–03.

14 Department for Transport, *The Future of Rail* (London: HMSO, 2004).

15 Department for Transport and Office for Rail Regulation, *Realising the Potential of GB Rail: Report of the Rail Value for Money Study* (2011).

16 Ibid., summary report, p. 42.

Conclusions

We have seen throughout the book that successive governments have been extremely active in 'reforming', reorganising and reviewing the management of the public sector, using all the four basic methods of governance: markets, hierarchies, clans and networks, with a preference for reducing the power of the professional clans and increasing markets and hierarchies with some emphasis on networks. Over the long run, if we look back three decades, the boundary between the public and private has shifted with the privatisation of the old nationalised industries and the public utilities, but since those transfers from the public to the private the boundary has changed slightly, mainly through the growth of outsourcing and contracting, a practice which probably accounts for just over a third of public spending on services.

As we have seen, one vehicle through which the move from professionalism (clan control) to management (hierarchical control) is through a transformation of the inspection function into a method of control, and the establishment of a series of regulators for the privatised utilities to enable governments to control various aspects of the services, including price and quality. At the same time, networks at local level were established as a co-ordinating mechanism, especially in areas regarded as being in need of regeneration.

Is it possible to evaluate the impact of all these active interventions? One challenge in answering this question is the fact that successive governments have held back from making overall evaluations of the major changes. Individual initiatives have had evaluations, such as the single regeneration budgets; the use of PFI/PPP as a way of building schools, hospitals, prisons and infrastructure; the value of school inspection, and we have seen some of these throughout the book. The more over-arching changes have not been the subject of formal evaluation: the division of the whole of the Civil Service into policy functions in the departments and serviced delivery in the Agencies or organisations working under Agency principles; the division of the whole of health and social services into 'commissioners' and 'providers'; the creation of a centrally designed system of performance management reaching down from Whitehall into every school, hospital, clinic, prison, old persons' home in the country.

As we saw in Chapter 6, one fundamental problem in public management is the difficulty of establishing an independent valuation of outputs. Without such a valuation, measuring efficiency, defined as unit costs of outputs, is very hard. The difficulty of establishing what is exactly the cause and effect relationship between what government agencies do and outcomes on the ground also makes outcome evaluation difficult, as we saw in the impact of government actions in the criminal justice field; for example, extra spending, more staff, changed management structures and practices could not be linked to changes in outcomes.

EFFICIENCY

However, it is possible to make some remarks about efficiency. First, there are periodic estimates of productivity, using proxies for the value of outputs.

For example, the Office for National Statistics has estimated NHS productivity 1999–2005.[1] Depending on whether adjustments are made for quality and for the impact of the relationship between NHS and private inputs, productivity over the period has either fallen or grown slightly. The results are shown in Figure Con. 1.[2]

Figure Con. 1 probably does not allow us to attribute the changes to anything that the government did over the period to the management of the health service. The slight changes, such as they are, could be the result of technical improvements, staff effort or better management. What the figure does show, however, is that there was no great, discernible improvement over the period. Our definition of 'reform' requires us to see a measurable improvement in the volume or quality of services or in the relationship between the state and the citizen to be sure that a real reform has taken place.

To take another example, higher education, we can take a crude measure of productivity: the number of students and the number of academic staff. In the decade from 1994/5 to 2003/4 we saw a growth in total student numbers from about 500,000 to 2.2 million. Over that period, the total number of academic staff increased from about 114,000 to 150,000, including an increase in part-time staff from 12,000 to 43,000. We can ask questions about the quality of the student experience as a result of the increase in the student:staff ratio, but the increase in productivity is clear. Does this imply, using our definition, a 'reform'? There is a measurable increase in throughput and that is matched by the numbers of qualifiers. The higher education sector over this period was not subject to the same sort of 'purchaser–provider' reorganisation that we saw in the NHS, but it was subject to a financing regime that required the admission of the student numbers the government had decided, as part of its policy to increase the higher education participation rate to 50% of the relevant cohort.

Apart from the creation of special, more autonomous schools, school education reform consisted of reductions in the role of the local education authorities, a centralised national curriculum and devolved management for schools. We saw in Chapter 4 that the performance of the school system, as measured by the Key Stage tests, improved quite significantly for the first three or four years of the performance management targets, with a slow annual improvement thereafter. The same was true for the performance at GCSE, where the targets were the proportion of pupils attaining grades A–C in a selection of subjects: an early rapid improvement, followed by a levelling off. If the improvements in pupil performance in the tests constitute a measurable improvement in the quantity or quality of service, then the changes in the management of the school system qualify as a reform, but they were carried out at a time of increased expenditure. Attribution of the improvement to the management changes, as distinct from the expenditure changes, is not straightforward.

NHS productivity is calculated by dividing the volume of NHS outputs by the volume of NHS inputs and observing the changes on a yearly basis. Following the information provided in earlier sections, there are currently three sets of productivity estimates of interest:

- NHS productivity without quality adjustment
- NHS productivity with quality adjustment but no allowance for private/public sector complementarity
- NHS productivity with quality adjustment and an allowance for private/public sector complementarity

Using the different input measures and the outputs volume series for the period 1999 to 2004 without quality adjustment, NHS productivity is estimated to have fallen between 0.9 per cent and 1.5 per cent per annum, as shown in Figure 9C.

When quality adjustment is applied to NHS output, but excluding any allowance for private/public sector complementarity NHS output growth during 1999 to 2004 increases by an average of 1.1 per cent per year. Applying these quality adjustment indicators therefore improves NHS productivity growth figures for the period to between an average increase of 0.2 per cent and a fall in productivity of 0.5 per cent per annum, as shown in Figure 9D. The adjustment for quality has the effect of changing a falling productivity trend into one that is relatively flat.

When an allowance for private/public sector complementarity is applied to quality adjusted NHS output, productivity is estimated to have increased by 0.9 per cent and 1.6 per cent per annum for the period 1999 to 2004.

Figure 9c: New estimate of NHS productivity, excluding quality change for NHS output, 1995–2004

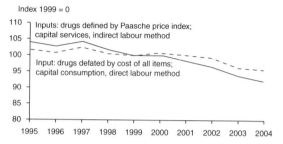

Figure 9D: NHS productivity based on output including quality change in NHS output but no allowance for private/public sector complementarity, 1999–2004

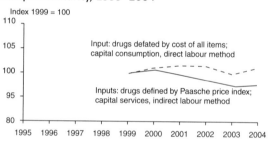

Figure 9E: NHS productivity including quality change in NHS output and allowance for private/public sector complementarity, 1999–2004

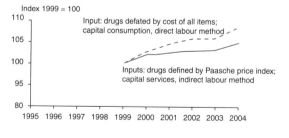

Figure Con. 1   Measurement of productivity for the National Health Service

Source: ONS, quoting UK Centre for Measurement of Government Activity, February 2006

If we look at the data from the criminal justice system that we saw in Chapter 4,[3] we see a large increase in spending and staffing in the police, courts, probation and prisons but a very flat time series of data on the numbers of criminals apprehended. These changes did occur over a period of apparent reforms: reorganisation of probation, changes in the management of the courts, a new performance regime for the police. The decreases in the reported crimes in the British Crime Survey may in some part be attributed to management changes, but may also be attributable, as we saw, to better security in vehicles and homes.

OVERHEADS AND TRANSACTION COSTS

Even if it is not possible to have a convincing measurement of the value of the outputs of the public services, we can make some assessment of the effective use of the resources allocated to the services. Most of the spending goes towards direct costs: the costs of staff, premises, materials and so on that are needed to directly provide education, healthcare, security and so on. Most of the reforms and reorganisation that we have seen throughout the book have concerned activities at one remove from the direct delivery of services, culminating in the 2011 healthcare reforms which were mostly about activities of commissioning and planning and financial transactions, rather than the business of doctoring and nursing. This applies to a lesser extent to the Agency arrangements: here the changes included discernible differences to the way that direct service providers are employed, managed and equipped with information technology and premises. The devolution of the management arrangements to the Agencies was designed to enable managers to better manage people and physical resources.

So, a test for success could be whether the changes in management arrangements divert resources away from the provision of services and if they do, does the expense on the layers of management and procedures add more value than they subtract? Two reforms that we have seen go in opposite directions in this respect: health and school education. The NHS's division into purchasers and providers created explicit and identifiable units, with costs, that are removed from the provision of services: they are about defining, costing, prioritising, commissioning, invoicing and paying for services. We do not know how much all this costs, but the House of Commons Health Committee revealed that they had seen an unpublished study estimating that 14% of the costs of the NHS were devoted to management and transaction costs. We do not have historic data to compare the old integrated NHS with the various versions of the internal market, but the impression within the NHS is that the transaction costs have grown. Incidentally the comparative figure for the United States healthcare system, where all health procedures require insurance or Medicare or Medicaid cover and therefore financial transactions, is thought to be 27%.[4] The 2011 reforms, with the requirement to purchase from 'any willing provider' and a common tariff imply more, smaller transactions and therefore more transaction costs.

The case of school budgets was the opposite: here the idea was that education budgets, administered through the Dedicated Schools Grant, should be spent on schools and not administration. Budgets within schools normally have to cover a very small number of administrative staff.[5] Outside the schools, in the local authority education department, overhead costs are strictly limited. For example, if we look at Birmingham City Council's budget, which we saw in Chapter 5, the school budgets added up to £729,932,000 in 2010–11, while the 'strategic management and support' budget line of the education department was £10 million, a sum less than the cost of school transport.

It would be possible to devise a 'purchaser–provider' division for education, with a set of people commissioning the schools to provide education according to a contract, with outcome targets and standard costs. In a sense that is what happens with the national curriculum, SATs tests and formula funding. Why is the arrangement for the health service so much more complicated, time-consuming and expensive than that in education? It is tempting to say that it is because of the complexity of what goes on in the provider side of the health service, with its variety of procedures, drugs, professions and facilities: schools are much simpler. But the complexity explains why anyone making a contract for healthcare should be cautious about whether the contracting process will add more value than it costs: we saw in Chapter 12 that contracts that have high complexity, small numbers of providers and information asymmetry are likely to be expensive, or are likely to produce best results if the contracts are 'obligational', rather than 'adversarial'. So, why are the NHS contracts designed as if they were complete contracts and essentially written as adversarial contracts? After all, the volumes are not predictable – nobody will accurately predict the numbers of procedures required in one geographical area in a year – even if the costs of a unit of treatment might be.

The financing and contracting model that is used for schools used to be applied in the NHS before the invention of the purchaser–provider divide: there was a formula based on demographics that allocated funds to regions and districts (different area scales at different times) and then adjusted according to the historical deployment of physical plant, since the hospitals tended to be concentrated in the cities. Budgets were then allocated to hospitals which would respond to needs within their budget, or if needs turned out to be higher than predicted, adjustments could be made. The whole administrative process probably cost no more than 3% of total spending.

Surely, incompetence is not the explanation for the creation of such a complex, expensive and ineffective system. A more likely explanation is that the whole apparatus was established to enable privatisation. In the case of local authority services subject to competitive tendering and privatisation by outsourcing, as we saw in Chapter 11, the first step was the purchaser–provider divide. In the case of Community Care the same was true: the transfer of ownership of both domiciliary and residential services to the private sector was made possible by dividing social services departments into 'purchasers' and 'providers', thus enabling the purchasers to deal with any supplier. The whole division of the NHS into the two parts enables the use of the 'any willing provider' criterion to choose suppliers of health care.

CONTRACTUAL RELATIONSHIPS

The other major element of the experiment with public management was the extensive use of contracts both within the public sector and between the private and public sectors for service provision. The market as a governance mechanism was implemented through a series of contracts, ranging from the Public Service Agreements, Agency contracts, service level agreements, contracts between the train operators and the track operators on the railway, building and maintenance contracts, Public–Private Partnerships, right through to performance contracts with managers and individual members of staff. What conclusions can we draw about the success of contracting?

In the case of the railways, both the national rail service and the London Underground railway, experience with contracting was both ineffective and expensive: the complex set of contracts to run the national rail service resulted initially in very large transaction costs, perverse incentives, poor performance and ultimately a dangerous railway. The Metronet experience resulted in contract failure and a government bailout of the banks who put up the loan capital for the refurbishment of the infrastructure.

In many cases of ICT contracting, as we saw in Chapter 7, the result of the contracting process was failure to deliver, enormous cost overruns, very long delays, poor performance of systems and in some cases cancellation before completion of the contracts. In other, less public cases there have been successes, in website provision and maintenance, in transaction management and, in the case of the DWP, reasonably successful system implementation.

The use of PFI for the provision of infrastructure, prisons, schools and hospitals has been reasonably successful but, according to most of the evaluation, probably no greater success than more conventional financing and contracting approaches, and probably at greater cost. Where the contacts failed, as in the case of Metronet, the reason was mostly information asymmetry and unpredictable contingencies. Where they succeeded, as in the case of prisons and hospitals, the management of the contracts was done in such a way as to treat them as if the future was predictable, and this resulted in long-term commitments to buildings and facilities that could not be changed as requirements develop.

In the case of the NHS, the very high transaction costs probably did not generate better value than a more conventional hierarchical relationship. Apart from the questions of complexity and asymmetry discussed above, there was the basic problem of what would be the consequences of contract failure. What if a Trust failed to meet its contractual obligations either in volume, cost or quality? While there were some early cases of mergers of weaker Trusts with stronger ones, the PCTs had little power to close down 'failing' institutions. The Coalition backed away from the idea of allowing failing providers to be closed, compromising with a set of procedures to follow if failure occurred.

As we saw in the case of Southern Cross, the provider of residential care, failure can have serious consequences for the users of public services, removing their care homes, treatment centres and so on from the landscape of served provision. Such consequences may, however, be an essential element of the market as a governance mechanism: if there is no chance of failure, why should owners, managers and workers strive to create success? The directors of Southern Cross walked away with their £35 million not as a result of success in providing social care, although they did that as well, but rather as a result of financial engineering with their sale and leaseback scheme. The banks that financed Metronet and the companies that put up the equity had little or no adverse consequences of failure. The companies that serially re-negotiated ICT contracts mostly generated increased revenue from rectifying their failures. In November 2011, the government announced a £1 billion, ten-year contract for a private firm, 'Circle', to run Hinchingbrooke Hospital, Cambridgeshire, an NHS hospital with a large financial deficit of £40 million. The contract places the risk of the deficit continuing with the company.

THE CITIZEN–CONSUMER

We saw that the relationship between people and public services is varied and complex. On a given day, somebody could be a patient at a surgery, a parent at a school, a passenger and a victim of crime. Each would bring a person into contact with public services, in a distinct relationship with the people providing those services. In each case, the person would have preferences about how they would like to be treated, and their rights and obligations. Each brings different ways of accessing those rights: consultation, the right to use a different service provider, redress if the service fails. Each relationship also implies a different set of obligations on the part of the service provider, which come from different sources: the doctor's professional skills and ethics; the school's governance structure and representation; the bus company's safety regime; the police service's code of behaviour towards victims.

The task of all public sector managers is to ensure that each encounter with someone using the service is conducted according to the right principles and procedures and in a way that ensures that the people using the service are guaranteed their rights, whatever the source of those rights. In recent years there has been an emphasis by government on the right to choose, as a benefit in itself, sometimes with the implication that the right to choose overrides the other rights that people may have. Various surveys of people's attitudes to and satisfaction with public services suggest that the users of public services have other priorities: service quality, convenience, dignity and respect may all override choice. A moment's thought will reveal that this is likely: as a victim of crime, do you want a choice of police officer or police service? As someone requiring urgent medical treatment, is choice a priority? If all the schools that your children can travel to are of poor quality, will choice increase your satisfaction? The right to choose or to switch service provider is one possible way of empowering citizens as consumers, but may be neither necessary nor sufficient. The right to redress, to compensation, to influence, to fairness, to respect are all important elements of what people want in their dealings with public services.

Most of the professions involved in providing public services have, as part of their training, an ethos about the way in which the users of the services should be treated. At the moment of the encounter between the service provider and the service user, those ethics are the most important influence. In many cases, the encounter is based on emotion, on both sides. The nurses, ambulance drivers, teachers, police in their daily encounters with the people with whom they deal are not working solely to a fixed pattern of actions determined by their training: they are also reacting, through their emotions, with the people they encounter. Manuals, targets and performance measures tend to elide this fact.

Where there are more mechanistic transactions, a more rule-bound or hierarchical approach may be appropriate. In these cases, a hierarchical, managerial approach to the relationship might involve a rule-book or manual of procedures for customer-handling, with the backup of the appropriate customer relationship technology, recording all transactions, storing and accessing relevant data.

THE UNIVERSAL DATABASE

An apparent ambition of the Blair and Brown governments was that there would one day be a single universal database where all the data about everyone would be stored and accessible to all public services. The national identity card scheme, a favourite of Gordon Brown, would provide the central database, accessible to all departments, smoothing the way to crime prevention and detection, eliminating benefit fraud, enabling service delivery through education, health, benefits, tax and all other encounters between the state and the citizen.

The ambition generates a picture of a few powerful individuals at the centre of government with access to a series of dashboards showing performance against targets for customer service, benefits accuracy, tax collection success rates, schools performance, health outcomes. Policy problems could be solved by the application of more resources here, a new target there, a change to the funding agreement, a new clause or target in the Public Service Agreement.

The cancellation of the identity card and the modification of the health service database have postponed this cybernetic ambition, possibly for ever. The future of ICT will more likely be more local systems, with connectivity between them when that produces evident returns. With luck, those who commission and provide ICT systems for the public sector will work together to create solutions that reflect the desired processes of interaction between the service providers and the service users, rather than an overambitious, universal, completely interconnected series of systems. When they do this, let us hope that both sides make realistic and suitably modest claims for what their systems will and can achieve.

THE FUTURE OF PUBLIC FINANCE AND FINANCIAL MANAGEMENT

We saw in Chapter 3 that the state of the economy and especially economic growth has most impact on the funds available for public services. The future of public finance depends therefore to a large extent on the future of the economy, the restoration of growth through competitiveness, as well as the fiscal policies chosen within that economic future. Figure 3.1 showed a 50% rise in public spending in constant prices from 2001 to 2009. The financial crisis seems to have put an abrupt halt to that rise from 2010: the question is, will public spending return to its upward trend if and when the recession ends and the deficit is under control, or will the decade to 2009 be seen as a 'golden age' of the public sector, with its legacy of school and hospital buildings, but a reversal of its increases in numbers of staff in the NHS, schools, police forces?

The answer to the question partly depends on politics: we saw in Chapter 2 that there are those who believe that there is a political future of a 'liberal consensus': will this consensus arrive at a position on the level of public spending that fixes it as a proportion of GDP? If so, what is that proportion likely to be? If it follows a long trend the answer would be somewhere near 40%, including services and transfer payments at roughly half each. An alternative scenario is that those who favour the small state will be in power long enough to reduce the scale of state spending and push the proportion down, perhaps by 3–5% points of GDP, mainly by not increasing the level of tax revenues in line with economic growth – in other words cutting tax rates when the economy grows. This scenario would lead, as it did in the 1980s and 1990s, to visible deterioration of the infrastructure, including the railway, schools, hospitals and a drop in service standards. The last time that happened it produced election results in favour of more spending. So, perhaps this is a likely scenario: a continuation of periods of austerity for the public sector, especially in periods of poor economic performance, followed by periods of real-terms growth in spending, particularly in periods of economic growth.

What is the likely future of the way that public money is managed? We saw in Chapter 5 that there has been a long evolution of the system, ending with multi-annual plans, outcome definitions in the budget documents and explicit agreements about service levels and standards as part of the financial allocations. The Coalition government has declared itself both interested in outcomes and not interested in targets. This is in line with trends in the development of performance budgeting elsewhere: in Australia, for example, states that have developed performance-enhanced budgets have recently moved away from targets for improvement towards service standards, on the premise that services cannot improve forever. It is not clear whether this is David Cameron's view: an alternative explanation may be that he does not want to use the same measures as the previous governments because he fears that standards may fall after the spending cuts.

It is difficult to imagine a reversal in the progress of financial management, to make the argument that budgets should only be based on inputs, with no accounting for outputs and outcomes, or that financial planning should revert to being a purely annual business. Already the number of targets and outcomes in the spending reviews and annual budgets were declining, and the system was becoming less overwhelming in its detail: the trend may well continue towards a smaller number of standards and outcome measures, but a continuation of the idea of performance-informed budgeting.

INSPECTION, AUDIT AND REGULATION

We have observed trends in internal regulation, by auditors and inspectors: generally audit and inspection have developed into part of the performance management process and away from being a process of checking on pre-determined standards. If there is a tendency towards a less active and detailed management from the centre, this trend could continue: the processes of audit and inspection can continue to develop into ways of outsiders helping managers to do better.

Regulation is different: the regulators are there to implement whatever policies the government has towards the regulated industries, whether on price, quality, investment, sustainability. If the NHS is privatised, in the sense of a much higher proportion of services being purchased from private providers, then the inspection process will likely become more like the regulatory regime in the energy and water sectors: indeed this plan is set out in the Health and Social Care Bill.

No doubt there will be more structural change – the House of Commons Public Administration Committee has already expressed doubts about the wisdom of combining all school and children's services inspection into Ofsted. A period of combining the inspectors may well be followed by a process of splitting them up again: more change at the top, while the everyday work of the inspectors will no doubt carry on as before.

NOTES

1 Office for National Statistics, *Productivity Handbook* (London: Palgrave Macmillan, 2007).
2 Ibid., Chapter 9, p. 135.
3 See page x [AT PAGE PROOF STAGE]
4 Steffie Woolhandler et al. 'Costs of healthcare administration in the USA and Canada', *New England Journal of Medicine*, Vol. 349 (2003), pp. 768–775.
5 The secondary school in London where I served as Governor and member of the Finance and Premises Committee had one bursar and one secretary to manage an annual budget of over £6 million. The bursar handled all annual budgeting, procurement, including catering, and monthly financial reporting.

References

Alcock, P. (2008) *Social Policy in Britain*. London: Palgrave Macmillan.

Association of Directors of Social Services and National Council for Voluntary Organisations (1995) 'Community Care and Voluntary Organisations: Joint Policy Statement', London: ADSS/NCVO.

Audit Commission (2003) 'PFI in Schools'. London: Audit Commission.

Audit Commission (2005) 'Early lessons from payment by results'. London: Audit Commission.

Audit Commission (2006) 'The Future of Regulation in the Public Sector', Corporate Discussion Paper. London: Audit Commission.

Bakker Karen J (2003) 'An Uncooperative Commodity: Privatizing Water in England and Wales', Oxford: Oxford University Press

Baldwin, R. and Cave, M. (1999) *Understanding Regulation: Theory Strategy and Practice*. Oxford: Oxford University Press.

Bale, T. (2011) *The Conservative Party from Thatcher to Cameron*. Cambridge: Polity Press.

Blakemore, K. and Griggs, E. (2007) *Social Policy: An Introduction*. Milton Keynes: Open University Press.

Bogdanor, V. (ed.) (2005) *Joined-up Government*. Oxford: Oxford University Press.

Bourne, J. (2007) *Public Sector Auditing – Is It Value for Money?* Chichester: Wiley.

Broadbent, J. and Laughlin, R. (2004) 'Striving for excellence in public service delivery: experiences from an analysis of the private finance initiative', *Public Policy and Administration*, 19: 82.

Bruijn, H. de (2002) *Managing Performance in the Public Sector*. London: Routledge.

Bryson, J. (2011) *Strategic Planning for Public and Not For Profit Organizations* (4th edition). San Francisco, CA: Jossey Bass.

Budd, A. (2010) 'Fiscal policy under Labour', *National Institute Economic Review*, No 212, April 2010.

Burnham, J. and Piper, R. (2008) *Britain's Modernised Civil Service*. London: Palgrave Macmillan.

Cabinet Office Agencies and Public Bodies Team (2005) *Public Bodies 2005*. Norwich: HMSO.

Cabinet Office (2005) *Transformational Government – enabled by technology*, CM 6683. London: HMSO.

Cabinet Office (2008) *Excellence and Fairness: Achieving World Class Public Services*. London: HMSO.

Care Quality Commission: introductory leaflet, undated.

Care Quality Commission (2010) *Annual Report 2009–10*. London: HMSO.

Central Office of Information (2010) *Reporting on progress, central Government Websites 2009-10*, COI 2010: report available at: coi.gov.uk/websitemetrics2009-10.

Chartered Institute of Personnel and Development (2010) *Building Productive Public Sector Workplaces*. London: CIPD.

Chartered Institute of Public Finance and Accountancy (2005) *Response to ODPM Consultation on Inspection Reform*. CIPFA homepage

Clarke, J., Newman, J., Smith, N., Vidler, E. and Westmarland, L. (2007) *Creating Citizen-Consumers*. London: Sage.

Clarke, T. (2002) 'New Labour's big idea: joined up government', *Social Policy and Society*, 1, 2: 107–118.

Cole, M. (2011) *Political Parties in Britain*. Edinburgh: Edinburgh University Press.

Communities and Local Government (2007) *The Single Regeneration Budget: Final Evaluation*. London: CLG.

Communities and Local Government (2010) *Housing and Planning Statistics, National Statistics, 2010*. London: ONS.

Communities and Local Government/National Statistics (2010) *Local Government Financial Statistics England*, No 20. London: ONS.

Comptroller and Auditor General (2002) *Using Call Centres to Deliver Public Services.* HC 134 Session 2002–2003. London: HMSO.

Comptroller and Auditor General (2003) *The Operational Performance of PFI Prisons,* HC 700 Session 2002–2003: 18 June 2003. London: HMSO.

Conservative Party (2010) *Invitation to Join the Government of Britain: The Conservative Manifesto.* London: Conservative Party.

Coombs, H.M. and Jenkins, D.E. (2002) *Public Sector Financial Management.* London: Thompson.

Crawford, R., Emmerson, C. and Tetlow, G. (2005) 'A survey of public spending in the UK', *Institute of Fiscal Studies Briefing Note 43,* June 2010.

Davis, H. and Martin, S. (eds) (2008) *Public Services Inspection in the United Kingdom.* London: Jessica Kingsley Publishers.

Deacon, R. and Sandry, A. (2007) *Devolution in the United Kingdom.* Edinburgh: Edinburgh University Press.

Demirag, I. and Khadaroo, I. (2010) 'Costs, outputs and outcomes in school PFI contracts and the significance of project size', *Public Money & Management,* 30, 1: 13–18.

Department for Children, Schools and Families, and National Statistics (2009) *National Curriculum Assessments at Key Stage 2, England, 2009.* London: ONS.

Department of Communities and Local Government (2010) *House Building Statistics 2010.* London: HMSO.

Departments of Communities and Local Government, Health, Education and Skills and Home Office (2007) *Developing and implementing the new comprehensive area assessment and associated inspection arrangements.* London: HMSO.

Department of Communities and Local Government (2007) *The New Performance Framework for Local Authorities & Local Authority Partnerships: Single Set of National Indicators.* London: HMSO.

Department for Education (2010) *A Technical Guide to Contextual Value Added (including English & maths) Key Stage 2 to 4 2010 model.* London: HMSO.

Department of Health (1997) *The New NHS, Modern, Mependable.* Cm 3807. London: DoH.

Department of Health (2000) *NHS Plan, a plan for investment, a plan for reform.* para. 6.3. London: DoH.

Department of Health (2003) *A Short Guide to NHS Foundation Trusts.* London: DoH.

Department for Local Government and Communities (2008) *The National Procurement Strategy for Local Government, Final report.* London: HMSO.

Department of Transport (2004) *The Future of Rail.* London: HMSO.

Department for Transport and Office for Rail Regulation (2011) *Realising the Potential of GB Rail, Report of the Rail Value for Money Study.* London: HMSO.

Department of Work and Pensions/Office of Government Commerce (2006) *DWP Jobcentre Plus roll-out: Integrated Supply Chain.* London: DWP.

Dove, M.H.I., Kushner, J., and Zumer, K. (2004) 'Privatization of water in the UK and France - what can we learn?', *Utilities Policy,* 12: 41–50.

Driver, S. (2009) 'Work to be Done? Welfare Reform from Blair to Brown', *Policy Studies,* 30, 1: 69–84.

Drucker, P. (1955) *The Practice of Management.* London: Butterworth-Heinemann.

Fukuyama, F. (1992) *The End of History and the Last Man.* London: Penguin.

Fulton, Lord (1968) *The Civil Service.* Cmnd 3638. London: HMSO.

Furmston M.P. (2006) *Cheshire, Fifoot and Furmston's Law of Contract.* Oxford: Oxford University Press.

Giddens, A. (1998) *The Third Way: The Renewal of Social Democracy.* Cambridge: Polity Press.

Glennerster, H. (1995) *British Social Policy Since 1945.* Oxford: Blackwell.

Goldfinch, S. (2009) 'Dangerous enthusiasms and information systems development in the public sector', in S. Goldfinch and J. Wallis (eds), *International Handbook of Public management reform.* Cheltenham: Edward Elgar.

Griffiths, S. (2009) 'The Public Services under Gordon Brown: Same reforms, less money', *Policy Studies,* 30, 1: 53–67.

Grimsey, D.and Lewis, M.K. (2004) *Public Private Partnerships.* Cheltenham: Edward Elgar.

Ham, C. (2009) *Health Policy in Britain.* London: Palgrave Macmillan.

Hartry, H.P. (2006) *Performance Measurement: Getting Results*, second edition. Washington DC: The Urban Institute Press.

Hayek, F. (1944) *The Road to Serfdom*. London: Routledge.

Heeks, R. (2006) *Implementing and Managing eGovernment*. London: Sage.

Helm, D. (2005) 'Editorial', *The Utilities Journal*, Vol. 8, March.

HM Inspector of Prisons (1999) *Report on Wandsworth Prison*. London: HMSO.

HM Inspector of Prisons (2006) *Report on Wandsworth Prison*. London: HMSO

HM Inspector of Prisons (2009) *Report on Wandsworth Prison*. London: HMSO.

HM Treasury (1961) *The Control of Public Expenditure (Plowden Report)*. Cmd. 1432. London: HMSO.

HM Treasury (2007) *Managing Public Money*. London: HMSO.

HM Treasury (2010a) *Public Expenditure Statistical Analysis*. CM 7890. London: HMSO.

HM Treasury (2010b) *The Spending Review Framework*. CM 7872. London: HMSO.

HM Treasury (2010c) *Spending Review 2010*. Cm 7942. London: HMSO.

HM Treasury (2011) *PFI data Summary*. HM treasury website

House of Commons Communities and Local Government Committee (2011) *Localism*. Third report session 2010–12. London: HMSO.

House of Commons Education and Skills Committee (2007) *Sustainable Schools: Are we building schools for the future?* London: HMSO.

House of Commons Health Committee (2011) *Commissioning*. London: HMSO.

House of Commons Public Accounts Committee (2009) *Building Schools for the Future: Renewing the secondary school estate*. London: HMSO.

House of Commons Public Administration Select Committee (2009) *Top Pay in the Public Sector*. London: HMSO.

Hudson, B. (2011) 'Ten years of jointly commissioning health and social care in England', *International Journal of Integrated Care*, 7: 11.

Jessop, R. (2002) *The Future of the Capitalist State*. Cambridge: Polity Press.

Jordana, J. and Levi-Faur, D. (2004) *The Politics of Regulation*. Cheltenham: Edward Elgar.

Keynes, J.M. (1936) *The General Theory of Employment, Interest and Money*. London: Macmillan.

King, P. (2009) *Understanding Housing Finance*, second edition. London: Routledge.

King, R. (2007) *The Regulatory State in an Age of Governance*. London: Palgrave Macmillan.

King's Fund (2005) *An Independent Audit of the NHS Under Labour (1997–2005)*. London: King's Fund.

Leadbeater, C. (2004) *Personalisation Through Participation*. London: Demos.

Le Grand, J. (2007) *The Other Invisible Hand: Delivering Public Services through Choice and Competition*. Princeton, NJ: Princeton University Press.

Mayer, C. (2005) 'Commitment and Control in Regulation: The Future of Regulation in Water', in C. Robinson (ed.), *Governments, Competition and Utility Regulation*. Cheltenham: Edward Elgar.

Ministry of Justice (2010) 'Compendium of reoffending statistics and analysis'. *Executive Summary Statistics*. London: HMSO.

Mitchell, J., Bennie, L. and Johns. R. (2011) *The Scottish National Party: Transition to Power*. Oxford: Oxford University Press.

Moran, M. (2003) *The British Regulatory State*. Oxford: Oxford University Press.

National Audit Office (1995) *Contracting for Acute Health Care in England*. Report by the Comptroller and Auditor General. London: NAO.

National Audit Office (2003) The *New Energy Trading Arrangements in England and Wales*. London: NAO.

National Audit Office (2007) *Information and Services*. London: NAO.

National Audit Office (2007) *Government On the Internet: Progress in Delivering*. London: NAO.

National Audit Office (2009) *Department of Transport. The failure of Metronet*. London: NAO.

National Audit Office (2009) *Performance of PFI Construction*. London: NAO.

National Audit Office (2010a) *A Short Guide to Structured Cost Reduction*. London: NAO.

National Audit Office (2010b) *Criminal Justice System: Landscape review.* London: NAO.

National Audit Office (2010c) *HM Treasury: Financing PFI Projects in the Credit Crisis and the Treasury's Response.* London: NAO.

National Audit Office (2010d) *The National Offender Management Information System.* London: NAO.

National Audit Office (2010e) *The Performance and Management of PFI Hospital Contracts.* London: NAO.

National Audit Office (2011a) *Information and Communications Technology in Government: Landscape Review.* London: NAO.

National Audit Office (2011b) *The National Programme for IT in the NHS: An Update on the Delivery of Detailed Care Records Systems.* London: NAO.

National Audit Office (2011c) *Highways Agency procurement of the M25 private finance Contract.* London: NAO.

National Audit Office (2011d) *National Health Service Landscape Review.* London: NAO.

National Foundation for Educational Research (2007) *Evaluation of the Impact of Section 5 Inspections.* London: NFER.

NHS (2005) *A Guide to the National Programme for Information Technology.* London: NHS.

NHS (2008) *Developing the NHS Performance Regime.* London: NHS.

Normann, R. (1991) *Service Management.* second edition. Chichester: Wiley.

Office of the Deputy Prime Minister (2003a) *Local Government Act 1999.* London: HMSO.

Office of the Deputy Prime Minister (2003b) *Best Value and Performance Improvement.* London: HMSO.

Office for National Statistics (2010) *Public Sector Employment.* London: ONS.

OFSTED (2008) *Report, Elizabeth Garrett Anderson Language College.* London: HMSO.

OFSTED (2011) *Framework for Inspection of Children's Homes.* London: HMSO.

Office of Fair Trading (2010) *Choice and Competition in Public Services.* London: OTF.

Office for Standards in Education (2007) *Review of the Impact of Inspection.* London: OSE.

Office for National Statistics (2007) *Productivity Handbook.* London: Palgrave Macmillan.

Owers, A. (2010) Speech to Prison Reform Trust.

Pollock A., Shaol, J. and Vickers, N. (2002) 'Private finance and "value for money" in NHS hospitals: a policy in search of a rationale?', *British Medical Journal*, 324: 1205–1209.

Prentice, G., Burgess, S. and Propper, C. (2007) *Performance pay in the public sector: A review of the issues and evidence.* London: Office of Manpower Economics.

Rawnsley, A. (2010) *The End of the Party.* London: Vintage.

Royal Academy of Engineering and British Computer Society (2004) *The Challenges of Complex IT projects.* London: RAE.

Royal College of General Practitioners (2004) *The Structure of the NHS Information Sheet No. 8.* London: RCGP.

Russell, B. (1935) *In Praise of Idleness.* London: Routledge.

Spicker, P. (2011) *How Social Security Works.* Bristol: Policy Press.

Sako, M. (1992) *Prices, Quality and Trust.* Cambridge: Cambridge University Press.

Sandry, A. (2011) *Plaid Cymru: an Ideological Analysis.* Cardiff: Welsh Academic Press.

Secondary Heads Association (2003) *Towards Intelligent Accountability for Schools: A policy paper on school accountability.* Policy paper. March.

Sheridan, P. (2009) 'PFI/PPP Disputes', *European Public Private Partnerships Law Review*, 2.

Silvestri, A. (ed.) Centre for Crime and Justice Studies (2011) *Lessons for the Coalition: an end of term report on New Labour and criminal justice.* London: Hadley Trust.

Simmons, R., et al. (eds) (2009) *The Consumer in Public Services: Choice, Values and Difference.* Bristol: Policy Press.

Solomon, E., Eades, C., Garside, R. and Rutherford, M. (2007) *Ten Years of Criminal Justice Under Labour: An independent audit.* London: Sunday Times and the Hadley Trust.

Stuart, A., Emmerson, C. and Kenley, A. (2007) *A Survey of Local Government Finance.* London: Institute of Fiscal Studies.

Thomas, S. (2006) 'The British Model: Failing Slowly', *Energy Policy*, 34, March.

Thorlby, R. and Maybin, J. (eds) (2010) *A High Performing NHS? A review of Progress 1997–2010*. London: The Kings Fund.

Vining, A.R. and Boardman, A.E. (2008) 'Public Private partnerships: Eight Rules for Governments', *Public Works Management Policy*, 13.

Water services regulatory authority (OFWAT) (2010) *Delivering sustainable water: Ofwat's strategy*. London: Ofwat.

Welsh Assembly Government (2010) *Budget Timeline*. Cardiff: WAG.

Williamson, O. (1975) *Markets and Hierarchies*. New York: The Free Press.

Wilson, D. and Game, C. (2011) *Local Government in the United Kingdom*. London: Palgrave Macmillan.

Woolhandler, S. et al. (2003) 'Costs of Healthcare Administration in the USA and Canada', *New England Journal of Medicine*, 349: 768–75.

Index

Page numbers in *italics* refer to tables.

Total Managed Expenditure (TME) 95, 96, 98, *99*
Total Place initiative 183
Train Operating Companies (TOCs) 247, 248, 249–50
transaction costs, overheads and 255–6
transactional dependence (contracts) 214–15
trust 218

universal database 259
Universities 68–9, 136
urban regeneration 234–5

values
politics and management 39–41
service design 161–2

Vining, A.R. and Boardman, A.E. 229
vouchers, cash and customer control 156–7

Wales 12, 13, 23, 38
finance 104, *106, 107*
health services 22
performance management 128–9
PFI highway project 235
Welsh Water 245
Wandsworth Prison, inspection reports 173–5
water supply and sewerage services 242–7
welfare state/system 60–1, 63–4, 88–9
whole services, competition for 200–1
Williamson, O. 212–13